Creating Interactive CD-ROM

for Windows™ and Macintosh®

Creating Interactive CD-ROM for Windows™ and Macintosh®

Scott Fisher

AP PROFESSIONAL
Boston San Diego New York
London Sydney Tokyo Toronto

This book is printed on acid-free paper. ♾

AP PROFESSIONAL
1300 Boylston Street, Chestnut Hill, MA 02167

An imprint of ACADEMIC PRESS, INC.
A Division of HARCOURT BRACE & COMPANY

United Kingdom Edition published by
ACADEMIC PRESS LIMITED
24–28 Oval Road, London NW1 7DX

Library of Congress Cataloging-in-Publication Data
Fisher, Scott, 1956–
Creating interactive CD-ROM for Windows and Macintosh / Scott Fisher
p. cm.
Includes bibliographical references and index.
ISBN 0-12-257565-2
1. Interactive multimedia. 2. CD-ROMs. 3. Macintosh (Computer)
I. Title.
QA76.76.I59F57 1995
006--dc20 95-10089
CIP

Printed in the United States of America

95 96 97 98 IP 9 8 7 6 5 4 3 2 1

Contents

Chapter 3 • Structure

Chapter 4 • Prototyping

Chapter 5 • Navigation

Chapter 6 • Module Design

Chapter 10 • Testing

Chapter 11 • Publishing

Appendix A • Tips and Tricks

Appendix B • Contents of the CD-ROM

Preface

What Can You Get from This Book?

In this book, I've made an awful lot of assumptions about you, your skills, the projects you're working on, and your experience with computers in general and with working in images in particular. I've done it so that I can focus on producing the tightest, most focused work I knew how to do, dedicated to one task: turning multimedia users into multimedia authors. With that in mind, here are a few of the assumptions I've made, and some suggestions on what you can do if they're wildly inaccurate for your individual condition.

Assumption 1: You want to make your own multimedia title. Most of the people I talked to, interviewed, and worked with for this book had very specific projects that they wanted to produce. Some of them had wildly creative ideas for entertainment titles, games, mysteries, love stories, or other entertainment-oriented titles. Most of them wanted to use multimedia to help them in their business, especially when that business involved teaching or training people. Teachers who have adopted CD-ROM technology for classroom use are particularly excited at the prospect of developing their own course material for the computer, or better still, of letting their students create their own multimedia projects. So are marketing professionals who want to create moving, interactive brochures that show their products in action, small-business owners who want to put their catalogs into CD-ROM for use in in-store kiosks, human-resources staff that want to put company orientation, background, and procedural information on CD-ROM, and other people who want to incorporate interactivity, animation, and digital video into a desktop presentation that helps make their job more rewarding.

From time to time, though, I'd meet people who said, early on, "Oh, I just want to learn a little about how multimedia works." Within a short period of time—often less than an hour—these people tended to jump up and say something like "I've got a great idea for a title! It's about these two teenagers who fall in love, but their families hate each other, so they secretly get married but they both end up dying tragically...." So if you don't yet have an idea, stick around and keep reading; the chances are good that you'll get one soon.

But given the assumption that you already know what you want to make, look at the examples in the book as pieces of the overall solution to the problems you'll face in designing and producing your own multimedia title. Some of these examples are simple pieces I produced to look like, or to represent pieces out of, other kinds of multimedia titles. Some of them are short proof-of-concept pieces that my multimedia students have made and graciously allowed me to include on the CD-ROM. And some of them were just too much fun to leave out.

If for some reason you don't already know what kind of multimedia piece you want to create, keep reading—one will come to you. Given all the examples, suggestions, categories, types, markets, and focuses that I present for multimedia titles, the chances are good that you'll find one that excites you. And if not, you'll learn a lot about how multimedia works and how the design team made some of the multimedia pieces that you have seen and enjoyed.

Assumption 2: You haven't got a lot of money to spend on development. If you have got a lot of money to spend, please contact me directly through the publisher, and I will be happy to help you spend it. But most of the people I talked to while producing this book still think that three thousand dollars, two thousand pounds, fifteen thousand francs, or whatever it is in the currency you use, is a fair-sized chunk of change. In that light, I've tried whenever possible to focus on inexpensive solutions rather than on full-blown Industrial Light and Magic packages and products. The good news is that some technology is becoming cheaper by the minute; most of the prices I mention in this book will be laughable by the time it sees print ("he paid *how much* for that?"). But between the drop in storage costs, the introduction of low-cost, high-performance processors from both Apple and Intel, and the expansion of the market for software to a size that permits economy of scale, you can assemble an effective multimedia production studio for what amounts to the down payment on a new car. If you already have basic computer equipment, you can probably do it for even less—though older computers (386 and earlier PCs, 68020 and earlier Macintoshes) will be less effective in handling the volume of data that multimedia requires.

Again, if this assumption doesn't fit you—if you're planning to set up a top-of-the-line multimedia studio and you've got a few million in venture capital to spend on equipment, software, and talent—please do not hesitate to call. I'll be happy to help you spend some of that money. On a more serious note, all the techniques, examples, products, and processes that I mention in this book work on high-end equipment as well as low-end equipment; they work faster, though not necessarily more easily or more effectively. You don't need a million dollars worth of equipment to produce a beautiful multimedia piece: you need talent, creativity, and vision. And in the multimedia industry today, vision will go a lot farther to get you money than money will go to get you a vision.

Assumption 3: You are already familiar with the basics of using your PC or Macintosh. I've had to assume that you know what a double-click is, that you know how to pull down menus and choose a selection, that you know how to close a window on the Mac and how to iconify it on Windows. I've assumed that you know the letters that your PC assigns to your various disk drives (and furthermore, that your 3.5″ floppy is A:, your hard drive is C:, and your CD-ROM drive is D:), and that you know how to navigate through the directories on those drives or through the folders on your Macintosh. I've assumed that you know you have to put the CD-ROM into the drive with the printed label facing up (if you didn't, you do now). And I assume that you know how to copy files to your hard drive, whether by the drag-and-drop method that the Mac and Windows use, or by typing the DOS commands if you prefer to work directly at the command line shell in your PC.

If you're not comfortable with these concepts, there are a lot of well-known reference books designed to get anyone comfortable with the basics of operating Macintoshes and PCs. In that case, keep reading this book for motivation—it'll tell you how to do what you really want, while you struggle with learning what to do when DOS tells you "Abort, retry, fail?" when you type the wrong disk drive in a command line.

Assumption 4: You're not into technology for technology's sake; you want to use it to do something else. I'm a fence-straddler here; I am attracted to cool new tech toys simply because they're new, but I don't really commit until I can see how it benefits me either personally or professionally. (As a case in point, I did not own a CD player until late in 1994. Most people back away from me slightly when I tell them this. I've got two CD-ROM drives in my home office, one on the Mac and one on the PC, and I've recently started listening to audio CDs on whichever computer I'm not using at the moment.)

As such a fence-straddler, I can assure you that the cool new tech toys I talk about in this book—video capture boards, image manipulation software, 3D modelers, and high-density mass storage units—are all pretty much required parts of the business of producing multimedia titles. If you want to use video in your title, you will need a way to convert it from the image on tape to the image on disk (Chapter 7 tells why these are different). If you want to use 3D animation, you'll need a solid modeling tool to draw the objects and you'll need some kind of animation program to make it move. If you want to keep these images close at hand, you'll need lots of disk space; video, even compressed video, eats space like no other form of electronic data you've ever seen. (Don't believe me? Take a look at some of the short video clips on the CD-ROM, then either Get Info on them if you're using a Mac or look at them in the File Manager on Windows, and see how much room it takes to store a comparatively tiny piece of video.)

Assumption 5: The acceleration of technology accelerates the acceleration of technology (or, for those of us who have programmed in Lisp at one time or another, the acceleration of technology is recursive). Faster processors make possible more complex programs, which require larger memory, which in turn enables the production of files that take more room on disk, which requires faster access speed, which requires faster processors, which continues the cycle all over again. What this means, first of all, is that performance gets cheaper every month. (Notice that I didn't say that computers get cheaper: what happens is that they stay about the same price, they just do a lot more for the money.)

More fundamentally, though, the acceleration of technology means that when I talk about performance, specifications, capabilities, and especially prices, most of what I'm typing is obsolete before I've even pressed the keys. A competitor, a new product line from the same company, or a more cut-throat reseller has probably already introduced something with the same specifications, capabilities, or other characteristics as what I've just written about, and it will either cost less or do more for the same price.

There are two ways to react to this situation. You can sit tight, waiting for prices to drop a little more, knowing that if you wait a month you can save maybe 20% on the cost of the equipment you want to buy today. On some purchases, that's wise; so far I've saved enough money on the price of the 1.05 gigabyte hard drive I've been meaning to purchase for the past two months that I'm now able to buy a 2-gigabyte drive for less than the 1-gig would have cost me last summer. On other purchases, it's not; sometimes the window of opportunity for your projects is only open for a short period of time.

And that introduces the second way to react to the rocketing capabilities and plummeting costs of technology: you have to think about when you must buy something today, knowing that it will cost 20% less in a few months or a few weeks, because you need to start working today on the project that this equipment lets you pursue.

Acknowledgments

Multimedia, everyone keeps reminding everyone else, is collaborative. As such, no book of this nature could be created in a vacuum; in addition to the people who provided equipment, grants, and support for the actual production, there were a number of people who provided creative and technical support for the samples, answered questions about products and packages, and otherwise provided guidance during the design, writing, and production of the book.

First, of course, are the great editorial and production team at AP PROFESSIONAL, headed by my editor, Jenifer Niles. It was a pleasure working with her again on this book, as I had on *Multimedia Authoring*, and she made sure that I had what I needed to get this book finished. Karen Pratt, also familiar to me from my previous book for APP, provided invaluable technical assistance about such issues as providing the fonts on the electronic media and other issues that made the production smoother than it would have been if she hadn't prepared me. And on this round, Cindy Kogut and Jacqueline Young provided invaluable support in the crucial final stages of production. Thanks to all of you for helping keep this book tight and (almost) on time.

I was also fortunate, living as I do in Sunnyvale, to have friends at Apple and Intel who provided me with equipment for my use during the development; I'm not looking forward to having to return it, but the equipment loans that they provided me made it possible for me to begin producing sample video clips on both platforms. First, to TeriAnn Wakeman, Mistress of CPU Compatibility for Apple Computers, a huge debt of gratitude for the loan of a Macintosh Quadra 630 with the Apple Video System capture card installed; in addition to giving me the ability to capture video, simply having the 630 made writing the book easier than it had been when I began the project, using my old Mac Classic II. Second, to Mike Gendimenico, technical marketing specialist at Intel, for arranging the loan of an Intel Smart Video Recorder Pro and for offering advice on the installation. It really was a snap to put the board into my 486, and again this is something I'm not looking forward to giving back!

But while I've discussed multimedia applications for entertainment and professional use, I found that the education community gave me some of the most exciting and engaging projects, ideas, and support. First, to the Sunnyvale School District's Multimedia Specialist Program and the program's director, Marie Scigliano, huge thanks for letting me participate in some of your training and in some of the classroom work with the specialists. Second, to Larry Liden, director of the Institute of Computer Technology in Sunnyvale, one of the Multimedia Specialist Program's supporters—thanks, Larry, for letting me do the "Multimedia Projects for Teachers" class. Working directly with people who are doing what the book teaches really helped me understand what they wanted to know.

Thanks also to teachers like Donna Haswell, Karin Van Klaveren, and Maria Matteis, who are using computers and multimedia to make their classes more exciting and to get all kids involved in the creation of their own media projects. I know that they share with me a belief that if we can get kids started creating their own media images while they're young enough, they'll be able to see "the man behind the curtain" (to borrow an image from *The Wizard of Oz*) and be less susceptible to media manipulation as adults.

Another team that helped immensely is the crew at AltaVista Technology: Jack Marshall, Keith Queeney, Chris McConn, Glenn Nelson, and Karin Vogler. We all hope their "horror story" about getting the files for their product, MediaWrangler, to the CD-ROM publisher will help others avoid the same kind of problems that Jack had during the week between Christmas and New Year's, 1994.

Last, thanks to my personal friends and associates who put up with me, listened to crackpot ideas at all hours of the day and night, kicked me in the backside when I needed it, and pulled me along when that was the right thing. To Chris Kantarjiev, for having been the kind of best friend who kept me on the track of the possibility that I saw for the book, for myself, and for multimedia: thanks again. To Chuck Clanton, for having "too many good ideas," I appreciate the visualization and creativity exercises you helped me with.

To Torrey and Bronwen, my daughters, thanks for having put up with a father who never let them play on the computer: thanks, my darling girls. Wait till you see how great you and your stories look on the CD-ROM!

And most of all, thanks to my editorial assistant, proofreader, initial audience, reality checker, dialog coach, cinematographer, alpha tester, purchasing agent, diet partner, chief cook and bottle washer: my wife Kim. I couldn't have done it without you, O best beloved.

Chapter 1

Guided Tour

Contents of the Book and the CD-ROM

It's easy to be drawn in by the power of CD-ROM and multimedia. Color, motion, sound, interactivity: you get all the capabilities of a Hollywood production and more, on your desktop and under your control. Imagine the ways that you could use this same power in your own work, for your own purposes, in your own titles. If you are involved in teaching, communicating, explaining, or otherwise conveying information to other people, chances are you have asked yourself how you can use the power of CD-ROM and multimedia yourself.

This book explains how you can do just that, using a comparatively modest computer setup—probably with little more equipment and software than you may already have, either at your workplace or in a home office. It offers specific tips on how you can use your PC or Macintosh to create, edit, and distribute multimedia productions for work, school, or entertainment. It takes you through the steps required to plan, design, create, revise, and publish your own multimedia presentations on CD-ROM. There are sample files on the CD-ROM in the back of the book, all keyed to the exercises in this book, so that you can build examples of multimedia documents using the components distributed here. Additionally, the book offers suggestions and exercises to help you get started on developing your own multimedia titles, and there's even a list of some organizations and individuals that can help you with some of the complexities you may not have envisioned.

Teach Yourself Multimedia

If you're interested in doing your own multimedia documents, you can benefit from this book. It's meant to be a first step into the world of multimedia and CD-ROM, a guidebook for people whose professional, academic, or personal world is changing to involve some aspect of the production of multimedia titles. For example:

- Teachers are using multimedia documents to involve their students in learning in ways never before possible. Students at all levels, from first grade through post-graduate, respond to learning through multimedia, for all the same reasons we're interested in it: it's exciting, enjoyable, and best of all directly under the user's control.
- Marketing and sales departments are finding that packaging a sales brochure on CD-ROM lends it power, detail, and emotional impact that neither a four-color brochure nor even a videocassette can begin to match. By putting the prospect in charge of the information—and surprisingly enough, by putting them close to the information on their computer screen, rather than far from it as when viewing a videocassette—marketers are achieving far better retention, penetration, and acceptance of key messages. Sales catalogs, product marketing information, and almost any other kind of communication can benefit from this new medium.
- Training departments—whether in companies that manufacture a high-technology product or perform a basic service—find that internal training, as well as customer training, can be more successful if the trainee is allowed to follow computer-based materials at his or her pace. Better still, multimedia's random-access abilities let the trainee search for topics of interest easily, rather than shuttling a series of videocassettes to get to the right point in the training material. Customers like CD-ROM training material not only because the material can be more entertaining but also because of the control that they have over the pace and repetition of key portions of the course. In addition, most customers report that CD-ROMs make the company that produces them seem more on the cutting edge, both of technology and of customer service.

These categories of CD-ROM and multimedia users don't even take into account the most glamorous: producers of entertainment and game-related multimedia, whether for publishers like Brøderbund and The Software Toolworks or for independent distribution. CD-ROM is in the same stage that desktop computing was in about 1982 or 1983: the prevalence of games and entertainment software got all the publicity and generated all the excitement, but now, ten years along, the vast majority of desktop computers spend their time working on spreadsheets, sending electronic mail, or publishing business documents. The spread of CD-ROM drives is expected to follow the same trend, and as the number of drives increases, it becomes economically viable to reach a larger and larger audience by putting your message on CD-ROM. The matter is simple economics. Software companies today find that it costs about as much to package their programs on one CD-ROM as it does to use two 1.4 megabyte diskettes—but the CD-ROM can contain as much information as 471 of those same diskettes. The opportunity to include more content, more detail, and more features (and therefore to be able to charge more for the product) makes CD-ROM a particularly attractive solution for software publishing. It makes it equally attractive for publishing information, particularly when that information works best on a computer.

At the beginning of 1994, Dataquest reported that there were more than six million CD-ROM drives in the United States alone. That figure was expected to double during the year, and preliminary reports seem to indicate that growth might be even faster than expected. This means that by the time this book reaches your hands, there will probably be between twelve million and fifteen million potential users for a CD-ROM that you design, produce, and market. For those of you planning to sell a CD-ROM as a product, this is good news because it increases the potential market that you might expect to reach. For those of you producing CD-ROMs as an adjunct to your company's or school's regular product or service, it's equally good news as it makes it more likely for you to reach a wider audience (as well as easier for you to sell your financial controllers on the benefits of spending time and money on the project).

From the technological standpoint, there's no fundamental difference between designing a travelogue of bed-and-breakfast spots in the Santa Cruz Mountains and designing an interactive self-teaching guide to the plants and animals of the region. Whether you're designing a CD-ROM for entertainment or simply using the entertaining nature of multimedia to back up a sales, education, or training presentation, this book contains concrete, hands-on suggestions that can save you money, time, and headaches as you design, produce, and distribute your first CD-ROM title.

Authoring Multimedia Documents Today

If you don't have enough cause in your life to suffer from anxiety attacks and blind, wheezing panic, scan through any issue of *NewMedia* magazine and look through the ads and articles at the variety of solutions for multimedia authoring. This is not to say anything even remotely negative about *NewMedia*: it's easily the best periodical on the market for people interested in keeping abreast of the newest developments in multimedia software and hardware. If you are or hope to be a serious practitioner in the multimedia field, you need this magazine. What is negative is the overwhelming selection of multimedia authoring tools. As I write this, there appear to be hundreds of software packages that you might choose for one or more pieces of a multimedia project. In some fundamental way, literally any piece of software on your computer could provide content for a multimedia title. (If you doubt this, consider that some of the images included on the CD-ROM in the back of this book were manipulated by a screen saver program. The only thing I can think of that's a bigger stretch than that would be to record the sound of a modem and use it as a special effect.)

Instead, this book is a hands-on guide to using a few of the most popular and predominantly inexpensive tools on the two most popular platforms: the Apple Macintosh line of desktop computers, and PCs running Microsoft Windows. It covers authoring tools at a range of prices and capabilities, from inexpensive ways to do canned slide shows with recorded audio tracks to sophisticated interactive tools that can be used for games, computer-based training, entertainment titles, or other professional-level applications. The most expensive piece of software I talk about in this book currently retails for $795; the least expensive is under $30.

The equipment on which this CD-ROM was produced was simple, low in cost, and typical of what many home, small-business, and educational computer users already have or can buy inexpensively. As with so many things, you can literally spend as much money as you have and then some on computer equipment–buying additional memory, disk drives, software, add-on boards, and the like. The purpose of this book is to show you what you can do with a surprisingly modest investment in equipment, provided you plan well, think your project through carefully, and concentrate on making your presentation's content as good as it can be.

How simple is the equipment? On the Macintosh side, I'm using the new Macintosh 630, running a 68LC040 microprocessor that's been internally sped up to run at 66 MHz (but the bus still runs at 33 MHz). This particular computer has 8 Mb of RAM, an internal CD-ROM drive, and a 340 Mb internal IDE hard drive. It also has the single most crucial component for creating your own multimedia titles: a built-in video board, supporting Apple's Video Player software. I'll talk a little more about this later, in Chapter 7. For now, I'll simply say that I got into the habit of going off to shoot video, returning home, and watching the day's footage on the Macintosh because it was so much easier than using my VCR. This characteristic, by the way, is shared across the entire Macintosh AV product line—even on the more expensive systems that can offer better video capture quality.

On the PC side, I took advantage of a bundled system and selected a Compaq Presario 860 CDS. This machine also runs its processor (in this case, a 486SX2) at 66 MHz, and like the Mac keeps the bus operating at 33 MHz. What this means for both machines is that computation-intensive operations—such as compressing video or performing complex graphical calculations—take longer than the newest generation of Pentium-based PCs or Power Macintosh computers, where the whole system is designed to run at 60 to 90 MHz. As the cost of Power PCs and Pentiums continues to drop, both of my 66 MHz machines will look like dinosaurs compared to the price and performance of later equipment.

In fact, it's worth pointing out that the Compaq cost about the same as the Macintosh Classic II 4/80—an original-size, one-piece Macintosh with a small screen, a 15 MHz processor, 4 Mb of RAM, and an 80 Mb hard drive—that I bought two years previously. Technology becomes cheaper every season; you may need to ask yourself whether the cost of purchasing something now will buy you an edge in the time it takes you to begin producing your multimedia title, or whether you can put off additional equipment purchases for a few weeks. Recently one Saturday morning I gave a short presentation to a writer's group on how to get started in multimedia projects, and I quoted disk-drive prices from the previous week's newspaper ads from a local discount shop. When I returned home to read the paper, I found prices that were nearly two hundred dollars less than I'd quoted that morning. (If the prices keep moving downward at this rate, by the time the book sees print the disk drive makers may be paying you to use their equipment!)

The Compaq came with the popular SoundBlaster 16 sound board from Creative Labs, which was compatible with all the sounds I ran through it. Video was another story, and Chapter 7 tells about some of the options for capturing, compressing, and displaying video in the PC world. The short answer is that if you want an inexpensive, simple-as-making-toast solution to capturing video (but picture quality and performance are secondary), the Macintosh 630 wins hands down. For education applications, simple entertainment pieces, and many other applications where theater-quality video isn't critical, the Mac's built-in video capture (using QuickTime software compression technology) is more than adequate even at comparatively low frame rates. The speed and simplicity of using the Apple product makes it a serious consideration for anyone who's working on his or her first multimedia or desktop-video presentation. On the other hand, if you want TV-quality video, you can get it from either platform—you'll just have to pay a little more for it. RasterOps' Movie Pak for the Macintosh and Intel's Smart Video Recorder Pro are the price/quality leaders as I write this, but we'll discuss them more in Chapter 7.

On the software side, the Macintosh still reflects its early lead in multimedia authoring by the number of authoring tools that are mature, full-featured, or easy to use. And yes, I said "or," not "and." The simplest multimedia system for the Mac is Apple's own Media Tool, a drag-and-drop system for connecting screens (instead of cards in the HyperCard model), adding interactivity, incorporating QuickTime movies, and pulling together sound, motion, pictures and text into a single presentation. It's the best solution for people who don't want to learn a programming language, but who can use a word-processing program, a draw program, or any other software.

With a little more capability at a slight increase in complexity for some users, Claris Corporation's HyperCard 2.2 and up supports enough additional utility to be an effective authoring system for even complex and beautiful CD-ROM titles. The runaway success story of the CD-ROM marketplace, Robyn and Rand Miller's *Myst*, uses HyperCard to control its interactivity. (You'll hear about *Myst* a lot in this book, not only because it's the best-selling CD-ROM to date, but also because I'm a dedicated fan of this particular instance of what I feel is a completely new form of entertainment.) At the cost of having to write scripts (which are really no more complicated to learn and implement than, say, a sequence of DOS commands), HyperCard's features make it a more suitable system for more complex operations such as user-profiling, interacting with external programs, taking notes, and even rudimentary database operations.

Unquestionably, the premiere multimedia authoring software on the market, however, is Macromedia's Director, now up to version 4.0. Director has a steep learning curve and tremendous power, but it provides a number of features that make it the tool of choice for people who want to do Hollywood-quality presentations. The current version supports more complexity, a greater number of cast members, and is capable of sophisticated two-dimensional animation effects. As such, it's a great choice for doing games, children's presentations along the lines of the Brøderbund

Living Books series, and even adult-oriented instructional materials that rely on animation as well as video to make their point. If you want a mul timedia presentation that looks and feels like a motion picture with interactivity, save up your money and get Director.

For the PC, one option—though declining in popularity as PC solutions mature—is simply to use any of these authoring tools on the Macintosh, then save the resulting multimedia title in a Windows version. All three tools support this technique by offering a Windows player; in fact, many of the examples included on the CD-ROM began as Macintosh files and were copied to the Compaq after I saved them in Windows format. This is great news for Macintosh owners who want to tap into the 85% and more of the CD-ROM drives that are connected to Windows machines. It's less happy for people who have PCs and want to do their own development without spending another $1279 (today's suggested retail price) on the Macintosh 630 I describe here. But let's look at the history of multimedia development on desktop computers.

In 1991, the PC world was plagued by compatibility issues to the extent that at the San Francisco multimedia expo, many PC vendors of multimedia products devoted half of their show floor staff to making sure the equipment worked for a few minutes between crashes. That gave impetus to the Apple multimedia tools users; however, it's simply not the case today (at least to the degree it was in 1991). Modern PC multimedia software and hardware can still be a little more dodgy than it is in the Apple world, if only because there are more vendors for the PC, but there are a number of standard hardware and software solutions that make multimedia authoring in Windows almost as easy as (and potentially less expensive than) doing the same work on the Macintosh and porting the runtime version.

The good news for the "Intel inside" brigade is that you don't have to buy an Apple to make your own multimedia presentations. If you liked the sound of Director's capabilities, you can now purchase Director 4.0 for authoring—not just playback—on Windows. Another high-end tool for multimedia authoring is Asymetrix Toolbook, about which we'll read more later in some of the case studies from multimedia developers who put together their packages on PCs. The advantage of the size of the PC market means that there are comparatively inexpensive tools, such as the simple but effective MediaWrangler from Alta Vista Technology. It can be used to do some simple storyboard-like presentations and allows you to define sensitive regions, open additional illustrations, connect to video or audio clips, and otherwise create effective multimedia documents (if not in quite as polished and high-powered a way as you can with the much more expensive Director).

The best news for cross-platform development, however, is that whatever system you choose, the situation is worlds better than it was even two years ago. Today, many major software companies support cross-platform versions of their programs that can even share data files. During the development of this book, I became quite accustomed to removing a floppy disk from one computer and inserting it into the other, then reading its data with the appropriate tool. (To give credit where credit is due, it's primarily Apple's PC Exchange software that simplifies this; the Macintosh can read and write PC diskettes as easily as it can read its native versions, and most Mac versions of popular software—Microsoft Word and FrameMaker being the two with which I was most familiar while developing this book—now contain filters for handling cross-platform data files in their own or, in some cases, other applications' formats.)

Using This Book

This book is designed to be used next to your computer, while you work on your own multimedia presentations. (One tip: go to a good kitchenware supply store and look for a clear plastic cookbook holder. It's a good way to keep the book open to the pages of interest while you use your hands.) The key to using the book successfully lies in utilizing the selection of templates and multimedia content pieces on the CD-ROM in the back of the book.

Most people learn best by starting with a proven, working example and then modifying it to make it do what they want. If you've ever taught yourself a programming language, you probably did what most people do: start with the example in the book, then change lines a few at a time until the program does what you want. Other skills are best acquired in much the same way: even the most creative chefs usually start by following a known recipe exactly, then modifying it to fit their own imaginations, their own tastes, or the wishes of their customers. The multimedia samples on the CD-ROM are designed to let you do much the same thing: start with a known working beginning, then add components and change things around. In the process you will learn to develop your own sense of style, your own creativity, and of course your own skills in turning visions into presentations.

Nearly every chapter in this book contains two kinds of information: concepts and tutorials. The concepts open each chapter and give you the background you'll need to understand the chapter's contents. For instance, Chapter 5 talks about navigation, and describes some of the instructional and cognitive theory behind designing ways to help your users find their way around your title. The conceptual sections of the chapter lay the groundwork for the hands-on lessons that follow, much like the lecture portion of a college course.

The tutorials follow, and are keyed to sections of the CD-ROM. This section of the chapter points out items of interest in the information contained on the CD-ROM. The example sections use the fixed, prerecorded ("canned," if you prefer) multimedia samples to show you what the concept looks like in one example. If you follow the steps outlined in the tutorial sections of this book, using the files distributed on the CD-ROM and one of the authoring systems I describe here, you'll be able to make your own multimedia presentations using the pieces included on the CD-ROM as a kind of do-it-yourself kit. Once you see how these work together, you can approach your own projects with the knowledge that you have created a successful multimedia title already. You'll know many of the pitfalls to avoid in the design and implementation of your own documents.

Finally, some tutorials let you try out some of your own ideas by working from a given starting point but suggesting new directions, proposing different content, or recommending further study. One benefit to distribution on CD-ROM is that you can't erase the original files, so if you want to modify the book's examples after you've copied them onto your hard drive, go ahead: if you wreck one beyond any hope of ever making it work again, you can just copy it in from the CD and start over. The tutorials are paced to some extent by where they fall in the book; early tutorials offer much more concrete suggestions and procedures, telling you how to do something, while later ones assume that you've been working along with the text and tend to be less specific. As a result, the tutorials become much less concrete as the book progresses, with the idea that you've been absorbing the basics and are probably ready to reach out on your own. (This also means that those of you who start with Chapter 9 may be a little lost; if something doesn't make sense, keep flipping pages backwards till it starts to sound comprehensible. As good as interactivity and hyperjumping is for its own purpose, there is a time, a place, and a reason for linear information design.)

Remember, no single book can be a comprehensive guide to using every multimedia authoring program available today. With that in mind, each of the chapters includes examples with specific instructions—lines of scripting code, screen snapshots of files, or other detailed information—about how to use a few of the most popular (and generally the most simple) authoring tools. If you have a tool other than those mentioned in this book, use the reference manual that came with your authoring software to determine the exact steps you need to follow for the package you are using. The basic processes are similar across most authoring platforms; there are differences in terminology, menu selections, and scripting commands, but the purpose is similar.

About the CD-ROM

The CD-ROM is set up to be used by both Macintosh and Windows systems. The information is duplicated (where necessary) across the two platforms. Whether you're using this book to learn how to author a document in Windows or on a Macintosh, the basic content is similar. (In some cases it's identical: there are several examples on the CD-ROM that I authored on the Macintosh, saved in Windows format, and copied to use with the Windows player.)

From the standpoint of this book, there are two kinds of files on the CD-ROM:

- examples, which are fully functional interactive multimedia documents that you can view, use, and examine all you like; and
- components, which are raw data: video clips, compressed sounds, digitized images, and pieces of text that you can combine into your own multimedia documents.

The components should be the most interesting in the long run. They're meant for you to manipulate, experiment with, and get a feel for what it takes to put together a working multimedia presentation. They're like the ingredients in a kitchen; the examples are classic dishes that you can follow, but if you want to be a creative chef you'll have to make up your own recipes. The exercises in each chapter use these components to show you ways to put media elements together, and also to get you thinking about your own sense of style and composition. On the other hand, the examples show you a few ways of combining components to achieve what are at times very different results from the same basic material. I'll call out specific examples from time to time, as well as point you toward some of the components that I have included in order to make a point in the text. You'll get the most out of this book if you have a CD-ROM drive from which you can watch the action on screen while you read along, but it's not necessary. One of the beauties of the old-fashioned paper-bound book is that you can read it in bed, on the train, on the couch, or wherever you do most of your reading.

About the Video Clips

The video clips on the CD-ROM are all stored either as QuickTime movies on the Macintosh, or as QuickTime for Windows or .AVI files on the PC. This is becoming the most popular way of encoding video, but it's by no means the only way. There's more discussion about video capture boards in Chapter 7.

Video can be the most expensive medium, whether to produce, to convert, or to distribute. It's one you'll want to learn to use wisely, and the video clips included here demonstrate that. The basic rule of thumb is to use video only when you have no other way of showing the information. Effectively, this means using video to convey motion or to convey information that can only be taught dynamically or through seeing a change over time. A "talking head" is probably the worst kind of video to include, with panoramic shots the next worst: both show only information that could be conveyed with a sequence of still images and audio narration underneath.

For many applications, still images with interactivity and voice-overs can convey information as effectively as video, at a fraction of the storage space and without concerns about performance glitches. That's why one interactive example is a short tour of the plant life in some of the microclimates to be found in and around the Santa Cruz mountains. For such an application, it's the interactivity and control over content that makes the presentation work. Obviously you don't need video to sense the beauty and grandeur of an old-growth redwood forest or a sun-drenched canyon. However, having motion helps show you how the scenery changes in a short period of time—useful information when the subject is how close together two microclimates really are.

About the Audio Files

There are several kinds of audio files on the CD-ROM. First are the sounds that I recorded and captured as the audio portion of the QuickTime movies. On the Macintosh, the audio portion of a QuickTime movie is recorded in stereo if it comes in as stereo input. Since most camcorders now have dual microphones, you can hear things moving from right to left on your computer (assuming you have stereo speakers or headphones, of course). Other sounds were captured in analog form on a number of different media—probably the least efficient was a microcassette recorder which I then played into the microphone of the computer. One benefit to complex authoring tools such as Director is that many of them support using the computer's CD-ROM drive as the source for an audio track, playing music from an audio CD. (When using recorded music be sure that you have legal permission to include it in your final presentation. It may be tempting to put some sounds from your favorite artist in your title, but be certain you've done your homework first. At the back of the book is a list of resources for obtaining rights for use in multimedia, as well as a list of royalty-free CD-based audio and video sources.)

About the Interactive Examples

In addition to the component files that you can use to build your own test-case multimedia documents while you learn how to put them together, there are a number of short, finished interactive examples that you can use to see some of the principles demonstrated in this book. I used a number of tools to create these examples. Some tools are easy to use; some have a steeper learning curve. Some let you do only simple interactivity, combining different media elements into a linear playback document, while others let you define elements of interactivity dynamically during the authoring process, either as structural elements of your document or as arbitrary elements of the display.

On the Macintosh, you can run sample multimedia documents that I created using HyperCard, Apple Media Tool, Microsoft PowerPoint, and Frame Technologies' FrameMaker 4.0. Note that FrameMaker is something of a special case: it originated as a desktop publishing system and is still the tool of choice for many writers, publishers, and other people involved in generating high-quality, complex printed material However, with the release of version 4.0, Frame added easy interactivity with a full-featured set of hypertext functions intended to support electronic document distribution—for example, publishing reference manuals as interactive on-line help rather than as printed books. Additionally, Frame 4.0 provides a programmer's interface to external applications, which can be run at the push of a button. And finally, developers of Frame documents on the Macintosh can include QuickTime movies within the pages of their Frame files, just as they were previously able to import graphics and illustrations for use in brochures, books, magazines, and catalogs designed and published in Frame. This makes Frame, surprisingly, a highly effective tool for developing multimedia documents. It's a snap for making electronic books—that is, documents that look and work like printed books but have interactivity, video, and links to external applications. But if you think of Frame only as a glorified word processor that's only useful for creating manuals, catalogs, and other printed publications, you'll be surprised to see some of the on-line applications I've developed and included on the CD-ROM enclosed in this book.

There's one catch: you'll need your own working copy of FrameMaker or its on-line display-only version, FrameViewer, to see these documents in action. Worse yet, so will your audience if you choose to use Frame as your multimedia authoring tool. As FrameViewer costs about $200 per user, it's easy to hide the cost of FrameViewer if you're designing interactive training for a complicated computer system that costs your clients upwards of a million dollars, but if you're trying to sell a computer book for about $30, it's a little more difficult. However, Frame Technologies estimates that there are over 200,000 currently active license-holders for FrameMaker, meaning 400,000 people use the product regularly and upwards of 1,000,000 people (by their accounting) actually have access to a Frame license.

In fact, the issues of licensing and distribution rights for software used to view multimedia titles is a significant one, which I cover in more detail in Chapter 11—purely a coincidental number. Yet if you don't pay attention to the licensing agreements of your authoring and display tools, your organization could find itself involved in a Chapter 11 of an entirely different kind.

The examples on the PC use many of the same authoring media as those on the Macintosh, with a few notable exceptions. It's an odd thing to consider, but many professional multimedia developers use Macintoshes to author their documents, but then release their products on the PC. (One side benefit is that those of us who work in cross-platform environments now find very few incompatibilities in working with Macs and PCs in the same office.) Many of the examples enclosed on the CD-ROM were thus authored: I captured the video using the Apple Macintosh 630 with its easy-to-use RCA jacks (just above the keyboard port on the back panel), digitized them into QuickTime movies, then converted them to QuickTime for Windows and copied them to my Compaq.

However, Intel's Smart Video Recorder Pro board (suggested retail $549) provides a fast way to capture incredibly high quality video images directly on the PC. And it comes bundled with Asymetrix's Video Editor, a sophisticated way to combine video and audio inputs from two of each kind of source, composing a single output from them.

Another PC-native authoring tool used for a number of the examples is a simple but effective multimedia database product called MediaWrangler from Alta Vista Technology (suggested retail $299). The real surprise of this product is that it provides HyperCard-like interactivity—the ability to define sensitive regions anywhere on an image—with no programming, scripting, or typing of any kind.

Furthermore, this takes any image type you can throw at it on a PC—bitmaps, TIFFs, JPEGs, GIFs, text images, or whatever you happen to need. It also supports simple but moderately powerful database access tools so that you can categorize your images and search them by keywords, making it a good choice for interactive catalogs. MediaWrangler's biggest limitation is its lack of a built-in page design or screen layout tool. But because it will import any graphic file that you can store on the PC, you can use it with the output of something like PhotoStyler or some other image composition software. Best of all, there's a demo version of MediaWrangler included on the CD-ROM published with this book. You can't save your multimedia documents after creating them, but you can use the component files distributed on the CD-ROM or you can import your own images, text, audio and video. You can thus practice the exercises included in this book and try some of the alternatives suggested for your interface design.

Tutorial: Running the On-line Examples

For details on using all the examples on the CD-ROM, see Appendix B. which includes suggestions for using the on-line examples included on the CD-ROM.

Basically, you should need to do very little. On the Macintosh side, you'll have to make sure that you have a recent version of QuickTime, Apple's video compression and display tool. Most of the Apple video was digitized for display at either 256 colors or "thousands," as Apple calls it on the monitor selection.

What difference do these settings make? To find out, follow these steps:

1. Choose one of the video clips from the CD-ROM by opening the folder marked Video. To save time, choose a short one by setting the View menu selection to by Size and picking one of the video clips at the bottom of the list.

2. Copy the selected video clip to your hard drive by dragging the file from the CD-ROM to your hard drive. Make sure you have enough room on your disk. (This step isn't entirely neces-

sary, but the video performance is enhanced by running off your internal hard drive.)

3. Pull down the Apple menu and select Control Panels. From there, double-click on the Monitors control panel.
4. When the Monitors control panel opens, choose the button for Colors and select 256. (Be sure you have selected the button, located at the bottom of the panel, that reads Rearrange On Close; this makes your changes immediate, rather than requiring you to restart your computer.)
5. Run the video sample that you copied to your hard drive in Step 2. Notice the colors: they're a little blocky, not bad but not as smooth or as natural looking as a television video display. When the clip finishes, leave the file on your monitor.
6. Repeat Step 3, but this time when the Monitors panel opens, choose Thousands from the list of settings. (If your monitor does not support more than 256 colors, or if you are using this on a grayscale monitor, you will not be able to continue.)
7. Now run the video clip again. Notice the difference in the smoothness of the colors, in the realism of the shading, especially in skin tones (if you have chosen a video with people in it).

This is just one example of the kinds of choices you can make when you develop multimedia projects on your own computer. In later chapters in this book, you'll learn how to copy these video clips into a number of popular authoring tools, and how to design presentations using these clips. You'll also learn how to make your own video, how to design a good presentation that follows your vision rather than following the technology, and how to package the overall presentation on CD-ROM in a manner that makes it easy for your customers, students, or business associates to use your multimedia project when it's done.

Perhaps most important, you'll take the first steps on the road to managing your own perceptions of media. I'll close this chapter—and bring you into the underlying "author's message" of this book—with an anecdote. My wife and I were sharing an enjoyable gripe session about some ridiculous Hollywood project we'd read about—I can't remember exactly which project, but it had something to do with making a feature film based on yet another 1960s cartoon series. We were both lamenting the lack of vision, of creativity, and of originality in the entertainment industry, and complained about how imitative that industry has become now that billions are at stake in the production and distribution of every picture. After a few seconds of this, we chuckled over the way we were idly tossing off barbs at an industry that, if nothing else, is financially very powerful, and I made the self-deprecatory comment, "Everybody complains about the media, but nobody does anything about it."

And then I imagined a narrator's voice-over saying in a booming baritone, "UNTIL NOW." Computer-based multimedia really presents the opportunity to democratize the generation of media content in ways that haven't before been possible. It puts the power to create, manipulate, and distribute images, messages and content into the hands of almost anyone who has the vision to share and the dedication to do what it takes to carry it out. You may have only a modest project in mind, perhaps a brochure of your company's products or a CD-ROM to be used to train people in departmental procedures. Or maybe you're a teacher using multimedia projects to get your students turned on to the possibility of bringing their own dreams to life in the heads of others.

If these sound like what you want to do, then click OK—or rather, turn the page and let's dive in to the first step in the process: identifying the design skills you need and beginning to plan your production.

Chapter 2
Preparation

The Design Team and the Production Plan

Every great work begins with a vision. To some extent, the degree of greatness (or at least of satisfaction on the part of the original visionary) depends on how closely the finished product adheres to the original vision, which in turn depends on how clearly the visionary can explain what he or she only imagines, so that other people can contribute, assist, participate, and eventually share the same dream.

This chapter describes the process of defining your vision. It outlines the importance of a good production plan for managing the design and construction of your multimedia document in the kind of organization you're likely to require. Because the best multimedia documents arise out of someone's vision, this chapter talks about how to visualize the title in ways that will make it more real to you during the planning stages, and also make it easier to track how effectively you are following that vision. The importance of understanding your audience follows: they are, after all, the people responsible for paying you, either directly if they are clients or customers, or indirectly if they are students or trainees whose instruction is the primary focus of your job. Required skills lead to identification of the members of the design team—all, once again, based on the initial vision you have for the document. The chapter closes with a checklist of questions to ask yourself as you visualize your document in more concrete terms, as well as a suggested contents list for a typical production plan.

Colleagues and Collaboration

Defining your vision in terms of multimedia implies not only transmitting this vision to others, but also determining what skills you'll need to produce your document. This means identifying the people, talents, and resources you'll need to draw on to make your project happen. Likewise, this book assumes you are working within some constraints of time and budget—that you are producing multimedia training materials that need to be available when the product ships, developing a stand-alone presentation for a trade show that's coming up on a specific date, or scripting a teaching aid that needs to be installed in the computer lab by the time the students arrive in September. In such cases, you'll need to come up with a concrete plan that helps you define the milestone dates, the tasks to be completed, and any associated equipment, consultants, or other outside resources required to complete the project.

If you've never gone through a multimedia production before, answering the questions required to come up with this plan may well be the most important thing you learn from this book. I like to say that one day spent just thinking about a project is equal to four days spent working on it without having thought about it ahead of time. The numbers may differ for you, but the basic rule is sound: diving into a project without having considered its structure, its components, or the people and things you will require to complete it will cost you time, money, and sleep in the long run.

Having a plan not only helps you track where you are in the production of your vision, it also helps you convey that information to others—for example, to the management or administrators of your organization, to the publishers of the multimedia title on which you're working, or to whatever person or organization you're accountable to for the work you're doing. Doing a production plan early can also help with the proposal stage of your multimedia document for the same reason: a good plan, one that shows you've thought your project through and considered most of the risks, costs, and details beforehand, can help you get approval, funding, or other necessary resources before you start.

But before you can start a detailed plan, you need to articulate your vision for yourself, for the core team who will be working with you, and in a strange sense, for the project itself. Anyone involved with a project that results in the creation of some work, whatever the medium—in film, in music, and (I assure you) in books—has experienced the sense that the project seems to take on a life of its own. As a project gathers momentum, it develops a kind of internal consistency, based on its growing store of informational content, that can make it seem as though the project itself contributes to the process of its own creation.

In a sense, that's true: after a certain stage, there is enough structure and enough detail in a project that it is easier to decide, if nothing else, whether a proposed component doesn't fit—like a scene in a movie or a verse in a song that just doesn't go with what's already been done. A good plan can help accelerate this process, can help you and your colleagues jointly visualize the final product, and can breathe life into your creation a little earlier than if you were to begin working from a vague idea and you just let things sort themselves out.

But before you can plan, you need to dream, to imagine, to visualize. You need a mental image before you can articulate its components. Fortunately, that's a lot more fun than writing a plan, and it's a great way to begin to create your multimedia project.

Your Vision for the Document

What do you see when you imagine the finished product of your upcoming multimedia project? What does it look like? What does it do? Who is going to use it, and what do you hope they will get out of it? For the time being, ignore the question of how you're going to make this all happen—that's what the rest of this book will show you. At present, you're dreaming, imagining, visualizing: start thinking about what you want people to see when they slip your CD-ROM into the drive and run the player program.

What kinds of pictures do you want it to have? Will it have photographs of people, places, and objects, line art that describes relationships or processes, or fantastic computer-rendered scenes like those in *Myst*? Is there a particular emotion you want to convey to your audience? Even if your document is a fairly straightforward training or education title, the look of its pictures—and for that matter, the overall layout of its screens, menus, and any other visual elements it may have—will have an emotional impact on the people who encounter it. Engage your audience's emotions and they will absorb almost unimaginable quantities of information. (If you doubt this, ask a couple of soap-opera fans to describe the running plots, intrigues, and relationships in their favorite series. Then ask them how to program their VCRs. Which is really more complicated? Engage the emotions, and the memory will follow.)

In addition to the emotional appeal of your document, what do you want it to cover? For training, commercial, and educational multimedia—what I call nonfiction multimedia—there's often far less latitude, simply because you're dealing with an external information set, whether that set is part of a school curriculum or the features of a product you're demonstrating. Still, you'll need to think of the scope of your document, and think of it from the user's perspective. Let's cover the user—your customer—first.

Who's Going to Buy This, Anyway?

Defining your audience will help you define the document's scope, particularly if you're developing a nonfiction title. What you anticipate from them—their knowledge, as well as any prior experience you can assume they have with the topic—can help you decide how much information you need to put into your document.

Remember also that interactive multimedia gives you the opportunity, in ways that linear media such as books and videotape do not, to make detailed, contextual information available at the touch of a button, without interrupting the flow of your main subject. Chapter 3 discusses this in more detail, and Chapter 6 includes a tutorial on revealing hidden details that lets you make additional information available to people who need it.

For educational material, audience identification will probably also include the age, grade level, and other details about the students who will be using the document. Even for a pure entertainment title, whether it's a game or a piece of interactive fiction, you'll benefit from spending some time thinking about the people you hope will buy and enjoy your title.

An understanding of your audience and their ability to understand or relate to your subject is crucial to planning your title's content (at least for nonfiction titles). Once you know who is going to use it, you can consider what they're going to want and how much they can digest at a time. This can help you make some fundamental assumptions about the structure of your title: how long its segments should be, what kind of media to include, and what language and vocabulary you need to use to reach your audience. Perhaps the most fundamental assumption you need to make at this point is whether the title will more closely resemble an encyclopedia with talking pictures, a television program that you can flip through at random, or a rich digital world in which objects perform when selected.

Skills You Will Need

Once you have an idea of what you're going to put together, you have to take a long hard look at your own abilities, including your output level. If you're driving this project as well as several others, you'll need to consider how much you can really produce by yourself. Where is your information source? Who is going to take the video? Who will design and render your scenes?

Of course, you may not need different people for each of these skills. Many times the graphic artist can also process the video, the writer may be able to code the scripts required to drive the document, and the composer may turn out to have a wonderful voice for the narration. But you'll need someone to do all those tasks, and more. Here are some of the jobs that someone must perform in order to turn your vision into a finished CD-ROM on a bookstore shelf somewhere.

- **Project manager or producer.** In some ways, the producer of multimedia documents is concerned primarily with the business of production: schedules, resources, conflicts, milestones, and making progress against the deadline. The best producers, on the other hand, have their own creative stamp with which they imprint their titles. Brian Blum, producer of several successful multimedia titles while at The Software Toolworks, stressed the need to envision the finished multimedia product over the ability to track schedules on his complicated flowcharts.
- **Writer.** The writer needs to be reasonably knowledgeable on the subject of the document, but he or she also must have a thorough understanding of structural, modular, and interactive writing and how this differs from most other kinds of writing. Writing for multimedia involves tracking all of the places to which a piece of writing can connect elsewhere in the document (whether that writing shows up as text on the screen, as narration for a video, or as the implicit writing that goes into designing the contents of a screen or a sequence). Chapter 3 talks more about how structure, information partitioning, and modular design affect the writer of multimedia projects. For a detailed look at the concerns of writers in multimedia, see my companion volume to this one, *Multimedia Authoring: Building and Developing Documents* (AP PROFESSIONAL, 1994).
- **Art director.** As someone who loves stunning visual design and who struggles desperately to create adequate visual design, I tend to put art directors higher in the chain than many people in the industry do. I think it's because I envy these skills the most: the ability to imagine visually and then to lay out, execute, and follow through with such details as color, shading, character design, and motion—all the thousands of physical and visual minutiae that separate an outstanding presentation from a decent one.
- **Animator.** In addition to someone who understands visual design, you'll need someone who is technically skilled at using computer-based tools to turn these designs into motion, into models, and into part of your interactive document. Your

vision will tell you some of the details, such as whether the animator will work in two dimensions or three, what specific skills and talents your animator will need, and what tools your animator will use to create your document.

- **Photographer—still and video.** The skill of being able to see extraordinary images in life and capture them in ways that excite others is an important part of any multimedia project that includes pictures of real objects. The skills involved in getting good, clear images mean that someone on your team is going to have to know about photography, and in particular about the specific requirements of photographs that you plan to use in an electronic document. These requirements include considering lighting, clarity, the ultimate resolution of the image if you're scanning from film, and encapsulating motion if you're using video. Chapter 7 devotes specific instructions to getting the best out of video, including ways to use your video camera to capture still images.
- **Programmer or scriptwriter**. No, this isn't the kind of script you'd use to shoot a movie. In multimedia programming, a script is a piece of code that defines some action or condition under which the document runs. For example, it's common to write a script that plays a particular video clip when the user releases the mouse button, or a script that draws shapes and produces words on the screen when a particular image finishes loading.

These are by no means the only tasks involved in a really complicated multimedia document. For example, I haven't included musicians, voice actors, the sound effects crew (also called Foley artists), or any of the specialists whose skills make the document sound as good as it looks. If you're working with something for which music is an important part of the aesthetic whole, you will need someone who is correspondingly skilled in audio. And of course, you'll still need to have all the administrative work done, from technical administration such as making system backups and keeping the equipment running through basic business administration like handling correspondence and buying supplies.

If nothing else, you'll understand why most people in this industry keep reminding newcomers that multimedia is collaborative—it takes many unique and specialized skills to make a really great multimedia piece. What this book will show you, more than anything else, is how to identify your own strengths and weaknesses, then to sign up people who can manage the areas that you can't. If you need a musician, the time to get one into the project is at the beginning, not during the last week before shipment.

Planning early is the best way to do what you really want, rather than having to settle for what you can accomplish in the time you really have. And as important as it is for you to identify the people and skills you'll need, it's equally important for a computer-based multimedia project that you identify the hardware, software, and other equipment you'll need to have before you can realize your vision.

Tools You Will Need

The exact tools you will need depend on your vision for your multimedia document—not the reverse. Don't put everything on video because you have a video camera, or use only three-dimensional models because you've got Macromodel or 3D Studio. Think about what you want your document to be like, and what you expect your readers to get out of it. Are you teaching about some elements of objects you find in nature? You'll want photographs, video, and possibly some line art and 3D model work to show the details or to highlight specific points. Are you creating a fantasy world for an interactive game? 3D modeling is probably the right choice, as long as it has a sophisticated rendering system. What about animation versus video—which one is right for your application? Again, refer to your vision. When you know what you want your document to look and feel like, you'll know what tools you need to acquire.

To some extent, you'll need a few consistent items no matter what your vision looks like. You'll need some kind of authoring system that runs on the platform you are using. For the Apple Macintosh, popular authoring systems include Macromedia Director, Claris Corporation's HyperCard, and the Apple Media Tool. For the PC, Asymetrix Toolbook has been the authoring system of choice, though the introduction of Macromedia Director for Windows is expected to change that somewhat.

You will probably need video if you're planning to do educational or training titles. This book focuses on low-cost solutions using camcorders running VHS-C or 8mm video through a selection of video capture and compression cards. You can get reasonable video quality with camcorders that start around $500 today. The easiest and least expensive solution for the Macintosh is Apple's own TV/Video System, which is included in many configurations of the Quadra 630. This board uses three RCA jacks on the back of the computer to accept video input from a camcorder; you can also use the 50-ohm coaxial connector (that's the screw-in socket that looks like the one you use to connect cable to the back of your television) on this board for input, but most camcorders support the RCA jack option. At a suggested retail of $249, this is a budget option that provides decent-quality video for education and training. Its chief limitation is that you can have size or performance, not size and performance.

The smallest video window (160 pixels by 120 pixels) gives you 15 frames per second, which is half the frame rate of broadcast television and just over half the frame rate of motion picture film; it's still smoother than the frame rate used on most Saturday morning cartoons, for example, which are shot "on twos"—meaning that they shoot at 24 frames per second but only draw 12 frames per second, simply repeating each frame twice. But if you want the next larger image, which is half the height and half the width of a standard NTSC image (that is, 320 by 240 pixels), you'll have to settle for 7 frames per second. This supports relatively slow pans on relatively static images, but not much more. Of course, you can get faster video capture systems, but they'll cost more.

For the PC, Intel's Smart Video Recorder Pro (at a suggested retail of about $550) may be the best reason to do multimedia on a PC. The Smart Video Recorder Pro captures half-size NTSC images (320 by 240) at a full 30 frames per second. It comes bundled with one of several video editors; early versions came with Video Director, an easy-to-use tool for editing transitions between video clips, for combining audio and video from separate tracks into a single output, and other simple video editing effects. If your vision includes fast, smooth video that really looks like watching television on your computer, this is the way to go. Of course, then you'll need to make sure that your target system includes a multiple-speed CD-ROM drive, and that your customers have enough memory and enough of the right hardware to match the speed of your video.

You'll also need the workstation itself. What should it have? Basically, you should buy the fastest processor, the most memory, and the largest disk drive that your budget will permit. If you've already got a PC or a Macintosh, consider at least upgrading the processor and adding RAM. On the Intel side, if you're not already using a 486 as a minimum, get one, preferably one of at least 50 MHz. The 66 MHz 486SX2 is a fast processor that requires no special circuitry on the board, but it comes at a price: while the processor operates at 66 MHz (that is, its internal clock ticks 66 million times per second), its external bus—the connection to the other components in your system, such as memory and video—only runs at 33 MHz. What this means is that the chip itself performs calculations at 66 MHz, but the information that it can get to and from the rest of the computer system can only travel half that fast. (When I was shopping around,

I made up the mnemonic that the SX2 in this chip's designation meant that it "Seems like it's X 2.") The SX2 is still a hefty performance improvement over a 33 MHz 486, and it's like the difference between a propeller plane and a jet compared to a 386, but there's still room for improvement. If you can handle the cost of upgrading to a 90 MHz Pentium system, you'll be happier in the long run, especially if you're planning to digitize a lot of video or render complex 3D images.

On the Macintosh side, the obvious solution is a Power Macintosh. Barring that, Apple's low-cost 630 is a dynamite platform for creating comparatively simple, video-based multimedia. We used it for nearly all of our digitization, in particular for the projects we did in conjunction with the Sunnyvale school district, mainly because Apple computers are still the prevalent system in schools. Apple's 630 also uses a 33 MHz processor that's been internally sped up to run at 66 MHz, also operating in a 33 MHz environment. But if you can afford the money, get a Power Mac, or upgrade your older Macintosh to use the new technology.

As for memory, how much is enough? You will need at least 8 megabytes of RAM on either platform, and more if you can afford it. One advantage of a large amount of memory, on the Macintosh with its MultiFinder at least, is that you can have several applications open at once, which speeds up the ability to capture images, data, and text in one program and insert or edit it with another. Screen captures, for instance, are much simpler on a machine on which you can run Apple's SimpleText to snag the desired portions out of the snapshot, and then simply click on the window that contains your graphics editor (or select it from the MultiFinder) and insert the image you selected.

Cost-saving Strategies for Multimedia Production

You can save money on equipment purchases if you think carefully about what to buy and when you will need it. Probably the best way to proceed is to start with a bundle, buy as much as you can afford, and then wait for opportunities to upgrade, improve, or add on later.

Bundles let you begin with a complete computer system, particularly important if you're planning to do cross-platform development; it means you can acquire a system with which you can come up to speed, if you're unfamiliar with the system. Macintosh users who find themselves wanting to pursue the large Windows market will find it easier to buy a complete, thoroughly engineered system all at once rather than putting it together piecemeal. This avoids frustration when you find that one upgrade is incompatible with something you did several months ago.

And as a general rule, buying the fastest processor, the most memory and the largest disk drive you can afford at once may cost a little more than waiting for sales, but if you buy carefully you can find thousands of dollars of software packaged with the system you purchase.

Once you have your basic platform, you can then add on RAM to make tasks easier and faster. Most systems these days come with 8 Mb of RAM; this isn't enough for multimedia work, especially if you need to have programs like Photoshop, Persuasion, and Frame all running at the same time to simplify pasting media from one application to another. The number that most developers agree is the best balance of price and performance is 24 Mb; it'll increase your ability to work without having to close applications, restart the computer, or use virtual memory (which has very unhappy effects on video capture).

You can also add on storage as you see your disk's free space shrinking. I talk about the continued drop in storage device cost elsewhere, but it means you can save hundreds of dollars by filling up the disk drive in your workstation first, then adding a fast SCSI external device later on. Two gigabytes won't be too much if you're planning to do extensive video or animation work; it's surprising how easily you can fill up 100 megabytes once you start editing files, leaving multiple copies, and keeping originals.

Speaking of video, the best approach is to buy the camera first if you don't already have one, get familiar with it, and learn to shoot decent pictures. Once you see what you're capable of, you may very well decide you need to hire a photographer. If the system you purchase doesn't come with its own video capture card or capability, you can decide later what video capture card you want, based on what you want to produce and how you want it to look. But the video quality will depend largely on the skill of the person with his or her eye to the viewfinder; if you're not experienced with taking video, start learning now and you'll end up with much better results.

The software you'll need varies first with the platform you choose and then with the kind of CD-ROM you want to create. Start designing your production first, and you'll see during the design phase when you need to buy what. I had a great amount of video before I decided what 3D package to buy, and I saved hundreds of dollars while digitizing numerous video clips and working with "real" images; likewise, the actual authoring package can wait, especially if you use some of the cheaper tools I talk about here to produce proof of concept pieces, samples, demos, or whatever. If you're aggressive, you may be able to show these demo pieces to investors, potential business partners, or others who can give you the financial backing you need to buy more expensive equipment.

How Long Will This Take?

One of the trickiest parts of planning any project is estimating how long it's going to take to complete it. This becomes even more complicated, not to mention more significant, when the project is tied to external deadlines such as the shipment of a product, a trade show, or the first day of a semester. The reality for freelancers is that deadlines are typically just as firm as they are in the corporate or the academic world, because with few exceptions, freelancers rely on the corporate world for distribution, publication, marketing, and production. Either way, whether you're putting together an elementary-school science program about the life cycle of bats or writing the Great American Novel as an interactive series of digital paintings with music videos and special effects, sooner or later you'll run into the need to deliver a finished product on a given date. This is vastly simpler if you think about it at the beginning of the project, at the design and planning stage, than if you wait till half the time has elapsed and you're stalled.

The problem is that this is the only area that nobody in multimedia likes to talk about. I'm not sure why; if you ask people technical questions about what software they used, how they shot a scene, how they compressed the video, how they indexed the movie or anything else, most multimedia developers will continue giving you rich details of the entire process long after you've fallen asleep. It's one of the nicer parts about the multimedia industry as it stands today: most of the practitioners are real enthusiasts, dedicated to promoting the art form as a legitimate way of conveying information, and therefore they'll share anything they can that they think will help other people buy into the concept.

But when you ask "How long will it take?," you're apt to meet a stony silence, or at best some fairly confusing and indistinct information. Part of this is legitimate: it's like deciding how long it will take to write a symphony. All creative projects face this issue; if for some reason the author gets stuck, the project stops till he or she gets going again. Part of this reluctance, I suspect, is also due to the fact that it's a new field and most of us who work in it still find ways to shorten the time while retaining quality, simply because we learn something new from every project. Similarly, because it's still new, we haven't encountered every possible flaw in project development. I know I'm sometimes reluctant to commit to a definite date when I've undertaken a completely new kind of project.

There's one other question I've asked myself, though, and that's whether some people are simply trying to avoid letting the client know how little time it'll really take. With some of the tools I've talked about in this book, you can put together final presentations, slide shows, interactive browsers, and even full multimedia books in much less time than the finished product would lead you to believe (depending on how much of the media is already available, versus how much you're going to have to create). The state of the software art is now such that it's possible for creative, professional people—not programmers—to build good-looking, powerful, effective presentations in a matter of a few hours to a few days, given the right experience and the right media.

So having given that huge disclaimer about scheduling things in this industry, here are several estimating rules used in two related industries—video production and technical publications—filtered through advice learned from developing multimedia projects. When using any of these rules as a formula for calculating your own project's duration, staffing level, or completion dates, remember to take into account your position on the learning curve, and that of your staff.

- Technical publications departments of major computer companies often use, as a planning tool, an estimate of three pages per day per writer to determine the staffing level and project duration. (All you writers who can crank out 25 or 30 pages a day shouldn't really feel all that smug—this daily page count includes time spent in meetings, research, the weeks that a project is out for editing, and the like. In other words, it includes not only the typing, but also the time spent staring out the window wondering what the heck to say next.)
- For estimating the production time for video, which has always been a collaborative field more like multimedia production, the rule of thumb is to estimate one day for every minute of video shot, edited, and produced. Again, this doesn't mean that the photographer shoots 60 seconds of tape and knocks off for the day: it includes time spent on retakes, on writing and revising the script, on mixing the sound track, and on editing the raw footage into a finished, polished presentation.

As much as these industries are related to multimedia, and as much as they feed the content and the tools that multimedia producers use, they're not exactly the same. You'll have to get a feel for how long it takes you and your team to create the kind of documents you want. The best way is to start with some of the examples and exercises given in this book, get a feel for how productive you can be, and then give it your best shot.

What Might Go Wrong?

We all know about the best-laid plans. The most successful plans—as opposed to the best, and there can be a significant difference between them—are the plans that take into account what can go wrong and have some contingency in place to deal with mistakes and problems along the way. Plans that consider the risks and contingencies involved in producing a multimedia title also make better proposals, particularly if you're making the proposal to a conservative organization.

In addition to risks, consider any dependencies that might affect the outcome of your plan. Are you counting on the new release of a particular software product to provide some needed function, such as search or bookmarks? This is a crucial dependency, which implies a risk. What will you do if the company lets its deadlines slip and releases the product three months late? Having a contingency plan for this eventuality can save you headaches, money, and maybe even your job.

Much of the art of planning is in anticipating potential failures and being able to adapt your original plan to take these into account. It's a sometimes ugly part of the planning process—few of us like to imagine problems with our creative projects—but it's one that can save a tremendous amount of difficulty later on.

Tutorial: Making a Production Plan

This tutorial consists of two parts: a series of questions and a suggested outline for your production plan. The questions will get you thinking, in fairly concrete terms, about your multimedia title. You can write your answers separately or you can make short notes here in the book's margins or under each question. (As an extra-credit exercise, consider how you might adapt this tutorial to interactive multimedia, and the ways you might be able to use the answers to help fill in the blanks in a prestructured production plan.)

The questions represent what I ask myself when beginning a project, as well as questions that a number of multimedia producers, publishers, and developers have contributed. These are all issues that you will face in preparing to design and produce your own interactive CD-ROM title.

1. What does your document accomplish? Does it teach, sell, demonstrate a product, entertain, or perform some combination of these?

2. What do you want your document to look like? Do you want it to look like a computer program, with menus and buttons and obvious controls? Do you want it to look like a book or a brochure, with text laid out around visuals and some kind of control for turning pages electronically? Do you want it to look naturalistic, representing some kind of environment with which you can interact through analogs of the real world, like clicking on a picture of a tree to find out more about it or clicking on the left edge of a picture to see what's in that direction?
3. What skills are your strongest? Are you a writer, an artist, a programmer, or a visualizer? Are you better at details or at concepts?
4. What skills (you knew this was coming, didn't you?) are your weakest? Are you incapable of drawing anything more complicated than stick figures? Does the thought of nit-picking the code required to implement a program fill you with frustration and loathing? Do all your pictures come out sideways and blurry, even with an autofocus camera?
5. If you could pick one other person to work with you, what skills would that person have to master to make your vision come into being?
6. How much information are you planning to put into this multimedia title? How much of it already exists? How much of it is likely to be in a usable form—that is, if you are planning to put a brochure in multimedia form, can you use the existing pictures and text and simply scan them into the computer? Are they already on the computer?
7. How much time do you actually have to spend working on this, given your current workload (assuming that you are taking on this multimedia project, as are so many people, in addition to your regular job as a teacher, marketing specialist, training coordinator, or whatever gives you the expertise you are trying to encapsulate)? How does this fit with some of the time-estimation techniques in the section entitled "How Long Will This Take?"
8. How much money do you or your department have to spend on software, hardware, and collateral material (training courses, books, and supplementary CD-ROMs) to shorten the learning curve?

All these elements will go into your production plan in one way or another. The answers to questions 7 and 8, in particular, affect one another intimately, though in a nonlinear fashion—more money usually means you can get things done in less time, but taking more time usually ends up costing more money anyway.

As a basic outline, your production plan should contain the following components:

1. A brief description of the project: title, synopsis, a little about the look and feel, and the highlights of the planned document. (If you are writing this as a proposal, be sure to come up with what editors call a "hook" in the opening paragraph—a compelling reason for the document's existence, a problem for which your document is the solution.)
2. An identification of the audience for your document—for example, users of your company's database product, students in the second year of college physics, or potential buyers of your multimedia design service.
3. A brief description of the document's scope, in terms of its size—the number of pages of text, screens of graphics, minutes of video, and other measures of its depth and, to some extent, complexity.
4. An outline or prototype storyboard for the document. This should include references to interactivity wherever required, as well as short descriptions or sketches of the contents of each screen, module, or other unit of your document's structure.
5. A brief discussion of some of the risks involved in the plan, such as waiting for unreleased software (even when it has been promised by the vendor!), dependencies on other projects for funding or personnel, the risk of new computer equipment not working properly for some time, and the like. Wherever possible, outline contingency plans in case one or more of the risks becomes a reality. Have a fallback position.
6. A list of the milestones for the production of your document—when narration needs to be written, when it needs to be recorded, when music production and graphic design needs to begin, and the like.

There are a number of project-management programs available for both the Macintosh and Windows platforms. You might wish to spend some money on a productivity tool like MacProject, one that builds automatic schedules, charts, and diagrams so that you can point to the areas of concern. For some organizations and some projects, this is overkill. I achieve good results using a simple spreadsheet to track my projects, but then since my multimedia work supports printed books, I track it by page count, which is easy for a spreadsheet to manage. You will gain the greatest benefit from the tools you use to track your projects by simply understanding everything that's going to go into your project—the scenes, the modules, the kinds of media, all the components—before you begin working on the project itself.

Fundamentally, the production plan is a blueprint of your title; the more detail you can put into it (within reason and a sense of the appropriate amount of time), the easier it will be to track your project and to convey your understanding of the project's status (as well as its vision) to other team members, especially to team members who join later in the process.

Review: From Vision to Visualization

This chapter discussed some of the important parts of planning your multimedia title: the skills, the tools, and the plans that make the difference between throwing something together and planning a complex project that realizes a vision. It suggested some of the people you might need to hire in order to make your vision a reality, or at least the kinds of people you'll need to consult if you make this multimedia document with only the staff you may have (or, if you're a teacher, if you have to make this document by yourself in what you used to jokingly call your "spare time"). It also offered a couple of schemes from related industries (technical writing and video production) that might help you estimate the time required to produce the multimedia document you really want. Finally, it asked questions to help you identify your own strengths and weaknesses, and outlined the basic contents of a multimedia document production plan.

In the next chapter, we'll move from the basics of multimedia planning to planning the basics of multimedia: the structure of on-line information and the first stages in visualizing your project. We'll see how a sixty-year-old technique for making motion-picture cartoons can be adapted to help you design, produce, and track interactive digital multimedia.

Chapter 3
Structure

About On-line Information

Whether you're talking about a multimedia entertainment title, the on-line help for an application program, a CD-ROM encyclopedia with video and audio clips, or an electronic catalog for choosing and ordering clothing, on-line information has one thing in common: structure replaces sequence as the underlying conceptual basis for its construction, interface, and use. The fundamental reality of electronic information is that you can get anywhere from anywhere else, with an ease and a speed that most paper documents can't begin to match (though there are exceptions). What this means for developers of interactive documents is that you have to consider much more than the basic flow and components of a document when designing for electronic delivery. You have to consider how the pieces of information fit, link, and connect with one another to create a network of learning inside the user's intelligence.

Some of the skills involved in this stage of document design may be new to you, so this chapter and some of the books in the bibliography can help you master the concepts of structured rather than sequential document design. This book concentrates on the application of this new kind of structural model to some of the types of documents you might put on a CD-ROM. It also introduces a concept that may be familiar to some of you, but that may also have a few new wrinkles even if you've used it in other forms: the storyboard, with a few modifications to take interactivity into account.

Fundamentally, understanding the structure of the information in your document involves the ability to see the component parts of a subject, to think in terms of how the micro-level components fit into the macro-level picture, and to analyze a topic for its internal dependencies and connections. There are a number of specific disciplines that teach these skills; I use the phrase "information partitioning" to describe the task of analysis and structural outlining that goes on at this stage.

One of the best tools for modeling modular document design is a modified version of the old animator's standby, the storyboard. This chapter shows you how to use a storyboard to keep track not only of the dramatic elements in a given point of view within the document, but also how each of the pictures in your storyboard can let you list the ways that you interact with this module, or at least the modules to which you can get from the one at which you're looking. The tutorial in this chapter is on making a storyboard, and takes you through the steps of designing a storyboard based on your house or apartment.

Before getting too far into storyboard development, however, consider the information that it represents. In traditional animation, the storyboard tracks only the sequence of images that make up the dramatic thrust of the film; originally, the storyboard replaced the shooting script in the early days at Disney Studios. But a storyboard for an interactive document needs to track more than the images that make up the visual portion of the title—a multimedia storyboard must also track the interactivity, keeping a record of where the user might come from and where the user might go, in effect tracking the relationship of every element in the title to every other element. In many ways, a multimedia storyboard is not so much a map of the document's flow, because the flow will vary from user to user, as it is a map of the document's structure. And because structured document design is still a relatively new field, it's worth spending some time discussing how this affects you and the storyboards you will design for your multimedia titles.

What Is a Structured Document?

Electronic document designers—not only multimedia designers, but those involved in the design of browseable databases, on-line documentation, and other electronically delivered forms of information—have adopted the phrase "structured document" to highlight the single most crucial design difference between an electronic document and a paper document. In designing a paper document, you (or your layout artist) need to consider the appearance of different elements: headings, chapter titles, body text, table and figure captions, column widths, all the elements that go into page layout. In the paper world, you might use typeface, type size, color (if you have the budget), white space, and other design elements to set off certain pieces of the copy for visual impact. Good design leads the eye to the important spots on the page, and sets up a dynamism and a flow that makes it easier for someone to read your document.

In the electronic document world, all these same elements apply in theory (if more rarely in practice). However, electronic documents mix in an additional requirement: the elements that lend this visual dynamic to the document's appearance must also convey—to the program that displays the document as well as to the human being who reads it—the element's position and, to some extent, its purpose in the document's overall design. In an electronic document, a section subheading not only indicates to the reader's eye that a new topic (but one that is subordinate to its predecessor) begins at this point, but it is also the key for the document browser, hypertext engine, or other electronic display medium that identifies this element in the entire document so that the user can find it, return to it, and can navigate with respect to it. Unless the program knows what this subheading is and where it falls in the document, it can neither display the information nor guide the reader to it in the first place. In this sense, the subheadings (as well as paragraphs of text, figures, and the rest) make up structural as well as aesthetic components of the document.

This should come as no surprise to careful writers, whether you have ever done an electronic document or not. Good writers of nonfiction have always used subject headings, chapter names, and other elements to provide cues to the reader about what's coming next, what information they can expect, and what function the following text performs. And good layout artists have done the same thing, using the appearance of text to set up a consistent mental image in the reader of what kind of information to associate with a given typeface, margin, or color. The only real difference is that in the paper world, the physical constraints of pages, binding, and signature sequence control the structure of the document. In the electronic world, in which interactivity makes it possible to move between any two elements in the entire document with equal ease, the writer needs to understand, control, and use the structure of document elements to let the reader know what's out there.

If you're adapting an existing work to the electronic world, you will probably end up using most of its implied structural elements—chapters, subheadings, and the rest—as the explicit structure of your electronic document. Good information design considers the user's search for knowledge at any point in the document, and to some extent the method of delivery doesn't matter. But not all existing works have the kind of structure that best suits electronic delivery. For example, you might end up working with multiple-page subsections within chapters for which there is no clear way to create subheadings or a table of contents that will cue the reader to the content. It's almost as much effort as designing a new work in the first place.

If you are designing your own document for electronic distribution, you need to consider all the elements that I discuss here (as well as in much more detail in the companion volume to this one, *Multimedia Authoring: Building and Developing Documents*). One of the key techniques that I use for determining structure in the design phase of an electronic document is information partitioning. In some ways, this is little more than a catchy phrase describing a way to write outlines; it's not difficult to learn, and you may well have been using the fundamental principles already—most careful writers do in one way or another. But to succeed in electronic information design and to make usable documents for distribution on CD-ROM, it's a concept that you'll need to master.

Matching Components with Connections: Information Partitioning

Information partitioning carries with it the inference that you will be separating the information into units that stand alone in some ways, but that are connected to the remainder of the information in others. Just as the partitions between cubicles in an open-floor office separate while joining, the partitions between information as you form your mental model of the subject are both separations and connections. It's this duality that you need to master for interactive information design: the way that information has context as well as content in the on-line world.

Information, in this sense, resembles an atom. Individual pieces of information are like individual atoms: they are distinct in some way, yet they aren't terribly significant. It's the structures they make up, whether atomic or informational, that give them significance. Information becomes knowledge when people can connect the individual facts they know in ways that add meaning to their lives, give them new skills, or otherwise enrich them beyond the simple possession of the facts. As you partition your information from a complete subject into individual atoms, remember that it's the connections between these atoms that make up knowledge.

By information partitioning, do I mean writing down the individual facts on index cards (or on records in a database) and sorting them? Personally, I'm never that organized, though I've known people who do much the same thing. For me, information partitioning means studying a subject, learning how it works, what it's made up of, and how it's put together, and then continuing to pick it apart mentally until I believe I have the atoms of information that I need to rebuild my understanding of the subject.

One technique that's useful during information partitioning is to look for pieces of information that contain other pieces of information within them. Keep exploring until your understanding is at the level of individual facts, discrete items, or information about a part or a step out of a procedure that has no smaller parts within it. This can help you identify the dependencies that exist within the information structure. Often, these dependencies will give you clues to how you will have to organize your presentation, document, game, or other multimedia document. In some ways, this is much easier for those of you specializing in nonfiction multimedia such as encyclopedias, how-to CD-ROMs, educational titles, or titles like *How Multimedia Computers Work*.

In nonfiction, you usually have the object from the physical world to which you can compare your information, or your understanding of the information. A CD-ROM about auto maintenance, for instance, might use as its information atoms the specific techniques for using various tools, or for removing individual parts from the car for repair and replacement. Each of these components of a car—oil filters, tires, air filters, battery cables, and spark plugs, to name a few common maintenance items—not only has its own existence, function, appearance and details, but it also has a structural role to play in the car itself, and therefore in the information. Partitioning the auto repair CD-ROM down to this level not only determines some of the atoms of information, but at the same time determines some of the network of connections between them.

Alternatively, you can divide the information in your subject into the smallest meaningful pieces: paragraphs, pages, perhaps even sentences for text-based documents like encyclopedias, catalogs, or even electronic magazines. Perhaps most effectively, you can partition your information into chunks that fit the human beings who will be reading it. Part of this is audience analysis: determining who you think will use your document and what they are likely to want out of it, even down to such issues as vocabulary use, sentence length, and other stylistic minutiae. Perhaps more important is an understanding of the human-factors issues that govern attention span, memory retention, and comprehension.

Attention Span and the Short-Term Memory

In the 1950s, psychological researchers in the aerospace industry determined that most people could store a fairly fixed number of facts for a specific period of time. The part of the brain used to store this information came to be known as the short-term memory; the number of facts was roughly seven, sometimes as many as nine and sometimes as few as four or five. Later, the number came to be expressed as "five plus or minus two."

As a "magic number" for human learning, five plus or minus two is a good place to start for determining the scope of certain components of your multimedia documents. If you require people to remember certain bits of information from one screen, card, or presentation to the next, you'll have more success if you keep the information to about five pieces.

Likewise, as the researchers found that the brain could hold this number of pieces of information, they also found that this information lasted in the brain for between 15 and 30 seconds before it had to be refreshed. The specific application was for people using printed manuals: the research led to a specification for manual design in aircraft maintenance operations that meant no one would have to remember more than five plus or minus two things to do for more than 15 to 30 seconds, the length of time it would take to look away from the manual, perform the task on the aircraft, and look back.

In multimedia nonfiction, you have a distinct advantage over the people working on those aircraft manuals in the 1950s. Whereas the mechanic on a jet had to look at the book, then turn away to perform the task, your readers will be sitting at the computer they're using while they're watching your multimedia presentation. This kind of close, face-to-face interaction with the material gives you an edge in reader concentration, in the amount and richness of the information you can convey in a single screen, and, if you design well, in the complexity of possible interactions with the user.

In multimedia fiction, of course, the aesthetics of your piece should rightly take precedence. There are other concerns for partitioning the information inherent in interactive fiction: advancing the plot, setting the mood, fleshing out characters, and creating an artificial environment in which the viewer can become lost. Interactive fiction still requires all the elements of a short story, novel, or screenplay; you just have to divide them into chunks that can stand by themselves and connect with each other in a fairly limited set of standardized ways.

On-line Reading Habits and Constraints

Readers of information presented on line approach it with a slightly different set of expectations, requirements, and even physical capabilities than readers of printed matter. Yet surprisingly few of these characteristics resemble watching television. Part of this is simply due to distance from the monitor. Some of the early studies into using interactive television as a way of broadcasting games discovered that people who watch television tend to do so from across the room, making them feel less involved with the information source; people interact far less with television-based games than they do with computer-based games, where they sit an arm's distance from the monitor.

Reading electronic documents follows the latter model more closely; readers find themselves wanting to control the display of the document to a much greater degree than they do the display of a television show (and no jokes about hogging the remote, thank you very much). Interactive readers of electronic documents bring the computer-game paradigm to the material, and expect a similar level of interactivity (if not necessarily the same fast pace) from the document.

Additionally, few of the specific characteristics discussed in this section relate to the design of interactive video, graphical documents, or other nontext elements of multimedia design. If you're designing a multimedia title that will be exclusively video, the issues of type design and text layout don't affect you and you can skip this section and jump ahead to "Modular Design for Interactive CD-ROM."

If you're already a professional who uses electronic publishing tools to create documents, you may well be too close to the problem that many people face as they approach electronic documents for the first time as readers. Technical writers, journalists, authors, and others who make their living pounding a keyboard connected to a computer screen are already familiar with many of the tricks for remembering where you are in a document, what you've already said, and to some extent what comes next. You can probably back up a page or more without having to think about what to do to make the computer display the information you want; you probably use section headings not only as cues for your brain about what follows but as cues for your eye to indicate how far below or above a heading you can look for a certain piece of information. In extreme cases, you probably know the keystroke or menu sequence required to bring up your program's search mechanism to look for a word or phrase that has eluded your other efforts to find it.

If you nodded your head while reading the last paragraph, then you have at least a basic empathy for the problems facing your potential readers. You, however, have an advantage. As the author of the material you have at least a passing familiarity with what you said and where you said it. The purpose of your document's structure is to replace some of this familiarity with cues that a new reader can use to find crucial pieces of information. To understand how to do that, you need to consider some basic information about how people approach electronic information.

Typeface and On-screen Layout

First, consider typeface. No screen made today delivers the kind of resolution, clarity, or detail that a printed page does. Typesetters deliver resolution at rates above 2000 dots per inch (nearly a thousand per centimeter); most computer monitors are closer to 100 per inch (40 per centimeter). This means that many elements you might have used on a page simply won't work on screen. One such element is the serif: the attractive little decorations at the ends of a stroke on characters in typefaces such as this one (Palatino, 11 point with 13 point leading). Serifs add a nice visual touch to books, but on many screens they do nothing more than add blur and eyestrain. You may want to consider a sans-serif font such as Helvetica, Geneva, or Arial for the displays you include in your document.

Likewise, type size is important for ease of reading on line. The clarity of a phototypesetter makes this 11-point type readable on the page; as I type this on the screen, it looks small and crabbed. Some typefaces are worse than others in this regard; in Times Roman at certain sizes, it's difficult to tell lower case e from lower case a when both are used in combination with certain other letters, making proofreading on line a chore at best. Most readers find that 12-point type is preferable for on-line reading, where glare and reflections can add to eyestrain. Many readers find that 12-point type is preferable for reading on the printed page as well, but 11-point type keeps the page count, and therefore one aspect of publishing cost, down.

If you are looking to publish a document that is primarily text, and you want a solution that includes the possibility of printing hardcopy versions on demand, check the tool you use. Frame Technologies' FrameMaker and FrameViewer products give you control of the magnification of the on-line document independent of the typeface and size. For example, you can design a document that uses 11-point type to keep the page count down when readers print it, but you can distribute the document electronically with the viewer set at 120% or 140% magnification, effectively using 14- or 15-point type for the electronic version. (Note that due to the size of the dots on a computer screen, some magnification levels make ungainly curves on the letter forms; if you adopt a solution like the one suggested here, test a number of settings to find one that looks the best.)

Now, how much of this 12-point type should you include in a module? Several concerns add to this issue. First are the human-factor concerns about short-term memory—five plus-or-minus two pieces of information for no more than 15 to 30 seconds. However, this is more a concern for paragraph design than for module design; a good paragraph needs about four sentences (a topic or lead sentence, plus two or three supporting sentences). For purposes of electronic text design, it's a good rule of thumb to try to keep about seven (plus or minus two) paragraphs for each subheading. In the world of structural document design, subheadings make good module markers, with the paragraphs between them containing the content of the modules. You can add more information if required, but a rough consistency will enhance the reader's sense of pace and flow in your material. (Chapter 6 contains a tutorial, "Revealing Hidden Details," that shows you ways for dealing with the need to include information beyond the basic flow of the module.)

Modular Design for Interactive CD-ROM

This chapter has already talked about modules as they relate to multimedia documents. While the term is becoming well known and the context here will provide a basic understanding, there are some specific elements of a module, as it pertains to all kinds of CD-ROM documents, that require additional study. These elements of a module affect the way you code it into your document, the way you determine its content, and the way you link it to other modules in your title. The module is the basic, fundamental structural element of your document.

So what is a module? We've talked about size—seven or so paragraphs of text, if you're doing an electronic book, or 15 to 30 seconds of video if you're asking people to remember a task and perform it. If you're doing an entertainment piece, a module might be stretched to include an entire scene from some structural viewpoint: for example, an exchange of dialog between two characters that establishes background, or a crucial plot element, or a dramatic confrontation. If you want an example of a module in a performance-based work of fiction, look at how Shakespeare constructs scenes within the acts of his plays. Every scene is self-contained inasmuch as it has its own flow, its own dynamism, and its own action; however, the scenes link together to form the acts, which in turn flow into the overall play. There are probably no better examples of structure, or of modules, in fiction than these. They encapsulate their message in context with the rest of the play in important ways that multimedia designers can learn from today. And unlike chapters in a book, the scenes in a play are meant to be performed—they have an inherent time element in their design that makes them particularly adaptable to interactive documents.

In addition, however, multimedia modules need to provide some kind of explicit linking, coding, and programmatic connection to the remainder of the document. In this way, a module is more like the source of its high-tech-inspired name: a unit of function in a structured program, also called a module. Program modules must not only contain their own functional unity, performing a discrete task within the overall structure of the application or system that they support; they must also support a standardized way of referring to the rest of the modules in the program, as well as permitting a similarly standardized form of reference to them by the other modules. The same conditions apply to modules within a multimedia document. This can mean a number of different things, depending on the tool you're using, each of which may or may not have a fundamental metaphor for handling modules.

HyperCard, one of the oldest and in some ways simplest multimedia authoring tools, uses the metaphor of a card as its way of identifying modules from a programmatic viewpoint. This metaphor assumes a stack of index cards such as a speaker might use to keep notes for a presentation; keeping notes on index cards implies limiting the amount of information you can keep on them to a handy size, and also implies that you can shuffle through them easily to get to the card you want, without having to flip through page after page of information. In a HyperCard document (called a *stack* to reinforce the metaphor of the card), each card has content elements that you add to it with text and drawing tools, and it also has control elements that you add to it by writing simple programming commands, called *scripts*, in the HyperTalk programming language. A HyperCard script might, for example, include what to do when the user presses a mouse button—some of the options might be to display another card, to run a sound clip, to show a QuickTime movie, or to perform a short piece of animation.

More sophisticated multimedia authoring tools, such as Macromedia Director, don't contain such built-in concepts of modules as the cards in HyperCard. In Director, you control the elements of your display, called *cast members* in the more theatrical metaphor of Director; cast members can be video clips, animations, sound bites, or static screens that display like scenery in a motion picture. Any individual Director document can contain up to 32,000 cast members (in version 4.0). In such a metaphor as this, where there is no innate module design scheme like the cards in HyperCard, it's up to you to design your document so that it has structure, interactivity, dramatic closure within the thematic elements, and all the other components that make up a good play or motion picture—as well as writing the programs that control its display. This is the main reason that authoring complicated multimedia titles is always described as collaborative: you really need a variety of fairly specialized skills to put together good multimedia documents. (And we haven't even covered three-dimensional modeling and graphic design yet!)

In short, whatever authoring tool you use, you'll be responsible to some extent for the size and content of the modules you design. In designing these modules, you'll need to keep track of the ways you get to them from other modules, the places you can go from each module you design, and the types of media you use in each. While there are many ways to do this, one of the most effective is to revise the classic storyboard to track pathways in and out of the scene and to provide starting and ending points for video sequences, sound clips, music, and any other time-based media elements your title may use. These could be animation, morphing, graph generation, or a new technique that hasn't been invented yet.

Mapping Document Structure with the Storyboard

Originally, the storyboard provided artists new to animation with a way that they could use the skills and talents they already possessed to create a new medium. Today, multimedia artists need to make a similar adaptation, by starting with skills they already have and creating a new medium with them.

In this case, we're going to start with the familiar tool, the outline. We'll turn it into a storyboard, and then add a way of tracking the structure of the information to put into a document. The simplest technique that I use for mapping a document's structure is to outline it as though it were a linear book. I design the table of contents, list the subject headings and chapter titles, and then pin the entire contents listing to the wall above my desk. Then as I compose the document, I have a map of its entire structure visible before me so that as I'm working in one area, I can quickly look up to the cork board and scan for the area that acts as my reference. This reminds me of places where I devote more attention and more detail to a topic, so that when I mention it somewhere else I can provide accurate cross-references.

But that's in a book, where the fundamental assumption is that you'll turn pages in sequence and follow the order of the book. (You may not, of course, and if you refer to this book later, you'll probably want to find specific information quickly rather than read through the entire book for concepts.) In your multimedia documents, you may choose to adopt a linear organization; Chapter 4's first tutorial takes you through the steps required to make a simple, linear multimedia document. In such documents, a traditional outline works quite well to manage flow, content, and sequence.

But if you're striving for real interactivity—if you want to make something with a wider number of branches, paths, and options at every step—you'll need to map not only the flow, as in my table of contents on the corkboard, but also the network of connections between these elements. You may have multiple branches, multiple choices from individual screens, and multiple possibilities that the user might follow.

The best tool I've found so far for the initial stage of this design is the whiteboard. By drawing pictures, lines, and comments all on one easily erased medium, you can conceptualize interactivity much more quickly than with anything else I know. Figure 3-1 illustrates a typical piece of interactive storyboard design.

In this figure, the presentation starts with "The Basic Shapes," and introduces triangles, circles, and squares. When users select a shape from the first screen, they travel to an introductory screen that gives some basic facts about the shape, and then to another branching screen with different examples of each shape's use, history, or background. From each of these screens, the figure leaves off with the "etc." screens, which carry forward the detail of the multimedia document.

From this figure, you can see how a sketch on a whiteboard can map out the two fundamentals of multimedia design: sequence and interactivity. From the first screen, "The Basic Shapes," the user can select one of the three shapes; this represents interactivity, making choices from a selection of possible paths. But from the next screen, which describes the shape that the user selected, there's only one possible direction—meaning the document becomes sequential at that point. (In a later chapter, we'll talk about mixing sequential and interactive structure in the same document. Briefly, you need to understand that some multimedia tools permit only sequential document design, creating digital "slide shows" rather than interactive documents. If you're planning to have any interactivity, you'll need to make sure that the program you use to author your document supports it.)

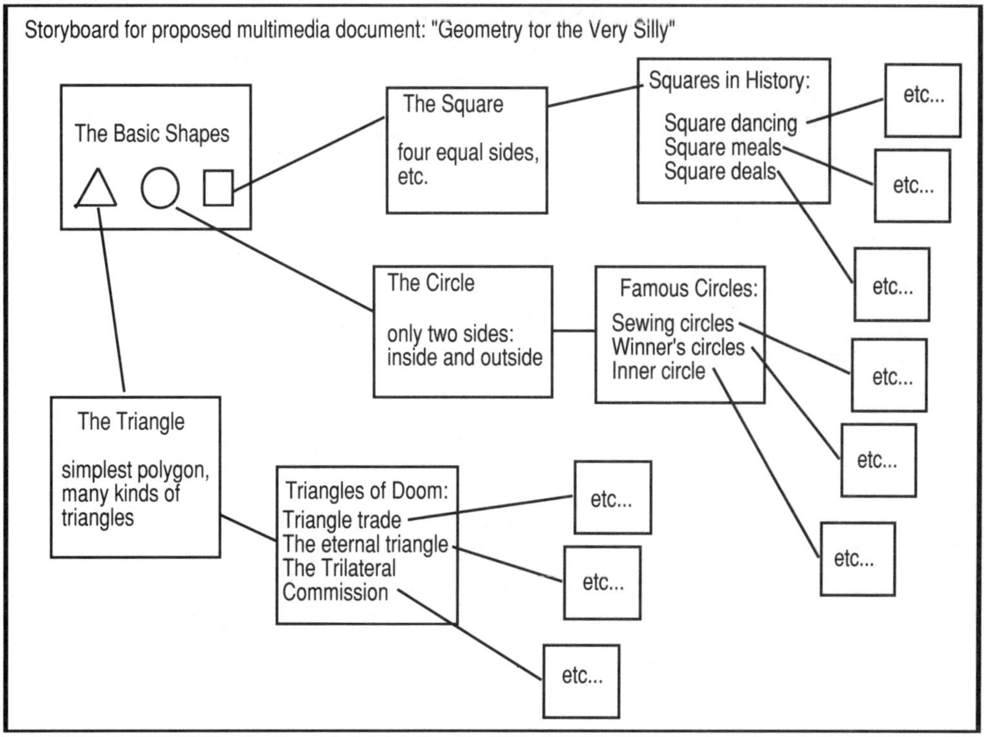

Figure 3-1. Mapping the network of connections in an interactive document

That's the basic concept of the interactive storyboard, however. When you refine it as you develop your document, and bring graphic artists into the project (or begin to work on the project yourself), you may do something more like a traditional storyboard, where there are sketches pinned to a wall with bits of dialog underneath them, or at least with references to the master script. Cork boards have an inherent advantage for designing interactive storyboards as well: you can pin pieces of yarn to indicate the links from scene to scene, and as the storyboard grows or moves, you can move the pins. Consider the possibility, too, of covering one wall in a conference room or a hallway with cork tiles. This would give you effectively a very, very large storyboard that your team could use as a central reference point. And of course, with some of the tools mentioned in this book, you might even begin to develop your storyboard electronically.

Tutorial: Making a Storyboard

Storyboard design is fundamentally simple: you don't need an artist's technique to sketch out a storyboard. All you need is the ability to imagine your story visually, because when it comes to the actual art work, you don't have to know anything more than which end of the pencil to put on the paper. You can create a highly effective storyboard with nothing more than stick figure art, circles with labels in them, and blobs of shape—as long as you can recognize your vision. With modern computer-illustration tools, this is especially true today; the initial sketches should be enough to fix your vision of the scene in your imagination. You can then use computer tools (such as your video camera, for example) to create pictures to guide your creative staff during the design and production of your title.

This tutorial takes you through the steps of storyboarding an interactive home tour like the one that you'll prototype in Chapter 4. For this tutorial, you might want to look at some of the sample files included on this CD-ROM. You might also want to generate your storyboard in some kind of computer-based draw program, but that's not necessary; you can use a pad and paper, or a whiteboard, or some other drawing medium to sketch in the storyboard. This tutorial teaches content and information management technique, not the ability to use a program or a pencil.

If you like, you can run D:\MWRANGLE\MWRANGLE.EXE, then browse the image files using the Camera button, to see some of the views that this storyboard was meant to use. However, as an exercise in visualization, try it first without looking at the pictures (except for the ones in the book).

The setting: You are designing the storyboard for a guided tour of a house that's being presented digitally. The first screen of the tour is to be a drawing of the house's floor plan; the idea is that as people click on pictures of the individual rooms, the digital tour displays photographs, video clips, or audio narration that highlight the features of that room.

Your storyboard needs to track the following components of the document you're designing:

1. Begin with your first scene. Where does the document open? In the document you're creating for this tutorial, you will want to start with a picture of the floor plan of the house. So sketch out a rough floor plan (use your own house, your apartment, your parents' house, or Alcatraz if you like).

2. Now, consider possible choices your users might take. Note them on the floor plan, and for now, write them down as a bulleted list next to the drawing. You might, for instance, include destinations such as living room, dining room, master bedroom, bathroom, kitchen, back porch, or any other elements of interest in the house you've drawn. This stage should be much like brainstorming: just throw ideas at the page, write them down, and then sort them later.
3. After you list all the destinations people might get to from the first screen, put each one on a separate sheet of paper (or on its own region of the whiteboard if you're using a whiteboard, or on its own card if you're using HyperCard.) If you're feeling particularly organized, number them.
4. From your list of possible destinations, imagine the scene that would greet people when they go into each of the rooms from the floor plan. Is there a particularly interesting lighting fixture over the dining room table? Is the hearth intricate? Is there a marble tub in the master bath? Make a quick and simple sketch of the most interesting feature of each room that guests would see when they walked into each of the rooms. Most important: visualize it as you would see it when you first walked into the room.
5. Now, for each of the rooms, consider where else your users might go. From the dining room, how would you get to the kitchen? From the master bedroom, can you see the back yard? Identify each destination from the list you created in Step 3, sketch them out, and on these destinations, include the name of the room that you left to enter this one.

You now have a storyboard that defines not only what pictures you'll need to take to make your digital tour, but also one that defines the structure of your information. This one was relatively simple, because you were using an actual structure—your house, apartment, or some other physical object—on which you based your document's design. When the information you're designing is in the form of a multimedia game, a piece of interactive fiction, an encyclopedia, or a work designed to support classroom materials on science, math, or reading, the connections between topics won't be as obvious as the doors and hallways in your house.

But the principles are the same. Now consider a storyboard designed to map the structure of a more abstract topic. Think of one—a reading lesson in an elementary classroom, the individual members of your company's product line, the possible actions that your character could take from a particular spot in a game. Let's review the same five steps, this time with the more abstract subject in mind.

1. Begin with your first scene. Where does the document open? Think of the setting if it's a dramatic title, or think of a strong visual component if it's a teaching or sales title. For example, in a multimedia product catalog, you might want to show all your company's products displayed on a showroom floor; for an elementary-school science lesson on plant life, you might want to show a picture of some recognizable plant like a sunflower. Whatever the subject, make a quick, simple sketch.
2. Now, consider possible choices your users might take. In the science lesson, you might want to discuss how the roots extract nutrients from the soil, how the leaves use sunlight to convert water and carbon dioxide into sugar, and how the flowers attract insects to pollinate the plant, creating seeds from which new plants grow. For right now, just make a list; brainstorm by coming up with everything you and your team can think of.
3. After you list all the information destinations that people might reach from the first screen, make a separate illustration for each of the units you have identified from your starting point. Again, keep them simple: just do the basic sketch that represents for you the fundamental element of the message.
4. From your list of possible destinations, imagine the information that you want to give your users as they encounter the module in question. What's the best way to present it? In video? In still pictures with audio narration? In text? In diagrams and animation? Think of what you want to say and how you want to say it. Remember, too, that while you're going to have to do all the things you define here, this is multimedia—you don't have to pick just one. If you want to have text with video and a voice-over on top of an image, go ahead!
5. Now, for each of the scenes, consider where else your users might go. From the roots (in the sunflower document), it would be reasonable for students to see what happens after the plant extracts water and nutrients, so you might want to let them go from the roots directly to the leaves. In a product catalog, you might want people to be able to see more expensive choices (and maybe even less expensive choices) in the same product family, or you might want to take them directly to add-on accessories or to the order desk.

As you can see, the same steps apply to analyzing your document's structure. There's more to the skill than this, of course; you need to consider your own sense of aesthetics, your audience's skill levels, and the actual degree of complexity in your subject. But these simple five-step procedures will get you started on creating a structural storyboard for your interactive document.

In the next chapter, you'll turn your structural storyboard into a prototype. If you haven't already loaded the CD-ROM to play with the examples, Chapter 4 will be where you fire up some of the applications and start creating your own multimedia documents, based on the tutorials you just went through. (This means that if you haven't done them yet, go back and do them now—they're part of the next chapter, which is where it really gets fun!)

Chapter 4
Prototyping

Building a Skeleton Document

The preceding chapter closed with a storyboard: a graphical representation of the structure of your document. This chapter turns that outline into a working model of an interactive multimedia document—a prototype.

Prototype documents are important, enough so that you should start one now, even before reading the rest of the book. The lessons you'll learn from constructing your first prototype multimedia document will help you avoid mistakes, make better decisions, and fundamentally understand the process of multimedia authoring. That's why Chapter 4 takes you through the steps involved in creating a couple of simple multimedia documents using several popular, easy-to-grasp tools that will help you get a feel for what it's like to put together this kind of presentation.

As you move from the storyboard to the prototype, your document takes a significant first step on the path to interactivity. For starters, this is the first time that it becomes essential for you to put your document on the computer: up till now, you can literally do all your design with a pencil and paper, perhaps with a video camcorder or a 35mm still camera to begin firming up your visual ideas and framing your screens or displays. More important, this is the first time you will be able to test your document—the first time you can really see whether your flow between structural elements works. If it works, that's great—you're ahead of the game. If it doesn't, well, that's one reason you build prototypes, so that you can try ideas that might not fly. Prototypes are often made quickly so that if you have to throw them away you won't waste a lot of time and money. At the same time, you want to construct them well enough that you can use them if they do work.

This chapter discusses how to plan simple interactivity even when structural or content elements may be missing, describes a few different approaches to implementing your design, and ends up with a tutorial section that shows you how you can use some of the component files on the CD-ROM to create your own interactive prototype documents. By the end of this chapter, you should complete the first example using the on-line components distributed on the CD-ROM, either using one of the tools described in this book or your own choice of authoring tool. (Again, if you are using an authoring tool other than those for which the instructions are given in this book, refer to the manual for your product to see exactly what steps you need to perform to accomplish the steps described here.)

Perhaps the most important decision you need to make when designing your prototype is whether you need interactivity or whether a linear structure is the right choice. While most of the observations from Chapter 3 regarding short-term memory and on-line reading habits are the same for interactive or linear documents, the assumptions you can make in each kind of document differ. Linear documents can be much simpler to construct, because the authoring tools typically support this kind of linear design—in which each screen follows its predecessor without having to detect user input and select a different screen that is out of the linear path of the document—fairly automatically. Also, most traditional training focuses on linear presentations such as speeches, papers, articles, outlines, or books. It's natural, or at least second nature, for people to think in terms of what comes first, what comes next, and what follows smoothly from one subject to its successor. Interactivity requires a new way of thinking for many people, and while it's not impossible for most people to pick it up, it can take some practice for the skills to become second nature.

Additionally, document components in the world of paper have a different paradigm than document components in the interactive world. The second half of the word "interactive" gives a clue: components of an electronic document are active, taking a role in the guidance of the user through the author's flow, structure, and organization, whether linear or fragmented. The details of navigation are covered in Chapter 5, and Chapter 6 discusses audience analysis as it pertains to the kinds of visual elements you will want to include. Let's look now at how visual design and element selection affect the construction of your prototype document: how to consider the function of a document element, and how that affects the way you format that element within your document.

Document Components: Function versus Format

As discussed in the previous chapter, one difference between traditional paper document design and on-line design is that paper documents have a passive relationship between the format of a particular piece of information and its function within the document's structure. In interactive documents, the relationship is much more active: the format or appearance of a piece of information in an on-line document can help define, for the user, what it does when you click on it.

One simple example is the video window control bar that displays across the bottom of Apple QuickTime movies (Figure 4-1). This format information—the bar, the controls for playing the movie, and the shape of the window itself—is also a way of identifying that window's purpose.

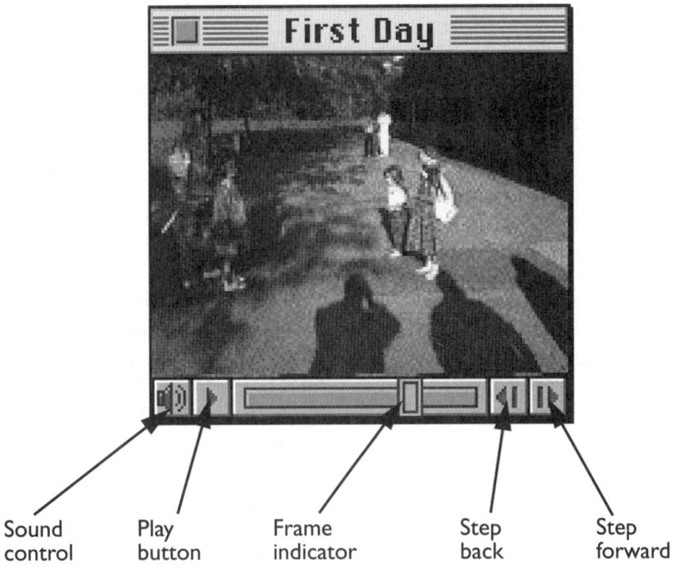

Figure 4-1. A QuickTime movie with its control bar

In Figure 4-1, the form that the movie takes on the screen tells the reader that it's a movie, with a play button, step forward and step backward buttons, and an indicator bar that shows the current frame.

But as important as these visual elements are for your presentation's function, there's a more critical sense beneath them: the function that each block of your document serves in forwarding your overall purpose. In writing for print, one operates under the fundamental assumption that pages proceed in numeric order and that readers follow these pages in the order in which the publisher prints them. Of course, individual readers may choose to jump around (particularly after they're familiar with a topic, about which Chapter 6 says more), but in paper, this sequence is an underlying design paradigm.

In interactive computer-based documents, the underlying design paradigm is that you can move instantly between any two elements of the document. It is therefore up to the document designer to choose which elements the readers can see and select at any given step of the way. Furthermore, because there's no linear paradigm in interactivity, the designer of an interactive document needs to consider things that the designer of a linear document can take for granted, particularly when it comes to what I've called prerequisite information, or what Hollywood calls "the back story."

Scriptwriters talk about the back story when they discuss what happened before the opening credits in a film. The audience doesn't see it, but it informs the characters in the movie with their motivations, their drive, their reasons for behaving the way they do. Probably the most vivid example of back story in Hollywood history is *Citizen Kane*: the film opens with a long traveling shot moving up the mountain of Xanadu, past the wreckage of incredible wealth, to where Charles Foster Kane lies dying; he drops the snow globe, utters the puzzling word "Rosebud," and expires. The rest of the film is devoted to filling in the meaning of "rosebud," which at the point the film opens is in the back story; the dramatic action is essentially pulling the back story into the present, and part of the beauty of the film is that none of the characters ever quite gets it.

(By the way, if you haven't seen *Citizen Kane*, put the book down now and go rent it. Not only is it a fabulous motion picture, but in many ways it's the first example of interactivity, produced 50 years before computer multimedia made one-on-one interactivity possible. *Citizen Kane* does more to define what interactivity and hyper-links are really about than most modern CD-ROMs do. The real story in *Citizen Kane* unfolds not on the screen, where Welles shows us only bits and pieces at a time, but in the audience's minds as we follow the "links" from character to character. This is why eventually the audience understands what Rosebud means, while the characters walk away at the end admitting they'll probably never know.)

In linear fiction, the author can always keep track of what the reader does or doesn't know about the back story at any given time; this lets the author build in dramatic irony, foreshadowing, and all the other elements of story design that go beyond simply telling the events as they happen. But fundamentally, the author knows how much back story the readers should know because the author has told the readers already. In interactive fiction, there's really no way of knowing how much the readers already know because there may be more than one way of coming to a particular point in the story.

In nonfiction writing, such as you might be doing as part of a project in curriculum development, reference, training, or marketing, the analog to fiction's back story is prerequisite information. In an on-line tutorial, for example, you will probably want to force linearity on your users so that they complete Step 1 before beginning Step 2; in an interactive brochure, you may want your potential customers to see an overview of your entire product line before they select the individual components that interest them, if only so they can make a reasonable selection. All this is information that your audience needs to know before they can proceed with a reasonable use of your document.

This may be the single most important function that your prototype serves: the control of revealing prerequisite information. If you're developing interactive fiction, your prototype lets you develop the pathways through the information that reveal just the amount of back story you want your audience to know at any given time. If you're working on a teaching document or some other nonfiction application, it lets you see what your audience will need to know before they get to a given block (or module) in the document. Your prototype lets you see how the information connects within itself, what you need to explain somewhere else, and how to present your audience with ways to get there. (Chapters 5 and 6 deal with these issues explicitly: Chapter 5 details how to guide your user through your document, and Chapter 6 talks about specific types of users and ways you can optimize your document for one or more of these types.)

For now, however, let's return to your prototype document, to what may be the first work you've done in interactivity. As with so many other subjects in this book, the first recommended step to developing interactivity is to plan it.

Planning Simple Interactivity

One way to plan an interactive document is to work out a list of which screens you expect you will need. Many people still use pencil and paper for this stage; it's easy to change, easy to throw away, and you can flip from sheet to sheet to see what you've already decided.

The simplest form of interactivity is page-turning. To use the Hypercard analogy, interactivity lets you select any card in the stack, or more specifically, it lets the author decide from which of the cards in the stack it is appropriate for the reader to select. In the simplest case, the author can narrow the field to one selection: the next card.

In addition to HyperCard, Apple Media Tool, and dedicated authoring systems such as Asymetrix Toolbook and Macromedia Director, both the Macintosh and the PC have simple, sometimes inexpensive packages for creating such next-card documents. These programs are often called presentation tools, and were originally developed for creating 35mm slides for conferences, overhead transparencies for meetings, and—almost as an afterthought, at least at first—electronic presentations on the computer screen itself. As the availability of computer screens grows, and as multimedia spreads to many fields, for many people these electronic presentations are becoming the most significant type of output. The issue, as always, is not the tool, but the nature of the information, its purpose, its inherent structure, and the reason you're creating the document.

Linear Multimedia: Presentations and On-line Brochures

Many times, for many reasons, a linear document is the right choice. Often, the sequence of information is significant enough to make interactivity relatively unimportant. In such cases, presentation tools such as those discussed here—Aldus Persuasion and Microsoft PowerPoint are two popular varieties—will let you create effective "slide shows" using a variety of computer-generated media, with simple on-screen animation as well as imported graphics and QuickTime movies. (Persuasion, however, adds interactivity to its capabilities, and as such you'll see a lot more of it in forthcoming examples and tutorials.)

Later in this chapter, you'll have the opportunity to see how to build such a linear presentation using PowerPoint. PowerPoint has another advantage over many more sophisticated multimedia authoring tools: the runtime version is free. This means you can use PowerPoint for giveaway documents such as electronic brochures, self-paced presentations, and other marketing materials (as well as making it much simpler to include PowerPoint examples on a CD-ROM included in a book).

Additionally, presentation tools can serve as a good way to do quick prototypes of simple documents, or sections of simple documents that you are planning to expand in greater detail with a more complicated tool. Often, the ability to see how things go together can help you develop the more complex, interactive document. With simple, easy-to-use tools such as PowerPoint, you can easily try a number of combinations from the same media, testing out flow possibilities in something that approaches real time.

How easy is something like this? Here's a timeline for the production of a linear—but large—presentation made for back-to-school night at Cherry Chase Elementary School. This project was actually an alpha test for the book. It involved my editorial assistant and wife, Kim Fisher, who did the camera work, consulted with me on initial document design, and performed the in-camera and digital video editing as well as using PowerPoint to author the document. We also had the gracious assistance of Donna Haswell, first-grade teacher at Cherry Chase Elementary School in Sunnyvale, California, who is one of Sunnyvale's 27 multimedia specialists trained as part of the Sunnyvale School District Education Foundation (SSDEF).

9:00 a.m.	Load video camera, walk to school
9:20 a.m.	Recess over: begin videotaping children for presentation
9:40 a.m.	Return home, begin capturing movies of 28 children
11:45 a.m.	Discover limit of 10 QuickTime segments per any single PowerPoint presentation; restructure slide show
2:10 p.m.	Walk to school with box of diskettes containing presentation file, QuickTime files, and PowerPoint Viewer
2:25 p.m.	School out: load presentation onto school Macintosh and show teacher
2:26 p.m.	Reattach teacher's jaw after it drops to floor

This exercise really taught us several things: first, that while simple tools such as PowerPoint have their limits—you can't really do a game, an interactive novel, or even a product catalog with it—they are useful for making professional-looking linear multimedia presentations with an absolute minimum of fuss, time, and effort. A more important lesson, perhaps, is that telling people about what multimedia means is like telling people what it's like to jump out of an airplane or take a ride in a race car. No matter how much you prepare them, the experience itself is more dramatic than they were expecting—if you do it right.

So how did we make this simple but effective presentation?

"I have to say that the real time-intensive part was capturing the video just so," Kim said later when we discussed her presentation, "and I'd have a lot to say about doing it again." Here are some of her suggestions, based on the finished product (which is on the CD-ROM as PowerPoint files for the Macintosh, named "Back to School 1," "Back to School 2," and "Back to School 3").

Leave lead time on your videotape with each subject. "I didn't have a lot of lead time with each kid," Kim said. This meant that some of her edits initially ended up with one or two frames from the subject immediately before or after the one meant for each slide. To avoid this, on a later shoot she started running the video camera for just a couple of seconds before having the child introduce him or herself. "It gives me more time to capture the right moments."

Rehearse your material for smoothness. "I think I needed to have each kid run through it once before I did it," she added. A lot of this depends on the child in question; some of the kids (as you may notice on the presentation) are naturally quiet and shy, while others speak up clearly.

Read the factory manual. It's tempting, because PowerPoint is so simple (and because I'd used it for its simplest purpose, making overhead transparencies), to think that it only does what's superficially available from the top level of menus. However, after the first prototype document was finished, we found that PowerPoint supports frame-by-frame editing of QuickTime movies—we could remove unwanted frames, trim the clips, and otherwise make more precise edits on the computer than we could in the video camera. We also found ways to do the fly-on, dissolve, and pop-up animation elements used in some of the screens of the sample document. (You'll see these demonstrated in some of the examples used with Chapters 4 and 5.)

What are the limits of a presentation package like PowerPoint for designing multimedia documents? The most crucial one is that you can't interact with multiple areas of the screen—users can't make choices, select options, or take different paths. For example, if you want to let your readers choose A, B, or C from a list, you need something interactive. However, you can use a presentation package to present A, B, and C in order. (Once again, Persuasion does let you do this, which is why the early tutorials that teach you how to design for interactivity use Persuasion.) You can decide whether to display each screen automatically when the preceding frame finishes, or you can let the user click the mouse to control "turning the page." And with the ability to do fly-on, dissolve-in and dissolve-out, and pop-up of individual elements, you can animate text buttons and graphics, as well as incorporating any outside animation or video that you have captured as a QuickTime movie. (On Windows platforms, as of the time of writing, you can't incorporate QuickTime for Windows; you can, however, include single-screen snapshots either from video, scanned in from a photograph, or created on the computer. And as QuickTime for Windows catches on, it's reasonable to expect that Microsoft will add support for QuickTime to this package.)

Tutorial 1: Creating a Linear Multimedia Presentation

The following tutorial uses the recorded data files on the CD-ROM and, with a presentation tool such as Microsoft PowerPoint, takes you through the steps involved in creating your own multimedia document. This document is linear, meaning you can't make choices about what screen to display next. Before you discount this completely, remember that plays, motion pictures, television shows, and videotapes are all linear. This is the simplest kind of multimedia document to prepare, and if you have a simple message or if the sequence of steps with which you build your document is important to you, choosing a linear design can still be quite effective.

The instructions given here assume that you have access to the Microsoft PowerPoint presentation tool. If you are using something with similar capabilities such as Aldus Persuasion, the menu selections will be different but you will have access to the same basic functions for building your linear multimedia document.

1. **Choose New from the File menu.**

   If you wish, choose Apply Template from the File menu and choose one of the background templates that you like.

2. **Title the first slide.**

   Put the mouse over the title area and click once (with the left mouse button on PCs) to select it, then type a title. (For now, it can be as unimaginative as "First Slide.")

3. **Pull down the Edit menu and select Include.**

   You will see a pop-up menu displaying the following options:

   Picture...
   Movie...
   Object...
   Outline...
   Date
   Time
   Page Number

   Choose the type of element you wish to include. For this exercise, select Movies (if you are using a Macintosh) or Pictures (either Macintosh or PC).

   PowerPoint displays a dialog box from which you can choose a media element.

4. **Select a media element.**

   For the Macintosh, select one of the QuickTime movies on the CD-ROM incorporated at the back of this book. These movies are all in the folder labeled "QuickTime for CD-ROM."

   For the PC, select one of the pictures from the directory entitled D:\FGRABS. These are all framegrabbed images that you can include in a PowerPoint application. (If the current version of PowerPoint for the PC now includes the ability to include QuickTime movies, you can choose one of the movies in the directory D:\QT4WIN.)

5. **Position the movie where you want it.**

   PowerPoint gives you a box with four "handles," indicating the corners of the media element you have selected.

   Move the box by dragging it with the mouse, or resize it by selecting one of the handles and dragging it up, down, right, or left.

   To maintain the same aspect ratio, hold down the SHIFT key while you drag the handle.

   When the box is the size and location you want it, let up on the mouse button and you will see the image (in the case of a QuickTime movie, the first frame of the movie).

6. Assign a transition behavior to the slide.

From the Slide menu, select Transition.... Select one of the transitions; for now, choose Box Out. You can then choose to assign a duration to your slide or you can click the radio button that causes this slide to remain on the screen until you click the mouse button.

Note that in PowerPoint, the transition occurs at the beginning of the slide for which you are assigning it. To make a transition when a slide disappears, you must choose the appropriate transition for the beginning of the following slide.

7. Add a new slide to your presentation.

From the Slide menu, select New Slide. You can also type Command-L on the Macintosh to create a new slide.

Perform the same steps, this time choosing a different media element and using different text.

Continue with this process, adding elements to your slide show, until you have three or four slides. For now, this will be sufficient; you can add new slides later.

If you don't have Microsoft PowerPoint, you can still view the sample prototype distributed on the CD-ROM with Microsoft's free PowerPoint viewer. To do this, open the Tools directory on the CD-ROM (that's D:\TOOLS on the PC) and look for the file called PowerPoint Viewer. Double-click to launch the viewer, then select the presentation called Prototyping from the dialog menu that pops up.

For further study, look into your program's manual and find ways to animate text, to make graphical elements fly onto the scene from out of the picture, and otherwise to give life and motion to your presentation. As a useful trick, try this: create two adjacent slides with several common elements in exactly the same location on both slides, then choose a display effect that reveals the new slide incrementally, such as a wipe to the right or left, or an iris open. Notice how this gives the appearance of making the material on the new slide simply replace the material on the old one. It's an interesting and useful tool for adding visual interest to your presentations; use it, for instance, to retain the same graphic but to change text in bullet lists beneath or around it. The file "Ch4 Linear Example" demonstrates several examples of this. You can give the impression of an animated build by controlling the appearance of each slide in this incremental way even if your presentation tool doesn't support animation or fly-on directly.

Tutorial 2: Creating an Interactive Document

For interactivity, you need a tool like HyperCard or MediaWrangler at the low end, or Macromedia Director or Asymetrix Toolbook at the high end. Unlike the example you created in Tutorial 1, an interactive document lets the user make choices at every appropriate spot in the document. That is, there may still only be one choice—proceed to the next screen—for certain stages of the document, but at crucial points, the user can choose from one of several options. This can be as simple as selecting Yes or No from a pop-up menu, or as complex as presenting a table of contents from which the user can choose which chapter to read next.

For this simple prototype document, the instructions use MediaWrangler, which is probably the simplest tool available for developing Windows-based multimedia documents. As with the previous tutorial, you can choose from any of the available media elements while you are working on the sample document, so if you have a particular project in mind, you can follow this tutorial and also begin making your own prototype multimedia document with the same steps.

In following this tutorial, note that all interactive documents use the same fundamental abstraction for interactivity: you define an area on one picture that, when you click it, displays another picture, a video clip, or a sound; by defining different areas on the same picture, you can give your users multiple choices. This tutorial uses MediaWrangler's command buttons, user interface, and overall structure to build this interactivity; you could do the same kind of project in Apple Media Tool or HyperCard, for example, and the interactivity would be similar, even if the way you accomplished it was somewhat different.

In the following tutorial, you'll:

- open an image of the floor plan of a house;
- make "hot spots" in several rooms on the floor plan; and
- assign photographs of those rooms to the hot spots so that your users can take a tour of the house from their desktops.

1. **Make sure that the CD-ROM is loaded in your PC.**

   For the purposes of this tutorial, I'll assume that your CD-ROM's drive designation is D; if you've given it some other designation, use that wherever I use D.

2. **Run MediaWrangler.**

   From the Windows file manager, go to D:\MWRANGLE and select the file MWRANGLE.EXE. This runs MediaWrangler; in a few moments, you'll get the MediaWrangler menu and toolbar.

3. **Select the File menu and pull down New.**

   MediaWrangler displays a pop-up menu of documents you can create; select the first type, Roundup File. MediaWrangler then prompts you to give your roundup file a descriptive title. For now, give it a simple title such as Interactive Tutorial, then click the OK button.

4. **Choose a root image.**

   MediaWrangler then prompts you to select an image file to act as the root. (The "root" image is MediaWrangler's term for the home card in a HyperCard stack or for Screen 1 in Apple Media Tool: that is, it's the picture that shows up first when you run the presentation you're building.)

   For this example, go to the Directories pane and select the following path:

   D:\MWRANGLE\IMAGES\HOMETOUR\TEXASHME.

   From this path, choose the picture BLUEPRNT.JPG. This image is the blueprint of a house.

5. **Create your first hot spot.**

   In the middle of the house, look for the words "Dining room." You'll make this room your first "hot spot" (or MAP—short for "media area pointer"—in MediaWrangler's terminology).

   To draw a MAP, click the right mouse button once and the cursor changes to a pencil. Now draw the outline of the dining room, just inside the walls, by clicking once with the left mouse button on every corner. When you return to the first corner you selected, MediaWrangler closes the MAP.

6. **Select an image to associate with the MAP.**

   To do this, first click the left mouse button once inside the MAP. Then, click the Camera button from the tool bar; this opens image files for you to choose. MediaWrangler opens a directory window as in Step 4, but this time leaves the directory set to the one you previously selected.

For this tutorial, select the file named DINNRM.JPG. The directory window disappears, but notice that when you move the cursor over the MAP you created in the dining room, the cursor changes to a camera. This is MediaWrangler's way of telling you that you have moved the cursor over a MAP. To see what happens, double-click the left mouse button: Media-Wrangler displays a photograph of the dining room.

One of the features I like about MediaWrangler is its ability to draw MAPs of any shape, as long as they have fewer than 255 vertices (connections between the line segments that you draw with the mouse). To see why this can be useful, click once on the image BLUEPRNT.JPG to bring it to the top of the presentation. Now we'll create a hot spot that isn't a simple rectangle.

7. **Create an oddly shaped hot spot.**

   Find the kitchen on the floor plan—it's just up and to the right of the dining room. As in Step 5, create a MAP by clicking the right mouse button once, then drawing the corners of the MAP by clicking the left mouse button to select each vertex.

   Notice how MediaWrangler draws a line behind the cursor, stretching out toward the last place you clicked the left mouse button. Draw a closed shape around the inside of the kitchen to finish your MAP, following the outline of the doors and the notch that the pantry makes when it juts into the lower-right corner of the kitchen.

8. **Select the MAP, then associate an image with it.**

   Click the left mouse button once inside the MAP to select it, then click the Camera button from the tool bar. As in Step 6, select a picture from the list; this time, choose the file KTCHNCUP.JPG, which displays the kitchen cabinets.

   Now move the cursor into the MAP you just drew in the kitchen and see that it turns into a camera again. Double-click on the MAP and MediaWrangler displays a photograph of the kitchen cupboards.

There's more to MediaWrangler than this—just as there's more to every program I give as an example in this book. For instance, if you use Media-Wrangler to create your own multimedia presentations, you'll probably want to browse the image files by their "thumbnails," or small versions of the picture's contents. Likewise, you'll want to save, compress, and other-wise manage your presentations so that you can share (or perhaps sell) them. While all of these steps are important, for now we'll leave them until a future date and concentrate just on the steps covered here in designing an interactive prototype document.

Review: What Prototypes Teach You

The first thing you learn from a prototype may well be how to use the tool you've selected. If you've never used MediaWrangler or PowerPoint before, you've now seen how you can put together simple multimedia presentations with these two tools. In this sense, the prototype you built was really from your own understanding: you followed the steps involved in putting together a document, using the samples provided on the CD-ROM, but thinking in terms of the projects you want to create.

There are other advantages to a prototype, of course. Prototypes identify areas where you need additional resources or additional work: for instance, you might build a prototype before you shoot any video, as a way of identifying exactly what content you want to capture. Likewise, prototypes let you check your work for flow, interactivity, and good sequential presentation of information. This can be particularly important in interactive presentations, where your users can select any of a number of destinations from a single screen. Your prototype can tell you when you need to make connections between one screen and some other one that contains prerequisite information—a concept that doesn't really work in interactive multimedia.

Another benefit of a prototype, of course, is that it can flesh out a proposal. If you need to convince someone—whether that's a management group in your own organization or a client who's deciding whether or not to use your organization for a project—a prototype can demonstrate your competency better than anything you can say. If it's well done it can also light up your client or your organization with enthusiasm, which may free up more than just the basic resources that you are trying to convince them to assign to your project.

Prototypes can also serve as the first steps in your project's evolution. That is, while you sometimes have to throw a prototype away, it's more often the case that you can reuse large portions of your original prototype, simply adding detail and complexity (or perhaps removing complexity as your vision of the project becomes clearer). This can be particularly important if you're using multimedia in a school setting; the prototype is the first level of positive feedback that you provide to your students, letting them see their efforts on the screen.

Most people also find it much easier to work on a functioning example than to plug away at something that may not do anything visible for months, so a prototype is good for your team as well. It gives people a sense of what they're doing, it helps spread the vision around among the people who will be responsible for creating it, and it gives everyone an external reference against which they can check their own work—much the way storyboards are used in traditional animation. And if you're developing a multimedia project in the classroom, the prototype is a great way to show your students what they're working on, to let them see some results of their efforts, and to get them even more excited at what they can accomplish. Teachers are learning that as exciting as it is for kids to browse through CD-ROMs in the computer lab, it's even more exciting for them to create their own interactive documents. This is one reason why Roger Wagner's HyperStudio multimedia authoring tool skyrocketed from 18th place to third place in educational software in 1993.

In many senses, the prototype is really an embryo: it's the first steps that your project takes toward a life of its own. Once you have a prototype for other people to see, the vision stops being yours and starts being shared.

Chapter 5 Navigation

Guiding the User through Your Document

In Chapter 2, I talked about your vision for the document: not only what components you want to include in it, but also what images and impressions you want to convey to the user—the "look and feel" of your document. Chapter 3 introduced the concept of document structure rather than format as the guiding metaphor for design. Chapter 4 let you build two different prototype documents that used different ways of presenting information to your users, one in a linear, step-by-step manner and the other in an interactive, choose-as-you-go form. This chapter discusses one of the most important ways you reinforce your guiding metaphor, let your users know how they can control their position in the document, and ultimately how you can control your document's look and feel: the navigation technique.

Navigation is another word for the user-interface design of a multimedia document. In multimedia, navigation encompasses the point-and-click interface as well as the underlying structure. To a large degree, navigation includes what you see as well as how you see it. Navigation, in this sense, means not only the way you permit users to engage other media elements in your document, but also the way you let them look for those elements as well as the way you let them know where they are, logically, in the document's structure. One of the most important navigation tools for this orientation component of the problem is often called a road map.

Basic Models: Programs, Books, and Environments

To begin understanding navigation, consider three different fundamental models you can use in designing your navigation scheme:

- the document as a sophisticated computer program, with menus, scrollbars, active areas, and message areas;

- the document as an interactive book, with a balance between text and graphics, a page-oriented design that lends itself to a traditional table of contents and index, and the general feel of an electronic book; and
- the document as a synthetic environment, embodying some of the ideas of virtual reality, in which you interact with objects in the scene in a natural and direct manner.

Each of these approaches carries with it a different set of connotations for the user, makes a slightly different emotional impression on people as they work their way through your document, and in some ways has its own strengths and weaknesses for particular applications. Choosing the right kind of interface model—or perhaps designing your own that falls somewhere between these three examples—can help improve your document's usability, and therefore, to some extent, its popularity.

Some multimedia titles present themselves as a sophisticated computer program, one in which the user navigates through the information by selecting from menus, using command buttons, and otherwise operating the controls in another kind of computer program. This kind of interface design is often simple and natural to do, and can work well with subjects that are closely tied to the computer. For instance, training documents on using a computer application can reinforce the user's knowledge of the program they're learning by emulating its structure and usability in the multimedia training.

A program-oriented interface is also a simple way to index text and graphics together. One example of such a way to keep images (or video clips) and text connected is to have the text files and the graphics files linked together, so that when you finish one file, the program steps to the next connected pair. A very simple example of one such user interface is shown in Figure 5-1. Experienced Macintosh users will recognize familiar cues from every program they've ever seen: the menu bar across the top of the screen, the QuickTime control bar and buttons on the bottom of the video frame, and the command buttons labeled "More" and "Play Video" beneath each window. And although Figure 5-1 uses Macintosh stylistic elements such as the Chicago font, Macintosh-style window bars, and oval command buttons, it's easy to imagine how the same contents could be made familiar to Windows users by changing the font to Arial, the window border to a solid bar of color, square or "chiseled" buttons, and other visual cues that would let Windows users know what to expect.

There are many things to consider about the story being told in Figure 5-1, however. First, of course, is that it's visually boring. Yes, the layout is nicely balanced, with equally sized windows for text and illustrations. But the presentation is too symmetrical: there's no dynamism to it, no motion in the layout. (Compare this with the picture itself, in which Annabel and Murphy are about one-third of the way in from the edge of the screen; this kind of intentional asymmetry lends motion even to still images, and directs the eye toward a particular goal. We'll have to do something about those shadows, though.) Furthermore, the screen looks like a computer program, with obvious frames on the windows, command buttons, and other control apparatus that belong more in Word for Windows than in a story about a little girl's first day at school.

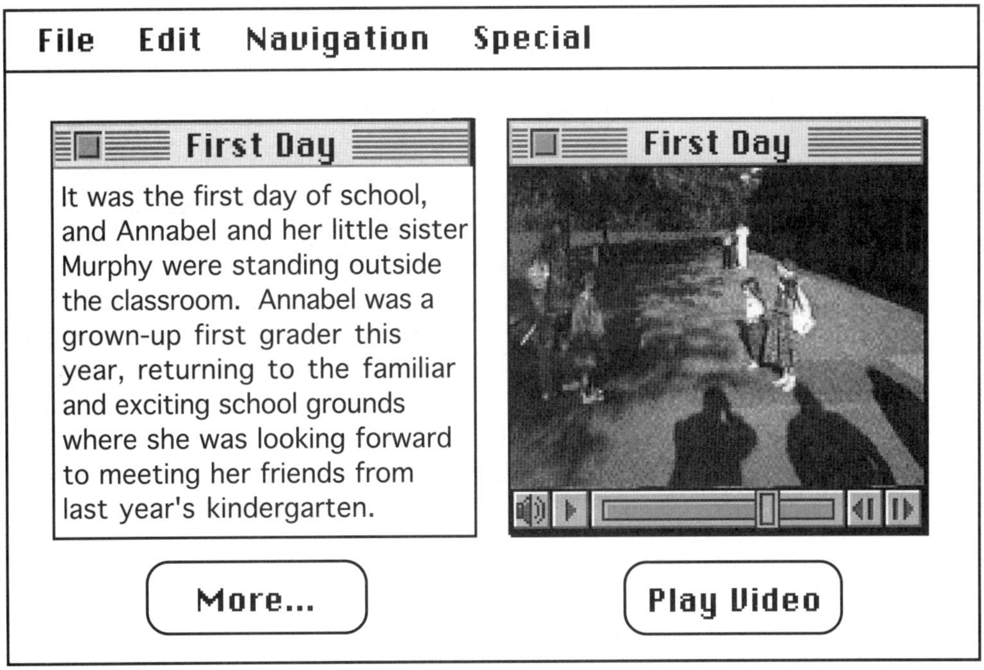

Figure 5-1. Storytelling with the computer model of interface design

In defense of this layout, it's obvious what the user needs to select to perform the various functions involved in running this program—that is, using this CD-ROM. The buttons are clearly labeled, the selections in the menu bar are in the familiar sequence (File, then Edit, then a pair of application-specific menus), and if there were more text than could fit in the left-hand window, it's obvious that there would be an elevator bar to let the user scroll up and down in the story. Additionally, it's easy to create and standardize. You can put text windows in most applications (HyperCard, Asymetrix Toolbook, and Apple Media Tool support this; you can even put it into a presentation package like PowerPoint). And if your multimedia presentation is rich in text, like the Mayo Clinic's *Family Health Disk* CD-ROM, you'll need a standard way of displaying text, either alongside a video window or within the same window (as in the case of the Mayo Clinic CD-ROM). However, for entertainment CD-ROMs, games, and interactive environments, this kind of user interface puts an artificial layer between the user and the information that distracts from the enjoyment of the experience.

Another way of presenting this information is to make it look somewhat like a children's book, one in which the visual elements are arranged a little more dramatically and in a more integrated way. Additionally, consider something I can't demonstrate on this page: using color. Many people find it difficult to read screens of colored text, but you might consider using a highlight color with good contrast against the background (without being so high-contrast that they appear to vibrate, like neon pink and neon green next to each other).

Figure 5-2 illustrates another way of laying out the same page of the story. In this illustration, the video playback buttons remain under the video image, though in a modified form, and the More button gives way to a graphic indicating where you click to see the next screen. (I've left the "2" in as a lesson; I originally put it there to indicate that if you clicked that corner, you'd see page two, and my first testers—including the actual first-grader who plays the role of Annabel in this story—agreed with me. Some people, however, think it's the number of the page being viewed. Things like this are why Chapter 10 outlines some strategies for testing your document before publishing.)

Additionally, the text—now much larger—has been made to flow around the illustration. On the plus side, it gives a sense of direction to the page layout; on the minus side, it means that this frame—and by extension, every frame—will have to be laid out individually, rather than using a standardized page template as in Figure 5-1. The question becomes whether you want to do an easy presentation that handles things in a standard way, or whether you want to take control over each screen and lay out your document the way you want it to look.

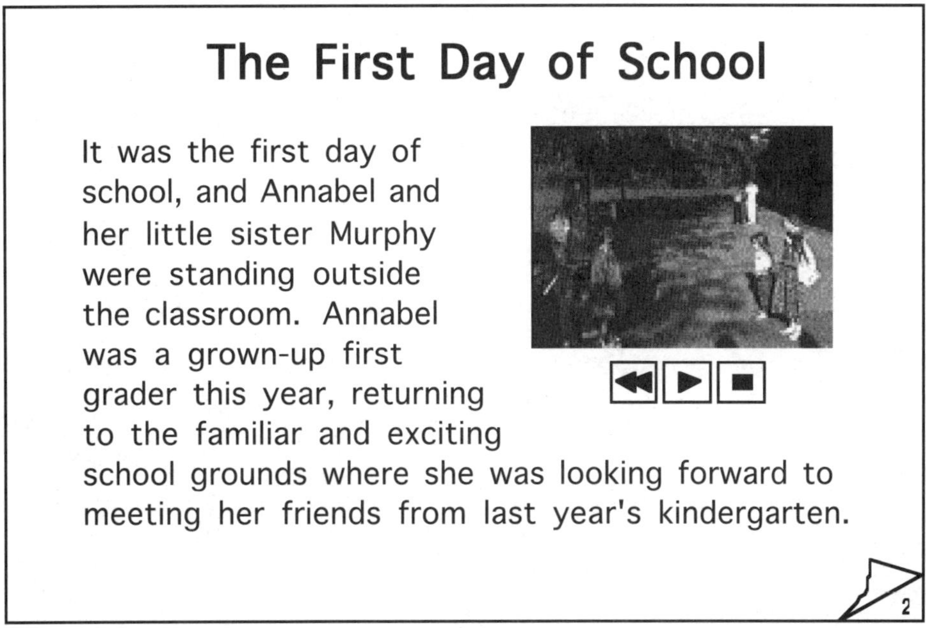

Figure 5-2. Storytelling with the children's book model of interface design

The third way of organizing a video screen is to lay it out naturalistically—that is, to set it up in such a way that the text seems to flow into and around the image, incorporating words into the picture, and even perhaps putting a more naturalistic play mechanism into the image. Figure 5-3 shows one way of using the same image, this time somewhat larger, giving a look that's more like a television show or a motion picture with embedded text in the image.

Notice several other elements of this version of the story of Annabel and Murphy. First, there's much less text in this screen than in the previous two; second, the picture is larger (and most of those shadows are missing; a little work with Adobe Photoshop or some other graphical retouching tool could get rid of the cameraman's head). Third, the text covers the heads of the woman and girl who are walking up to Annabel and Murphy, making it obvious that it's the little girl in the hat and her younger sister in blue jeans who are the main characters of this story. (If these other two characters are to take an active role in the scene, consider having the text disappear when the video starts.)

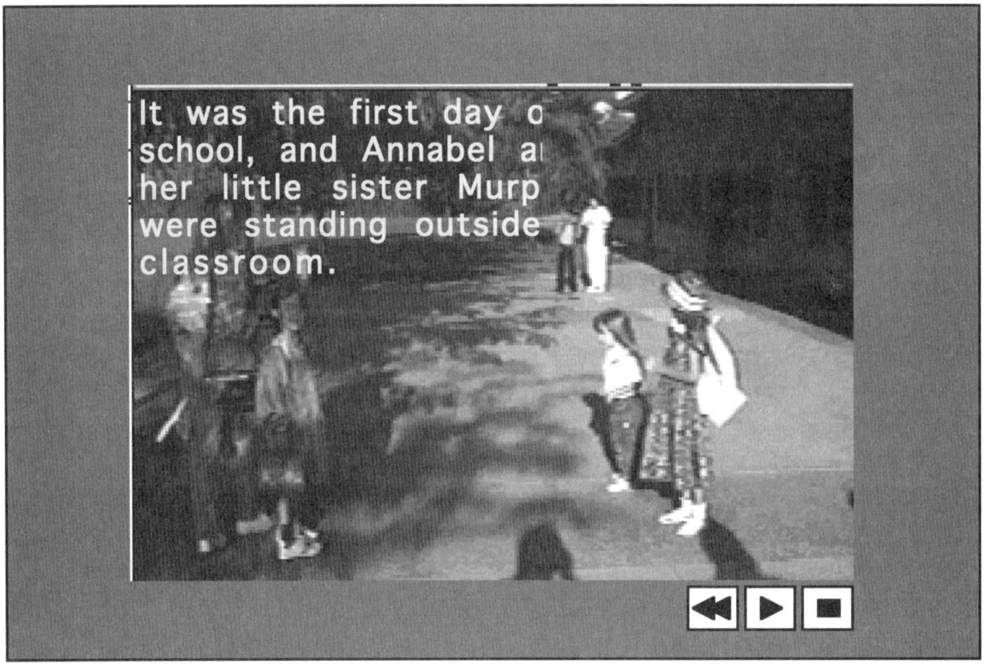

Figure 5-3. Natural inclusion of text and graphics in an environment

In this example, the same three buttons—a double left arrow for rewind, a single right arrow for play, and a square for stop—appear just outside the video area and offer the same commands with the same clarity as they do in Figure 5-2. However, this naturalistic presentation really lends itself to a subject in which the interactivity is much richer. In such an environment, you might make portions of the image mouse-sensitive, so that by clicking on the picture of Annabel (the girl in the hat) you hear what she has to say; clicking on Murphy lets you hear her comment. Although it's absent from this illustration, it would be simple to add a command to turn the "page." However, given the non-page-oriented metaphor behind this layout, you might want to make it a plus in the lower right-hand corner to see the next screen, and a minus in the lower left-hand corner to see the previous. Or, you could make it obvious (if not particularly slick) by labeling two buttons "Next" and "Previous," perhaps in right- and left-pointing arrows, respectively.

Layout questions such as these are the microcosm of navigation. That is, one can use different aesthetic and functional models to present your user with choices about actions to take from within a screen. Whether you use text buttons with clear labels such as More and Play Video as in Figure 5-1, or a sleek, graphically oriented TV-show-like interface as in Figure 5-3, or some other model that more closely represents the information in your subject, the last three figures demonstrate how you instruct your users in the intra-screen details of managing your CD-ROM title. The buttons, windows, and layout schemes shown here are like street signs and traffic signals, directing flow at an immediate level.

There's also, however, a higher level to document design, just as there is for navigation in the real world. Street signs can tell you that you're at the corner of El Camino Real and College Avenue, that you're at the intersection of 280 and 101, that you can make a left turn from the two center lanes, or that there's a bicycle lane to your right. But in addition to this information, getting to a destination requires a more global view of your position with respect to the destination itself. In travel, we use maps; in information navigation, we use what are sometimes called "information road maps," or more generally, information overviews.

Information Overviews

Just as reading a map while negotiating busy traffic is difficult, stressful, and possibly dangerous, you want to make sure that your users don't have to do any serious navigation while they are trying to make sense of an individual screen. To that end, develop a consistent way of letting your users have access to the information overviews in your document.

Information overviews are based on information partitioning (discussed in Chapter 3), but they are also—or in the best documents, they should also be—infused with a sense of the document's governing metaphor and style. At the simplest level, you can use the same three models for information overview that you used for the intra-module navigation aids shown in Figures 5-1 through 5-3: program, book, and environment. At a more complicated level, you can build an information overview that acts as a tutorial and helps reinforce not only your document's structure but also your user's understanding of the document. And of course, your information overview is a key to conveying a sense of the vision you have for your document.

First, consider creating information overviews for a document laid out like using a program. The most obvious way to lay out such an overview is to map it to the menu items of the program. This is a particularly useful technique for designing multimedia training documents to teach a program. This might be a map in the visual sense, whereby you actually use a simulation of the program's menu and let the user click on it to learn what each menu item does, to see a short explanatory video about how to use its features, or to enter an interactive tutorial about using it. Figure 5-4 shows one such way of mapping the interface of your document to a program menu.

In Figure 5-4, users interested in the operation of this imaginary program (borrowed from Figure 5-1) can track down items of interest from the program's user interface by following the user interface of the multimedia document. This particular example must be simple and static because it is printed on paper. But in a multimedia document, it doesn't have to be that way. You can use a more active approach, almost a cinematic one, while retaining the mapping to the menu. For an example of something you might do with an interactive tutorial for a program's menu bar, run the on-line example entitled "Ch 5 Program Interface Tutorial." It demonstrates how the information in your document can map to a program's interface dynamically, adding motion and text fly-ons to give life to the document. (We'll discuss how I made this example, once again using Microsoft PowerPoint for the sake of simplicity and ease of operation, in a few pages.)

In either case, the information overview follows the structure of the program menu. If you are not developing an interactive tutorial, you might still choose to use a program-like interface for your multimedia document for a number of reasons. It's generally simpler to standardize a programmatic information interface, with common menus, type styles, and user interaction. Furthermore, if you're dealing with experienced users of a particular platform, you can make some basic assumptions in your design about what your users know. In such cases, a program-like document overview can be the simplest to design because you make the decisions once and then apply them to the rest of the menus and controls with which your users navigate through the document.

Designing a book-like information overview conveys an entirely different feel to the user. It's worth asking why you should make a computer program work as though it were a book. There are a number of reasons, some purely aesthetic and others more practical. On the aesthetic side, you may wish to simulate the appearance of a book in the information overview because it works well with your material. For example, a multimedia catalog of works in a library might work well when presented in an overview that resembled a book. An entertainment CD-ROM dealing with spells, magic, and mysterious ancient wisdom might choose to use the appearance of a musty, leather-bound volume as its guiding metaphor.

Practical reasons in favor of the book metaphor deal fundamentally either with the input or the output. If you are converting information that has previously been published in book form—for example, if you are publish-

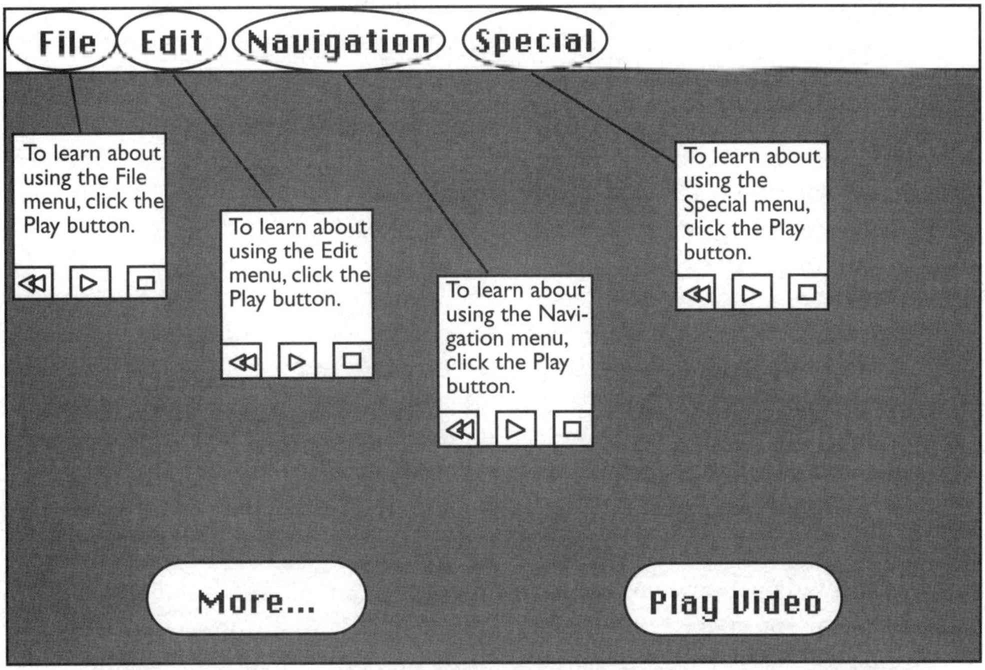

Figure 5-4. Relating the content of your document to the object it represents

ing a company's manuals, parts lists, policy and procedures documents, or other previously printed matter on a CD-ROM or in some other electronic medium, chances are good that the sheer size of the project will overwhelm you and your staff. You may easily have no time to design a fluid, pleasing user interface or information model to navigate through the document set you are publishing electronically. However, in most popular electronic publishing media, you can generate a table of contents automatically, and in some (Frame 4.0, for example) you can automatically create hypertext links to the chapter names, subheadings, and other structural elements in the document without having to insert them manually. On documents that cover thousands of pages, this can be an overwhelming reason for selecting an electronic metaphor that mimics paper.

Likewise, if your information is primarily text—such as Microsoft's *Encarta*, for example, or the Mayo Clinic *Family Health Disk*—you may choose to use a book-like metaphor for your document simply because it's essentially an electronic book, rather than a TV show with index markers and interactivity. This touches on the output-related reasons for selecting the book metaphor: familiarity and comfort. Most people who will use your program have probably been reading books since childhood (developers of educational multimedia for children and adult-literacy programs excepted, of course) and will be familiar with the table of contents and the index as ways of navigating through them.

You can sometimes split the difference between paper and electronic presentations by creating and using interesting screen layouts. Figure 5-5 shows one that uses some familiar cues from the paper world while taking advantage of the computer's ability to interact quickly. Here, the central portion of the document looks like a book, with facing pages (obviously a layout that either requires small type or large monitors). At the left-hand edge is a button or tab marked Table of Contents, and at the right is one marked Index, just where these elements are in a book. Familiarity may breed contempt, but it also eliminates frustration—that is, assuming that the familiar is carried through to its familiar, and logical, conclusion. (In the example shown here, I've included a typical page of text as well as a typical page from the table of contents, not because they are likely to appear on the same spread, but simply to demonstrate appearance.)

Additionally, this enhanced book metaphor includes a section across the top of the two-page spread headed by the legend "Jump to Chapter." The rounded "tabs" here, as with the Table of Contents tab and the Index tab, look somewhat like die-cut tabs that you might find in a reference book to support easy flipping back and forth between elements. In an electronic document that looks like this, you might click on any of these tabs to move directly to the chapter or section indicated on the tab. Additionally, in a thoroughly interactive electronic book, all the chapter and subject titles in the table of contents would all be interactive ways to navigate through the document—hypertext links that take you to the desired information in the book.

A refinement of this principle might be to display the tabs along the sides of the pages, just as they are in an actual book—some on the left and some on the right, depending on where you are reading. This kind of information overview provides two useful functions: in addition to the function demonstrated in Figure 5-5—that is, letting the user know what information is available— this latter variety of information overview lets the user know where he or she is in the information set. This function, of orienting the user in the document, is critical for certain applications. Figure 5-6 shows an example of this kind of layout.

Explicitly orienting the user in this way—by highlighting the tab at the left-hand by showing the chapters already read on one side and those remaining on the other—helps give users a sense of where they are in the document, a feeling of how much information they have already covered and what information remains to be explored. Additionally, cues like this

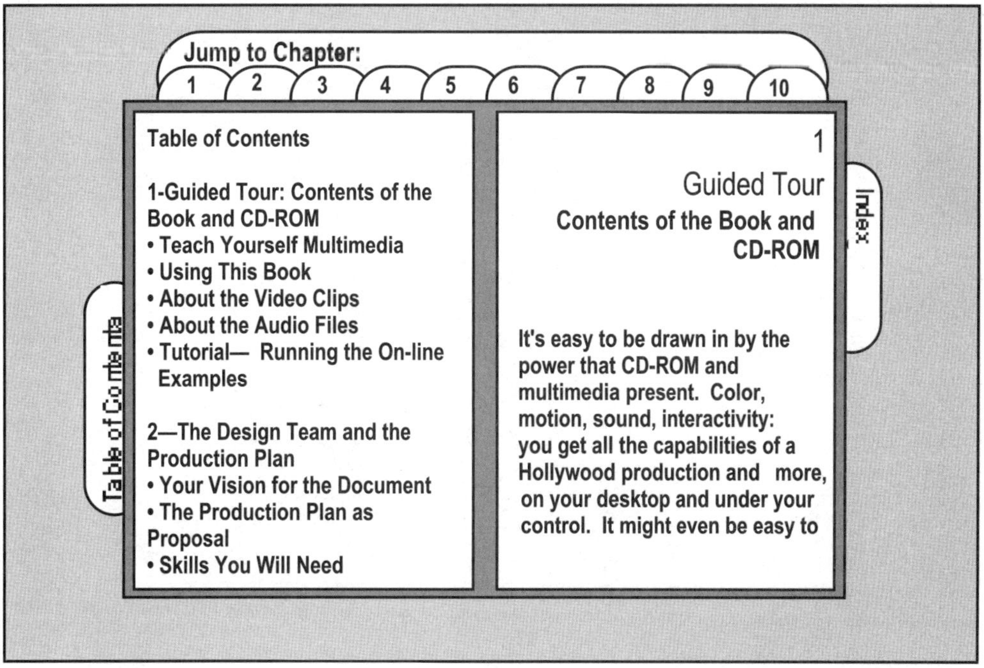

Figure 5-5. Enhanced book metaphor used to present information overview

can give kinesthetic learners—that is, people for whom physical input and physical cues are the keys to comprehension—an extra feel for the subject because it ties in with their physical experiences of using a book. Such people often, quite literally, "get a feel" for the information in a book by knowing roughly how much of the book is in each hand, just as some people use the position on a page or the chapter number in a sequence to remember information.

The third information overview model, that of the synthetic environment, presents the widest range of opportunities to the designer, and also presents the greatest challenges. It provides the closest means of matching your document to your vision, but it therefore assumes that you have a strong vision and a strong understanding of the information as well as the design.

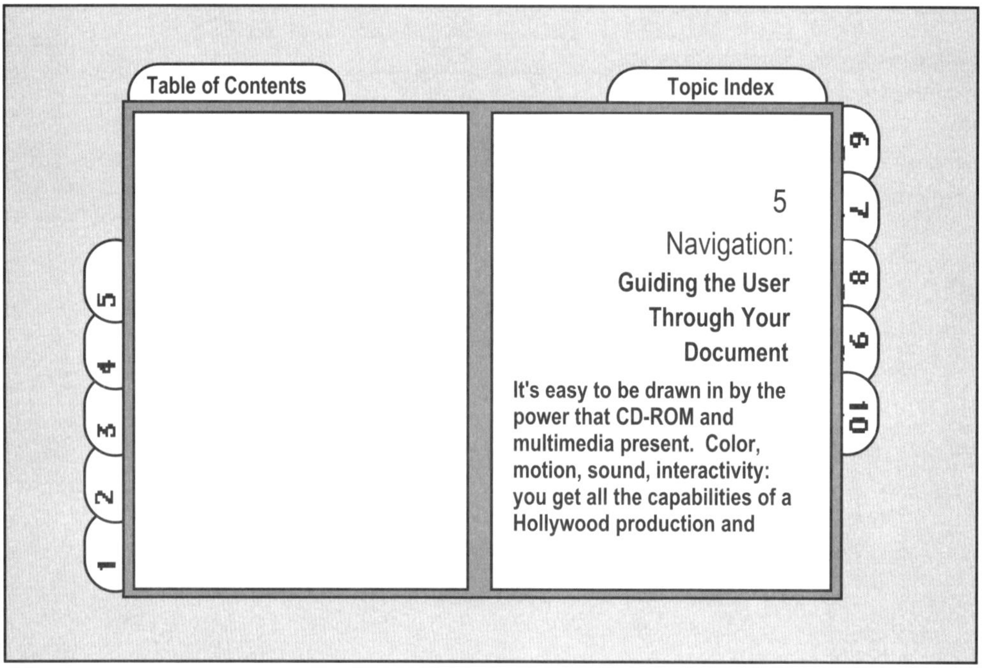

Figure 5-6. Enhanced book-metaphor overview, with explicit orientation

Reinforcing Concepts through User Interface Design

While talking about the information overview, I've often mixed it in with an understanding of the user interface of your document. This is an important concept to grasp: your information structure and the navigation model you select are essentially the user interface to your document, or rather to the information in your document.

Fortunately, this can actually make it easier to design your user interface, at least if you're working with a concrete object that has clear visual components and structure. One commercially available CD-ROM that does an excellent job of this is *How Multimedia Computers Work.* The interface to the CD-ROM is a three-dimensional rendering of a typical PC, with monitor, processor, mouse, keyboard, modem, speakers, and other components. To see and hear how a component does its job, you move the mouse to the component's picture and click. In a sense, the physical object (or its visual representation) serves as its own road map.

The underlying principle is fairly simple: as your users gain familiarity with the CD-ROM, they are simultaneously gaining familiarity with the object itself. The converse of this is also true: as your users learn more about the object's structure, they are also learning about how the CD-ROM works. This makes it easier for users to find things in your document: as they become more familiar with the object, it becomes more natural for them to follow its organization within the multimedia presentation you are designing for them. As a teaching and training tool, it's a highly effective way of closing the feedback loop to let each component of the education process—the teaching document and the subject being taught —work synergistically with each other to reinforce learning.

Does this sort of thing work well in games and interactive fiction? Once again, the answer depends on your sense of aesthetics and your audience level. If you're designing a game for young children, you want your user interface to look as much as possible like the thing it represents. To begin with, if you're designing a game for three- to five-year-olds, you'll need to put the basic controls in graphics, with sound support, and not in text-based menu items. (Though that may not be a hard and fast rule; recently I told my three-year-old to pull down the File menu in a program she was playing with, and she knew exactly what I meant and went to the correct part of the screen.) Brøderbund's *Living Books* are a successful example of this kind of game design; a sophisticated user (say, any first-grader who's used a *Living Book* more than about twice) can easily see which items on a "page" are sensitive to the mouse, and knows what to click. The fun here happens when the object does something unexpected, like the various pieces of paper pinned to the cork board behind the teacher in *Arthur's Teacher Trouble*. If you click on the flyer advertising choir practice, the three children's faces sing the triad of a major chord, after which the cat in the "Lost Cat" flyer above them joins in on the octave with a scratchy "meoooow!" It gets big laughs every time from my kids.

For games, then, it's important to make the controls obvious enough that your audience will be able to see that they're controls, but there should be an element of surprise in what the controls do when you click them. That element of surprise is what creates laughter, enjoyment, and what keeps people coming back to the game. For older players, the rules may differ, depending on the effect the game is meant to have. If the game is a mystery, like Sierra Online's *Gabriel Knight* games, half of the enjoyment is in figuring out which of the items in a scene really are important. There's a scene in *Gabriel Knight II: The Sins of the Fathers* (and this doesn't give away any of the mystery) in which Gabriel visits his grandmother's house and goes up to the attic to look through some of his late father's possessions. Because it's a mystery game, you know that something in the attic is a clue that will provide important information about the voodoo murders that Gabriel is investigating—but you don't know what it is, and even if you make the right guess, it's only one piece in the puzzle.

Perhaps most important for educators and training developers is the degree to which designing your own multimedia projects lets you combine games and learning to an unprecedented degree. Multimedia provides such a rich source of stimulation that the "ah-HA" feeling you get (when you solve a puzzle, as in *Gabriel Knight*, or when you click on the picture of the staircase in the library on Myst Island—and I'll say no more, except that my hair actually, physically stood on end when I did that for the first time) is a powerful way of ensuring retention. Educational software designers talk about "the sweet spot" in learning games: kids enjoy watching Saturday morning cartoons, but they need to learn. The best educational games are those that find this sweet spot of balance, where there's enough activity and interactivity to keep even the most jaded MTV audience responding, while still providing useful information in a way that the kids will retain.

Paying attention to the way you design and lay out your screens can help you find this sweet spot. Look for ways to reinforce the fundamental concepts you're trying to teach by connecting them in some way to a physical object. Figure 5-7 (from one of the examples) demonstrates this. In the example, the initial screen is based on a sketch I made while explaining the components of a video capture and display system for a seminar I was teaching. Each of the major areas in the diagram is a sensitive area that plays a video clip—something I couldn't do on the whiteboard when I originally drew the illustration.

For this book, the example in Figure 5-7 shows two ways that the layout of your information reinforces the underlying message. On the surface, the message of the example is how you capture video on a computer and later display it on a monitor. However, using this subject as an example in this chapter is also setting up a connection—a kind of psychological hypertext link, if you will—between the subject of this chapter and the subject of the next one, which is about how to capture and get the best use out of video. This is what I mean by reinforcing the structural understanding of your subject.

Links and How the User Finds Them

We've glossed over some of the ways you make links—that is, the sensitive items in a screen—obvious to your users. In a typical multimedia document, you may need to put links in text, in graphics, and even in video. (Yes, it's possible to put a hot spot in a video clip, or, more specifically, on the screen in a location where a video clip will be playing. I'll explain more later in this chapter, and of course you can look at the exam-

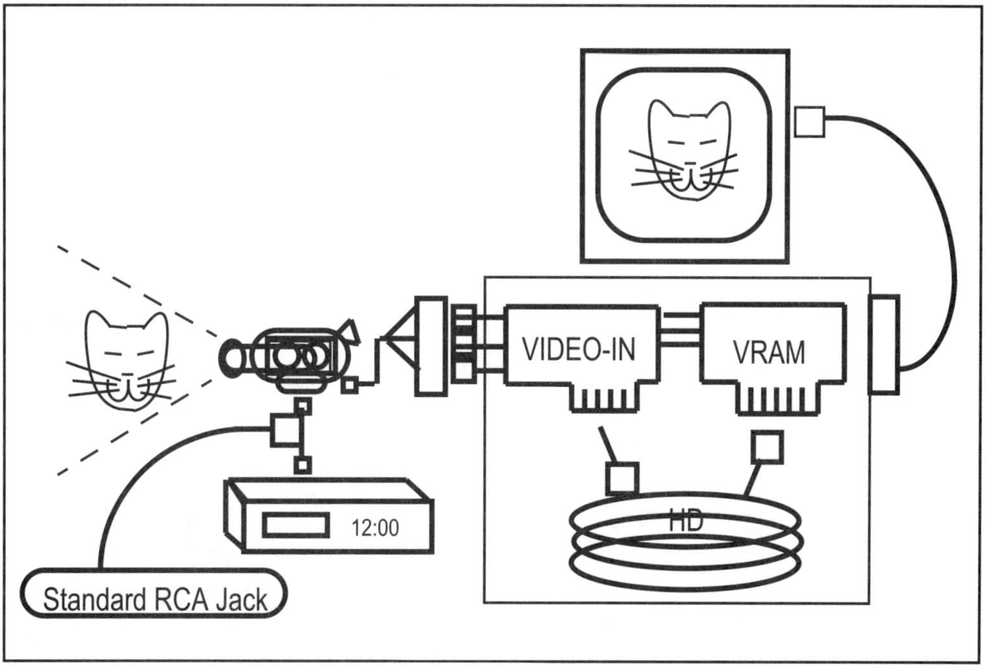

Figure 5-7. Block diagram as user interface design

ple on the CD-ROM.) Each of these media presents its own problems, but there are some conventions developing in the CD-ROM market, and a few common-sense rules that can help.

In the text portion of a multimedia document, there are three basic schemes, depending on whether you'll be displaying in color or black-and-white:

- putting a box around the text that stands for the cross-reference or link;
- underlining the cross-reference or link (sometimes with a double underscore to make it more apparent that it's not simply being underscored for emphasis); and
- displaying the link in a highlighted color.

Users of Windows programs with well-designed help files will be familiar with the last two. In fact, for help files created with the superb RoboHelp program from Blue Sky Software, you automatically get a different kind of highlighting for each of two different kinds of links: pop-ups and jumps. A pop-up is the kind of link often used for glossary entries. You click on the unfamiliar word and the definition displays in a small window that sits on top of the rest of your document, without changing it. When you're finished looking at the pop-up, you make it go away (in Windows, simply by clicking the mouse).

Pop-ups fill much the same structural need as footnotes: they provide additional information within the context of the main flow of the material, but they're self-contained. Jumps, on the other hand, are cross-references to another chapter (or whatever unit you choose to use for your basic modules in the document). A jump replaces the contents of the text window with the contents of the new module; you can "flip back" to the one you were looking at before, or you can follow another jump to another location. RoboHelp automatically uses a dashed, single underscore to signify pop-ups, and a solid, double underscore to signify jumps. In addition, both kinds of links display in the highlight color you've selected for Windows (by default, it's bright blue).

As a practical, technical note, consider the following different ways of highlighting text on a screen. Claris Corporation's HyperCard and Macromedia Director both support, among other ways, the use of text as a bitmap. There are advantages to this from a design standpoint: you can make the text into individual stand-alone blocks, particularly in Director, which you can then animate and make sensitive as hot spots or links. However, for someone used to a word-processing program that allows you to highlight text to modify, delete, or insert additional letters into it, it can be confusing. Having the text stored as a bitmap means that you can't go back and edit your text: once it's there, you can change the individual pixels, you can erase it, you can draw over it (and in Director, you can also draw under it), but you can't, for instance, correct a spelling or insert a word where text already exists. Furthermore, when you specify a region as the source for a jump in HyperCard, you're actually drawing a "button" directly on the screen, at fixed coordinates. Taken in context, this is an advantage; since you can't make the text move anyway, it's just as well that the buttons you define aren't really associated with the text but rather are placed where the text happens to fall beneath them. In Director, on the other hand, you can assign the sensitivity to the drawing element that includes your text; if you move the text around on the screen, the sensitive region moves with it.

Hypertext tools based on or derived from word-processing and publishing tools—for example, RoboHelp and FrameMaker 4.0—simplify things tremendously. To make a hypertext link to another topic in RoboHelp, you simply put the cursor where you want the link to appear and click on the Jump button from the RoboHelp tool bar. This opens a window containing all the topics currently in your document; you can then type the text you want to appear highlighted in your document, select the topic you want to jump to when the user clicks on it, and when you're done, click OK and the link is added to your document. If you later go in and add or remove text before the link, it doesn't matter; the link is associated directly with the text, not with the screen location.

FrameMaker works in a similar way, but with a little more flexibility. The procedure is as follows:

1. Select an existing region of text.
2. Pull down the Markers option of the Special menu.
3. Select Hypertext as the marker type. This pops up the following dialog box:

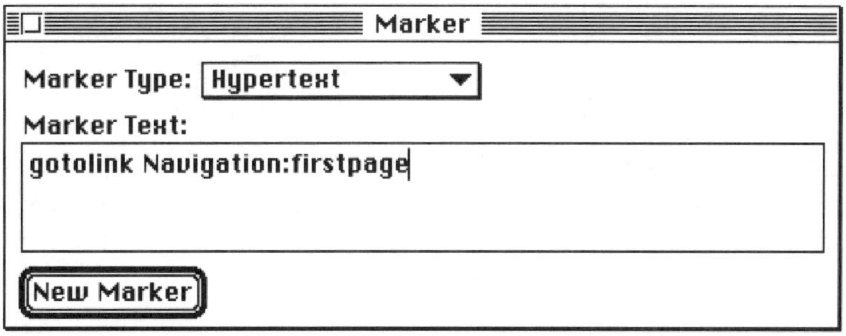

4. In the Marker Text box, type in one of Frame's hypertext commands. In the example shown here, this is how you define a jump (with the gotolink or openlink commands).

By the way, don't make the mistake of assuming that on-line help and multimedia are two different things. They're identical in virtually all fundamental ways: modularity, information overviews, linking, and interactivity are all shared by the on-line help for a Windows program and a QuickTime-based multimedia adventure game on the Macintosh. And for multimedia projects that depend heavily on text—such as encyclopedias, the reference portion of training or education documents, or any topic that's best served in text—tools such as RoboHelp (or its counterpart for the Macintosh, QuickHelp by Altura Software) are invaluable for seamlessly creating interactive text documents that you can embed into your video and graphical projects.

What about putting links into pictures? There are a couple of ways that are becoming standardized. The best way is to use graphic design to make the link objects in the scene stand out. Figure 5-7 shows a simple way of doing this, by using a heavier line on the sensitive portions of the illustration. The block for VRAM and the video capture card stand out because their borders are darker than the rest of the lines in the illustration. For games and entertainment you may wish to make the difference more subtle to enhance the enjoyment of looking for clues.

The ways you accomplish this vary from tool to tool. In HyperCard, because text and graphics are both varieties of bitmap, you simply draw a button around the portion of the image that you want to make sensitive; you then have to script the action that you want the stack to take when the user clicks this button. (The HyperCard Script Language Guide that comes with the Hypercard authoring package covers this in detail. The booklet *Getting Started With HyperCard,* which is part of the same kit, is a good, simple tutorial that will have you creating interactive stacks in less than an hour.) FrameMaker works basically the same way, but you need to add a text column over the part of the picture that you want to make sensitive, and then insert a hypertext command as previously described. (Chapter 27 of FrameMaker's manual discusses hypertext commands in detail.)

But many picture elements aren't rectangular. The tutorial at the end of Chapter 4 describes one of the tools on the CD-ROM, MediaWrangler from AltaVista Technology. MediaWrangler gives what is as far as I know the industry's most flexible and detailed control over the shape of your hot spot (what MediaWrangler calls a "MAP," short for media area pointer; in this business, you either love the jargon or you stay home). MAPs in MediaWrangler can be any shape, as long as they have no more than 255 points in the resulting polygon. To draw a MAP, you click the right button on the mouse and the cursor changes to a pencil. Click the left button once to start your MAP, and as you move the mouse you'll see a colored line stretching out from the cursor. Each time you click the left button again, the line will "stick" to the image. When you're done, double-click the left button. Now you can associate a media element with that hot spot, or MAP; the next time you or a user double-clicks on the MAP, MediaWrangler pops up the image, runs the video clip, or plays the sound that you associated with it.

Tutorial 1: Adding a Link to an Image

This tutorial uses Aldus Persuasion to add links and hot spots to your document.

Aldus Persuasion lets you add interactivity and navigation to your presentations by including a Jump button. To see the Jump button, make the Tools palette visible; the Jump button is in the lower-left corner, highlighted here:

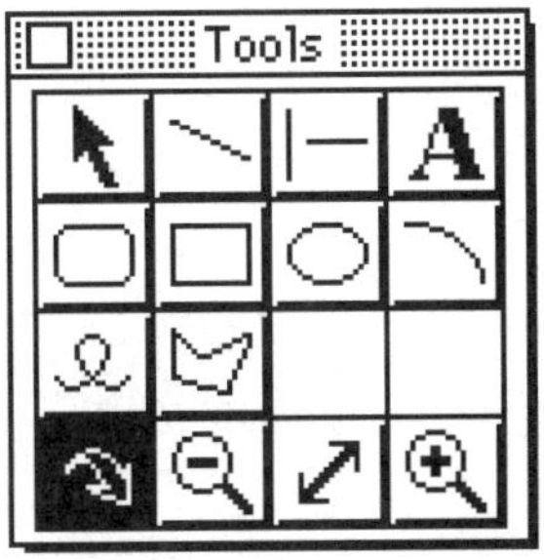

Here's the procedure for adding a jump to any region on your screen.

1. **Select the slide on which you wish to put the jump.**
2. **Determine the location in the text or graphic at which you wish to position the jump.**

   The stylistic issues around button design are interesting enough that I'll talk about them in the review at the end of this chapter; for now, just identify a region on the screen from which you want to make your users able to click for a jump.
3. **Click the Jump tool from the Persuasion Tools palette.**

   Now, the next location you click on the screen will be the approximate spot of your jump.
4. **Put the cursor over the area you wish to make a jump and click the mouse. (On the PC, click the left mouse button.)**

   Persuasion adds the Jump badge, with "handles" to indicate that you can resize and reposition the jump. If you need to move or change the shape of the sensitive area, you can do this now or at any other time you are editing this slide in Persuasion.

Tutorial 2: Making On-screen Navigation Buttons

To make on-screen navigation buttons in a document, you want to make sure they're in the same place on every screen. This tutorial demonstrates two methods of doing this, one in Persuasion and one in FrameMaker.

Adding a "Choose a Name" Button in Persuasion

The document from which this screen snapshot was taken deserves a little explanation. It is a multimedia report generated by the students of Donna Haswell's first grade class at Cherry Chase Elementary School in Sunnyvale, California. (A portion of this report is included on the CD-ROM.) Each child studied some way that animals adapted to winter. The class as a whole filled out a matrix with information including the animal's name, where it lived, what it ate, and some interesting fact about the animal. The students then used a charming beginning multimedia program called Storybook Weaver to write and illustrate the reports about the animals they had selected.

It was a collaborative effort. In addition to the 27 students who contributed their reports, my wife, Kim Fisher, contributed the navigation for this presentation, based on a design and a prototype that I had constructed.

On the school's Open House night, the report ran in the classroom, displayed on the television as well as on the computer, so that parents and siblings could see what the students had created. The program would run as an automatic slide show, displaying every child's report for 30 seconds, then advancing to the next report. We also designed it so that at any time, the children could click on a button to choose a name, then select their own name from a screen containing the names of every child who had contributed.

This meant that the "Choose a Name" button had to be visible on every screen. Here's how to do this using Aldus Persuasion:

1. **Add the text "Choose a Name" to the lower-right corner of the screen in one of the children's reports.**

   The children were already familiar with looking to the lower-right corner for information on navigating and managing the other computer programs they use. Additionally, we made the text magenta so that it would stand out in contrast to the blue-and-white colors selected for the background of the slides.

2. **Place a Jump button over the text.**

   This was performed just as explained in the previous tutorial.

When we finished, the screen looked like this:

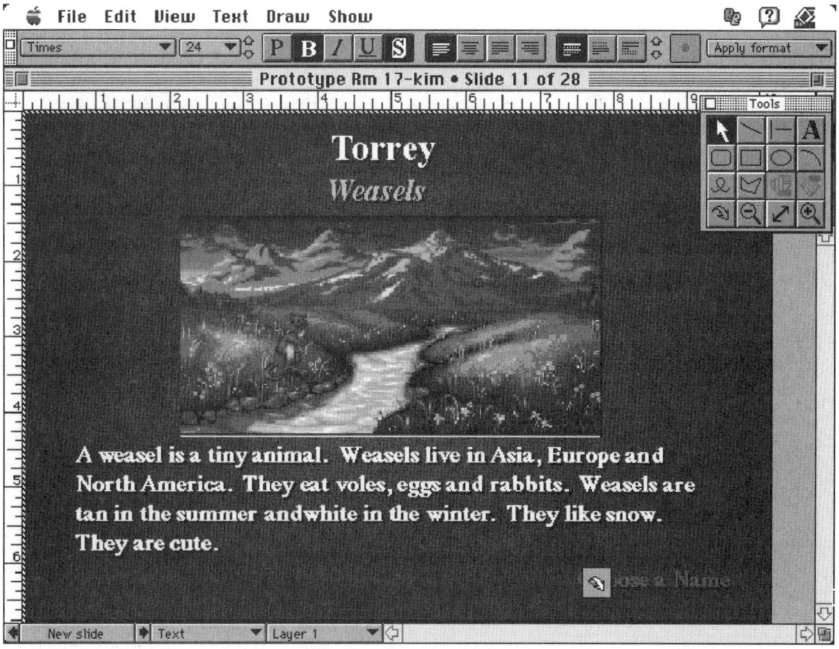

You can see the words "Choose a Name" in the lower right-hand corner, with the Persuasion Jump badge over them. The next step let us add the button and text to any slide that required them.

3. **Place the cursor to the left and above the Jump badge, then drag the mouse to select the Jump badge and the text.**

   You can tell that the badge and text are both selected because you will be able to see the handles for each of the elements.

4. **Edit the Jump so that it sends the user to the main navigation screen.**

   To do this, hold the mouse down over the Jump badge and select Edit Jump from the pop-up menu that appears. This displays the following dialog box:

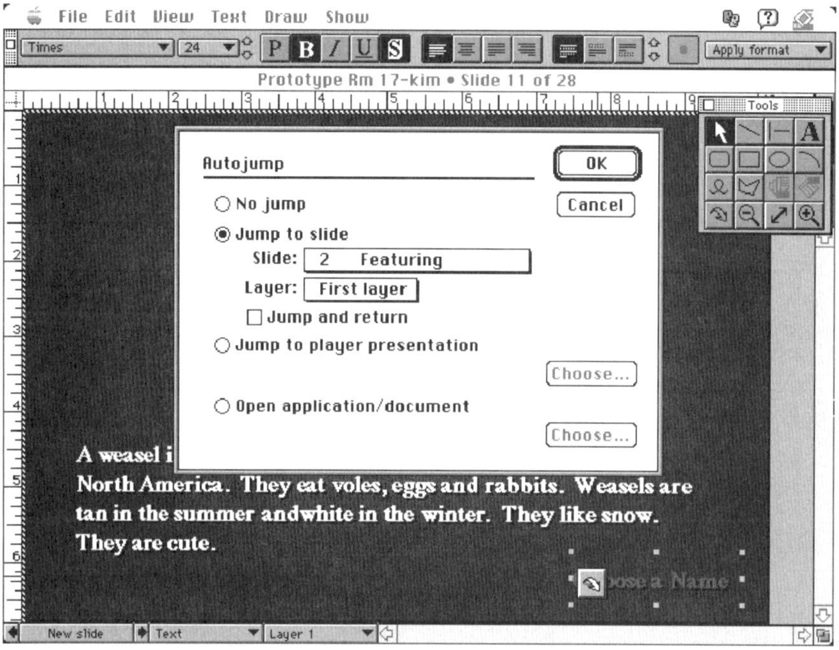

In Persuasion, when you hold the mouse button down while the cursor is in the box labeled Slide, a pop-up menu appears from which you can select the destination of your jump. In our presentation, the slide entitled "Featuring" is the slide that contains all the children's names, each with a Jump badge that lets them select their name from the screen containing the entire list. Select that slide, then click OK.

5. Copy the badge and the text by typing Command-C.

You have now copied the command button to the clipboard, ready to paste it into other locations in your document. When you copied the badge and its associated text, you also copied two additional pieces of information:

- the destination of the jump, in this case to Slide 2 entitled "Featuring"; and
- the on-screen location of the Jump badge and the text element associated with it.

Now you can paste the text and the jump into any slide in your presentation, and Persuasion automatically includes the destination of the jump and the location on your screen. This means that every slide that has this "Choose a Name" button will respond in exactly the same way, letting the children find their own name from a list on the slide entitled "Featuring."

Adding a Menu Footer in FrameMaker

Frame Technologies' FrameMaker 4.0 makes it even easier to add control buttons to every screen of your multimedia document. The following examples come from the CD-ROM version of my first book for AP, *The CD-ROM Guide to Multimedia Authoring*. This illustration comes from Chapter 1, "Learning to Think Multimedia:"

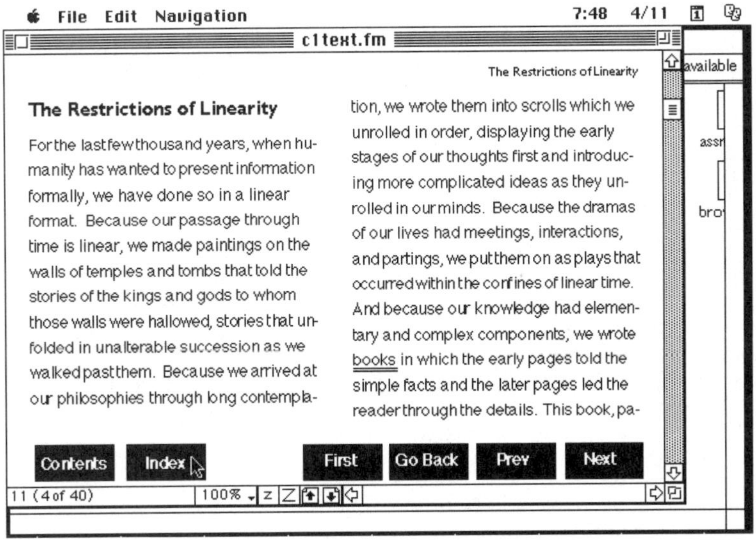

In this illustration, the buttons across the bottom of the display are in a footer that Frame displays on every page. The two buttons on the left take you to the table of contents and the index, respectively. The other four buttons take you to:

- the first page in the chapter;
- the last link you were viewing before you jumped to this one (FrameMaker keeps a stack containing the last 69 locations you viewed, and lets you step backward through them in the reverse order in which you selected them);
- the previous page in this chapter; and
- the next page in this chapter.

In keeping with what is becoming the common design for interactivity, I placed the Next button in the lower right-hand corner of the screen.

Here's how you add command buttons like these in FrameMaker. Note that the following instructions work on Macintosh, Windows, and Unix platforms; note also that some of the terms and instructions used in this tutorial assume you have some knowledge of FrameMaker organization.

1. Pull down the View menu and select Master Pages.
2. Make sure there is a text region across the bottom of the page, in which you would type traditional footer information such as the page number, document title, or whatever else you want to include at the bottom of every page.
3. Pull down the Graphics menu and select Tools. This pops up the following tool palette:

Text region tool

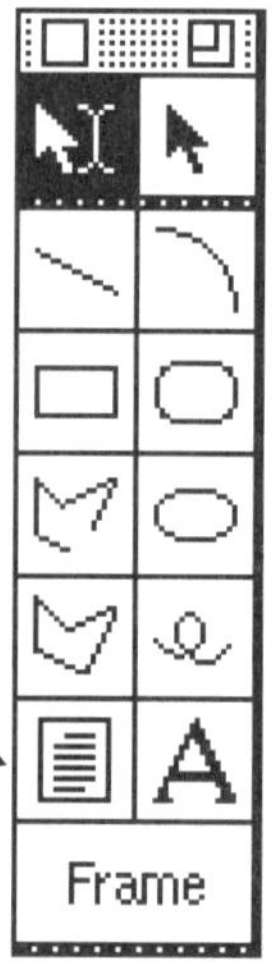

4. Select the text region tool and draw a new text region inside the footer.
5. Double-click inside the new text region to select it.
6. Pull down the Special menu and select Marker. This pops up the Marker dialog box.
7. From the Marker Type field, select Hypertext. Then, in the Marker Text field, type the words "gotolink firstpage."

The Marker dialog box should now look like this, except that the Edit Marker button reads New Marker the first time you make a new marker:

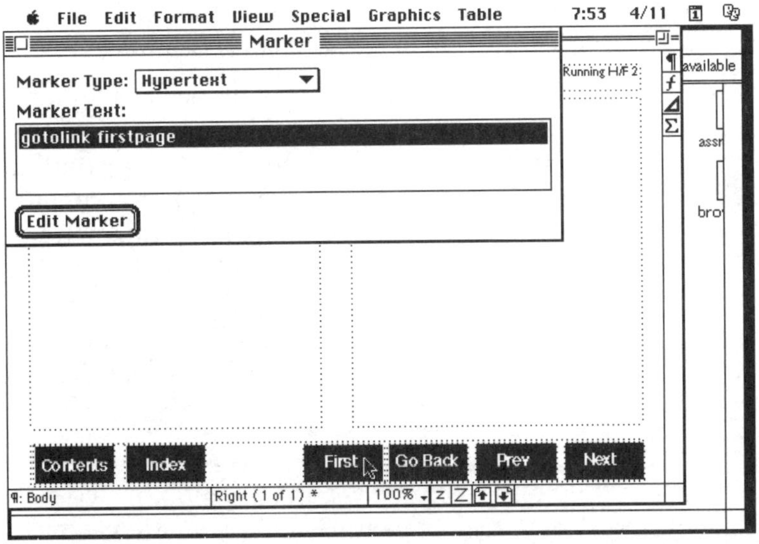

8. When you have typed in the hypertext command, click Edit Marker to add this marker to your document.

You can now drag this text region over any element in your footer. For the document used in this example, I drew blue boxes, then added white text over them. Then I added a text region as indicated in this example, placing this text region with the hypertext marker on top of the blue box.

FrameMaker handles hypertext by using commands that you type into the Marker Text box, as shown here. These commands let you determine where to jump when the user clicks on a hypertext link. In addition to a simple jump, Frame lets you decide whether you want to stay in the same window or open a new window.

You can also jump to a file other than the one being displayed. This way, if your document has several chapters which are in individual files, you can jump between the chapter files without having to concatenate them all into a single, gigantic file. Smaller files display slightly more quickly in FrameMaker, an important concern if you're planning to run on a computer with a lower-powered processor.

Review: From Macro to Micro

This chapter covered a lot of ground, moving from issues of overall information structure to where you put buttons on a page to make your document easy to use. This represents the range of the issues you face as a multimedia designer. It's not magic, it's not even terribly complex—as long as you approach it in small, easy-to-digest chunks.

We also looked at several models of user interface design: one that resembled a computer program, one that resembled a book, and one that resembled a movie with text and control buttons. As I've continued to study and develop interactive documents, I'm coming to the conclusion that the best ones look the least like any existing medium. Interactivity and digital multimedia make possible something that has never existed before, at least not outside people's heads: a way to connect any two (or more) objects in a representation of information. This permits you and your audience to link together familiar objects in ways that they have perhaps never been linked before.

In many ways, this defines the very essence of creativity. It is for this reason that interactive multimedia has such potential in the classroom—not because the kids like to look at pictures and play video games, but because the ability to produce their own multimedia documents gives them the power to connect thoughts and ideas in ways that no other medium has given them. It's a truism in education that you learn best by teaching; as the children in room 17 learned about their animals and put together their stories on the computer, they weren't simply repeating information they had been told to memorize: they were generating their own creative works in a way that connected facts for them at a deeper level than any other educational tool has been able to accomplish.

In spite of the novelty associated with the technology we use for its creation, the multimedia/nonlinear approach is in many ways the most natural for the human mind. The hard part is organizing the information in such a way that any other human mind can get at it. In the next chapter, I'll talk about some of the concerns you need to address in trying to reach other human minds. And although the title of that chapter is "Module Design," the real subject is the person who is going to use the module you design, and how that person's needs affect the way you put together your multimedia document.

Chapter 6
Module Design

Issues for the Rushed Reader

It's going to take some time yet before people pour themselves a cup of hot tea, wrap up in a cozy quilt, snuggle in front of the fire, and decide to relax with their favorite CD-ROM. Eventually, there's a good chance that CD-ROM-based information will become the prevalent form of entertainment, and that CD-ROMs will engender the kind of lose-yourself-in-the-story feeling that we now get from a favorite novel or motion picture. (To some extent, I confess I felt much of this the first time I explored Myst Island, but at present, the Miller brothers' *Myst* is unique in this art form.)

For the present, CD-ROM is used where it's economically effective: for conveying information on, with, and often about computers. Because you can't read a CD-ROM without a computer, the medium itself filters its audience. Because of the economics involved in recouping production costs, many CD-ROM projects currently are concerned with commercial and educational projects: subjects for which people are willing to pay to learn. That's not to say there isn't a huge market for entertainment CD-ROMs, from games to adaptations of popular novels to the new kind of music/video combinations that Peter Gabriel and he-who-was-once-Prince have produced.

But at present, nearly all of the people involved in producing multimedia for their own use are typically either teachers involved in creating courseware for their classes or other professionals involved in putting together multimedia presentations to inform or persuade an audience. The kind of people who use this kind of multimedia—I typically call it nonfiction multimedia—tend to have some specific needs, wishes, desires, and, for that matter, hot buttons, to a degree that's surprisingly consistent across a fairly wide user base. Users of nonfiction multimedia are typically involved because they want to get something out of it, something in addition to the enjoyment of clicking buttons and making things happen.

For instance, they may be learning to read with an interactive literacy program or finding out how to use a new application they bought for their personal computer. They may be looking up answers for a customer on their company's internal CD-ROM-based customer support application. But in all such cases, they are unlike users of entertainment multimedia. Users of nonfiction multimedia are goal-oriented, and this gives them several characteristics in common.

Three Audiences: Browsers, Scanners, and Students

In designing and producing electronic documents (as opposed to games) during the past decade, I've observed three fundamental ways that people use these documents. To help distinguish these ways, I identify the different kinds of users by three different names:

- *browsers*: people who are looking almost idly through an information set for topics that interest, appeal, or pique their curiosity;
- *scanners*: people who have a very specific task, almost a mission, and often a time frame within which they have to accomplish this task; and
- *students*: people who browse or scan, but who then look in great detail and are willing to follow cross-references in depth.

Each of these three kinds of user has very different needs, attitudes, and emotional states when they use your document. Furthermore, any individual human being who sits down to your document might belong to any of these categories at any time—and in fact may change from one category to the next at any time. This is one challenge for the designer of informational multimedia: you have to come up with a structure that meets the needs of three fairly distinct kinds of users.

What are the needs of each category of user, and how can you design for them? First let's talk about needs, about what each type of user really expects out of a document. Once you understand the psychology of user interaction that drives each of these user categories, you can develop a strategy for dealing with all of them.

Browsers are relatively easy to deal with. The typical browser acts like he or she is reading a magazine in the doctor's office. Browsers are looking for subjects of interest in your document, trying to find topics, entries, modules, or in some cases media types (a group of video clips, for instance, or all available sound samples) that pique their interest. Browsers may or may not have a specific goal, task, or project in mind; often they are reading for enjoyment, or otherwise engaging in a much less task-oriented pursuit. And lest you think that browsers, by their comparatively relaxed nature, are relatively unimportant, consider that browsing is the behavior engaged in by most people when they are deciding to purchase a book, magazine, or CD-ROM. It's one way of skimming over the surface of the content, looking for intriguing, useful, or pertinent bits of information on a topic that the browser wants to pursue; chances are you engage in much the same behavior when you're deciding between two books in the bookstore. If you lose the browsers, you may be losing customers.

Scanners, by contrast, are under the gun. Scanners are impatient, rushed, goal-oriented and task-driven. Scanners know what they need to know; often, they just don't know all the details—they have a good idea of the basic structure but they can't remember the order of the steps, for example. Scanners also typically have a certain amount of knowledge about the subject; sometimes it's enough to help them find things quickly, while other times it's just enough knowledge to get them into trouble by making assumptions about the information. When you think of scanners, think of someone on a customer-service hotline, someone who is getting an earful from an unhappy customer while trying to find the answer in an on-line database at the same time. Such a person has probably already been through internal training, probably knows some of the answer, but doesn't know all the answer or they wouldn't be using the document. Scanners need answers to specific questions quickly, without wading through a lot of unnecessary navigation. Note, by the way, that as more and more companies move to on-line documentation in a multimedia format for their internal staff as well as for customers, there's a good and growing chance that some multimedia project you end up working on will be used in just such a scenario.

Students bounce, to some extent, between the other two characteristics. A student has a goal, like a scanner, but doesn't already know the topic. A scanner knows some of the answer to his or her question, or at least knows that the answer is in the document somewhere. A student is absorbing information, acquiring the mental structure that your document provides while also following links, cross-references, and other navigational aids in a manner similar to a browser. Students typically (but not always) have the time to be more thorough than scanners, while they are more goal-oriented than browsers.

What Frustrates Each User?

It's worth considering how each type of user becomes frustrated with a document, so that you can avoid that fate insofar as it is possible. Browsers become frustrated—give up and put down the document—when they can't find topics of interest to them. It may well be that there are no topics in the document that they find interesting. If you don't care about hunting and fishing, for example, you're probably not going to find anything you want to read in *Field and Stream*, through no fault of the magazine's editors, writers, or art directors. Still, if you're browsing a CD-ROM about a topic that interests you, you'll get frustrated if you can't find topics, subjects, articles, or other clues about pieces of information that are contained within the document.

Scanners become frustrated primarily by anything that takes time. It's a well-known psychological anomaly that an individual's time sense changes under stress: if you think time flies when you're having fun, it goes hypersonic when you're looking for an answer while your supervisor is standing at your shoulder. While looking for answers in an electronic document under these stressful circumstances, people tend to become more impatient, to demand more immediate responses from the system, and to become frustrated when the document doesn't provide them with instant answers—not when they can't find what they want to know. It becomes the document's fault, and in many cases it is legitimately so.

Students become frustrated when the information is poorly organized, when there is no logical flow, or more to the point, when the information's structure does not follow the inherent structure of the subject. Students, remember, are still learning the subject at hand. Therefore, the document must reinforce the subject in any way possible; a structural approach to it is an important way to give students additional opportunities to learn and to internalize the way the subject is organized. Students dislike forward references—that is, cross-references to sections that they haven't seen yet. In the electronic world, where hypertext links and multimedia module selection takes the control of sequence and flow out of the author's hands and puts it into the user's, it may be the case that your students have stumbled across a module that best fits later in the information flow. You need to indicate this in the most nonintrusive way possible.

How can you indicate this in your document—how can you provide easy tags for all kinds of users to grasp while they follow your title? Here are some proven design concepts that work well with each of these user types. Some of them are complementary, meaning that you can use them in the same module to add informational benefit to more than one kind of user. Some of them are contradictory, meaning that you won't be able to pair them; in such cases, go back to your audience analysis or your structural analysis and decide where you want to put each solution. Often, reorganizing the structure of your document, or the default flow through it, will give you the solution you need for satisfying more than one kind of user.

(A word for game developers: Never mind. That is, if you are developing a multimedia game for which part of the play is discovering how it works or what happened previously—*Myst* is the most successful example of such a game in the CD-ROM market at the time I write this—you're more concerned with aesthetics, the user interface, and with the playability of the game than with information design. This section is predominantly valuable to developers of educational, training, and informational multimedia documents such as on-line encyclopedias, courseware, reference works, and other nonfiction documents. Note that many good entertainment documents can benefit from this kind of audience analysis and information design. But games have a different set of problems than the ones the information organizational tools described here are meant to solve.)

Designing for the Browser

Don't let the easygoing description of the browser lull you into thinking you don't need to design for this category's specific needs. As mentioned before, browsing closely resembles the actions of people who are evaluating books, magazines, and CD-ROMs for purchase. With that in mind, the browser may be the person who is looking through your title in a computer store or at a friend's home or office, making the decision of whether or not to buy your product. This means that in some ways, the browser can be the most important of all the categories.

Design for the browser really includes such issues as package design, marketing, sales, and to some extent sales training. When planned properly, a browseable user interface supports all these activities, as well as benefits from them. The rest of this section describes the way that your interface supports browsers, but let's examine some of the ways that browseability in the document can benefit from external design elements.

Perhaps the most important part of overall design that can affect the satisfaction that browsers experience when using your document is simply to help select the right audience. Cover design, packaging, and in-store support can help get the people who are interested in your subject to your title. The days are gone when people would buy nearly any CD-ROM simply because they had the drive and they wanted to play with something new. Now, just as with software, books, or magazines, you need to design a support scenario that helps select the right user for your product.

This includes the usual techniques: an appropriate list of features on the package, basic familiarity with your product by store personnel, and the rest of the product marketing details that you can learn from a marketing specialist or from classes and books on that specific part of the business. When you look at that information, however—specifically, marketing information about how to attract your target audience, how to establish product awareness, and how to "hook" potential buyers with the externals—be sure to feed it back to your interface design so that once your target audience is selected, they'll be able to find what the packaging has led them to expect.

Assuming that the people browsing your document are looking at it for the right reasons, how can you support their needs in your design? The most important answer is to provide some kind of overview, using clear and distinct titles, to the contents of your document. Browsers tend either to look in the table of contents or (in the book world, at any rate) to flip through the pages looking for subheadings that interest them. Later, browsers will occasionally find a paragraph—almost, but not quite, at random—and read it to see whether or not it touches on their needs. You can't control that level of detail (and indeed, in a visual multimedia document, you won't have subheadings or paragraphs that they can browse), but you can give your document a structure and an interface that assists these needs.

To begin with, develop a road map or structural overview of your document. This can be as simple and familiar as a table of contents, or it can be graphical and even animated to show the relationships between elements of your document. Browsers like to know what's available, without having to read through it in great detail. More important, they want to know how to get from where they are to where they want to go. In the book and magazine world, this is done with the table of contents, with key words at the top corners of dictionary pages, and with other visual cues. In electronic document design, there are several ways of doing this with interactivity, with animation, and with multimedia capabilities themselves.

One of the best tools for browsers (and for scanners as well, though we'll cover them shortly) is a pop-up navigation aid such as a table of contents, a graphical road map, or some other information guide. Many good multimedia applications have a button on every screen that either displays a map to the contents or the first screen of the program, if that is a kind of map. If your design includes a menu bar, tool bar, or some other display of the available command tools, at least one of them should let your users see (if not jump to) the overall navigation display.

What should be on this display? If your document is organized like a book, into chapters and subjects and subsections with headings and titles, then your first line of navigation is the table of contents. In this case, the titles and subheadings are critically important. Write headings that are clear, understandable, and concise. Most important, write headings that are distinct. You need to make clear to the reader not only what is in the section that the heading represents, but also what is *not* in a given section, through comparison with other headings.

For more visually oriented documents (or subjects), choose a visual representation of the information. For example, I designed a training document on how to use a company's product, a piece of electronic test equipment, for which an illustration of the equipment served as the introductory screen. Users of the document could select portions of the test system (which were also labeled with the title of the appropriate portion of the document), click on them, and see the contents of the training document as though they were inside the equipment at that point. The popular CD-ROM *How Multimedia Computers Work* (from The Software Toolworks, produced by Brian Blum) does much the same thing. The initial screen shows a three-dimensional model of a typical computer, with a monitor, a CD-ROM drive, external speakers, keyboard, and mouse. To see a presentation on each of these elements, you click on the element you want to see.

One problem with visual road maps that they don't share with the table of contents approach is that it may sometimes be unclear what is available for interaction. That is, in a paper book, the table of contents includes a page listing that tells you where the section starts; it's part of our basic literacy training to know that you turn to the page listed in the contents to see the beginning of the section. In this way, the table of contents entry is a visual signal that we can interact with in a known way. No similar visual signals exist for graphical road maps in multimedia programs that are as universally accepted as the table of contents. (The pull-down menu is probably the closest computer analog to the table of contents, as it lists in context a subset of the available functions at any given time; Chapter 5 talks about using pull-down menus as part of your interface scheme.)

There are several possible approaches. One, used in *How Multimedia Computers Work*, is to highlight sensitive regions as the mouse passes over them. For example, when you move the mouse over the main box of the computer containing the central processing unit (CPU), that entire box gets a kind of halo around it, as well as a title. This is good, in that it differentiates between the computer and, for example, the desktop on which it sits, but it has two related (if minor) problems.

The first problem is that it isn't completely unambiguous as to what you're supposed to do. Now, as graphical user interfaces become more prevalent, it's intuitive to try clicking the mouse on something. (In fact, a number of children's CD-ROMs have none of this kind of disambiguation; half the fun for my children in playing with the Brøderbund *Living Books* CD-ROM series is in clicking on all the items in a scene to see what they do. Again, for games and entertainment, this is a valid part of the sense of play; you might want to include it in a strict training or educational title as well, if it fits the tone you have chosen to take.) This minor problem is one that only faces people the first time they use the program, however; after you've clicked once on a highlighted object, it's easy to remember for subsequent uses.

Something that's not as obvious, however, is the issue of nested objects. I didn't discover for several sessions with the CD-ROM that there are smaller objects on the CPU that the program highlights separately when I move the cursor over them: the disk and CD-ROM drives, for example. Again, in this case the issue was very minor and I discovered these smaller sensitive regions by accident. But this was for a fairly simple, consumer-oriented CD that's predominantly meant as entertainment. If you are designing a training CD-ROM in which it is critical that your users see every available segment of information, make sure that you have some way of disambiguating the sensitive regions from the surrounding areas.

One specific technique for doing this is discussed in Chapter 8, "Animation." You can animate objects on an individual frame of your document, creating "layers" of visibility that reveal the different levels of detail to your audience. We'll also discuss this in the tutorial at the end of this chapter, "Revealing Hidden Details."

In short, then, browsers want to see lists of everything of interest. They want to know what their options are before they choose them. They like to be able to see an overview of the entire contents so they can see what catches their interest. They need enough information to be able to make a good decision regarding the selections they do make, and they'd like to be able to make these decisions virtually at any time, from within or outside any module in the document. And if they make the wrong choice, it's not as critical for them as it is for the next category, the scanner.

Designing for the Scanner

The scanner can be the toughest audience segment for multimedia documents. Scanners are tough on hardware and software designers because they want instant answers. You will know you've failed a scanner when you hear someone say, "It would have been simpler if I'd just looked it up in the manual."

Scanners are one reason that hypertext links can't be the sole solution. If you try to describe a network of hypertext links to a typical scanner, you'll get a blank stare, followed by veiled hostility. The manager of a customer support group for whom I was designing an on-line information system once told me, as I outlined the concept of hypertext, "I don't want to have to click my way through half a dozen screens to get to the information I want." And while I've used the word hypertext here, the same hostility would have applied if I had described it to him as a series of video clips, diagrams, sound bites, or any other media elements. Scanners want answers, and they want them immediately.

How can you stave off the impatience of a scanner? A couple of tools are the same as those you use for browsers: the table of contents and a good, well-planned topic index. Remember, the scanner has normally been through this information before; the customer support manager I quoted above certainly knew the subject. He simply didn't remember all the technical details for every part of the product his group supported. So you can put concise but complete lists of all the available information in a place that the user will expect it. If the list is under a button on every screen, scanners can give up on the path they're taking and choose another one if necessary.

Something else that scanners often ask for is search capability. People who have used computers to access text learn early on that the computer can search for a given word or phrase far more quickly than a person can. Such people often expect the same kind of search in a database of images, sounds, video and other non-text information. This is of course impossible, at least directly; no current image database lets you type in a component for which you're looking and automatically scan through all the images to find a match.

What you as the designer can do, however, is key your images to some text file through which the scanners in your audience can search. For example, you might have a topic index of pictures, in alphabetical order, through which your users can conduct an electronically assisted search.

When they find the characters they're looking for, there might be a hypertext link that displays the picture associated with that phrase or sentence, or that plays a video clip or a sound bite.

Something else that bothers scanners is having to retrace their steps to get to a previous location that was more suited to their needs than the one they're currently studying. This is why it's important to include an easy way for them to do so, such as a "go back" button or a history list. A "go back" button is quite different from a "previous page" button; both can be useful, but for different reasons.

A "previous page" button—and for now, let's talk about the document as though it were an electronic book—is like flipping pages backwards through a book. If you're reading page 117 and you click "previous page," you'll be on page 116. The multimedia equivalent of the same function might be to rewind a video clip, to go back to the previous screen, or to replay the element that comes immediately before the one that is currently on the screen.

In the interactive world, however, you have no guarantee that the element that precedes the one currently on display is the one that your reader was previously viewing. (In many paper documents, this was also the case, but there was no easy way to get back to a previous cross-reference.) Interactivity means that the reader of page 117 may very well have been reading page 43 or page 251 before getting to page 117. A "go back" button will take your reader back to the page he or she was reading before coming to the one that's on the screen now—wherever that was. And again, in the multimedia model, pages may have no meaning; you need to consider getting from scene to scene in easy ways.

Like browsers, scanners also want clear, easily distinguished headings and subjects. Scanners are interested in specific, detailed information about what's inside the topic in question so that they will be able to decide whether it will solve their problem. Scanners become frustrated by topics that are too much alike; similarly, they are frustrated by topic names that are too vague or general to be of use in deciding whether they will find the answer to their question—which is often time-dependent—in that specific section.

There are many functional similarities between designing for scanners and designing for browsers, as noted here. Perhaps the biggest difference is not so much in design of the interface as in design of the information itself, in making an effort to keep all significant information available at the top level of a module if your primary audience is scanners. Browsers and students will be more likely to click through that half-dozen screens to get all the information on a topic that interests them; scanners want a comprehensive synopsis right up front. (For suggestions about how to divide your information this way, see the tutorial section, "Revealing Hidden Details," later in this chapter.)

Designing for the Student

In some ways, students are the easiest to design for: they just want thorough information, well cross-referenced to related topics. Students are different from scanners in at least one fundamental way as well: scanners already know the subject matter to some extent, so you can often use this knowledge to help you design the information structure and the interface. Students, on the other hand, are by their nature still learning how the subject is structured. I often use the analogy of building a model in the student's mind as part of the teaching process. This in fact is one way in which game designers, teachers, and entertainment producers all face the same problem: in all cases, you need to approach the problem of constructing a mental image in the reader's head.

With students, however, the usability needs change rapidly from moment to moment. As students' mental models grow more complete, they start to gain some of the characteristics of scanners, most notably impatience with slow or difficult user interface components. When students act like scanners, they find better satisfaction in the same kind of guidance aids that scanners want, especially full-text search and retrieval mechanisms (where they're appropriate for the medium).

Design to Meet All Needs

There is one common element in information design for all three types of users: avoid surprises in the structure of your document. You can (and to some extent, should) build little surprises into the content; it keeps your readers awake and interested. But when you lay out and structure your documents, be sure that people get what they expect when they click on something.

If you're using text to guide your audience through your document, good headings are crucial to your success. The trick to a good heading is to add enough information that it's distinct, yet short enough that a reader can scan it quickly. Headings like "Overview" or "Introduction" are frustrating to scanners in particular, but they do little service to browsers or students either unless you tell your readers what you are introducing.

In multimedia, you have the ability to use illustrations, graphics, photos and movies to guide your audience through your document. Still graphics are a great way to show structural relationships between components of an information set, while video is a natural for showing sequential relationships. And because you can nest different kinds of information in the same document, you can shuttle back and forth between structure and sequence as required.

The exact balance between structure—by which I mean information that is connected in some hierarchical or topical way, rather than being dependent in a time-based way (such as removing the wheel of a car before you can fix the brakes, or plugging your computer in before you turn it on)—and sequence will vary from project to project, and from audience to audience. While it's by no means a hard and fast rule, you can find some guidance by considering that browsers and scanners are more concerned with getting structural, overview-type information at a deeper level, while students are more willing to jump into sequential, time-based information such as video, linear text, or audio at an earlier point in the document.

To put this into terms you have probably experienced: when you were first learning a computer program, you probably relied on someone showing you the detailed steps involved in performing some function, such as changing the typeface of a letter in a word processor or entering formulas in a spreadsheet. Later, you probably found yourself asking questions that had much shorter answers that reminded you of something that you already knew—such as how to copy a formula down the column of a spreadsheet, or what keystroke made the highlighted selection change from regular text to superscript. This is because when you were first learning the program, you were a student, and the sequence of information was more critical to you. You were still building the mental model of the information, and like any other model it needed a solid foundation, then a framework, before filling in the details. Later, when you needed a quick answer to something you couldn't remember, you were being a scanner (or perhaps a browser): you already knew where to put the information in the structure, you simply needed the information itself.

So in designing your documents, remember that the structural overview can be graphically oriented (as in the *How Multimedia Computers Work* CD-ROM) or it can be textually oriented (as in a table of contents or a bulleted overview). But remember that when you have the ability to mix video, audio, text, and illustrations all in the same document, you can jump easily from structure to sequence as the audience and the information call for. The trick is making sure your audience can find what they want—especially, but by no means exclusively, when that audience includes a large number of scanners. One of the simplest ways to achieve this, without resorting to complex tricks, expensive hardware, or even high-priced graphic designers, is simple: don't put too much on one screen.

White Space Is Free

Many people fall into the trap of assuming that screen real estate—that is, the amount of room on a screen that a text window takes up while people are reading it— is all-important. It's true, to some extent, that window size matters, and that too large a window blocks the part of the screen that may be running the program in which your students are really interested. People who spend too much attention on this issue, however, often end up designing modules that are nothing but compact, ugly blocks of text, difficult to read and impossible to scan. To some extent, and in some applications, the amount of real estate that a screen uses is significant, but for most users (especially scanners) it's not as big an issue as usability, finding items, or making decisions about whether to follow a given lead in the text.

If you've ever designed a slide presentation or a set of overheads for a corporate meeting, you have learned the importance of keeping your subjects short, concise, and clearly separated. It's even more true in multimedia, where you may not be present in person to answer questions about the bullet items on your slide. You must ensure that your audience understands each item clearly. One of the worst mistakes beginning multimedia and hypertext designers make is to pack too many bullets on a screen; if you can't distinguish each item from its neighbors, none of them is going to make much sense.

One reason why people want to pack information onto an individual screen is that we're trained not to waste paper. White space in a four-color brochure with photographs, glossy paper, and high-quality design is very expensive, especially when you've got a lot to say. If you've ever been involved in the production of a brochure, you know that white space wastes room on the page; if you're producing a magazine or newsletter, white space is wasted ad space.

In CD-ROM publishing, however, white space is free. You've got 660 megabytes of data to play with, and as long as you keep to the basic limits of the screen, you can limit your content to two or three subjects on an individual slide. A good guideline is the by-now familiar magic number, five plus or minus two. Having between three and seven items on a screen keeps the topics easier to understand, easier to scan, and easier to read if only because they're separated by a sufficient amount of space.

Of course, your structure should be reasonable after having considered information partitioning back in Chapter 3. Thus, if you present five plus or minus two topics on a screen, from which the user can select individual topics to pursue through the document, you will have already partitioned the information in such a way that everything on each screen is related. If you need to continue information on a second screen, that's better than overcrowding an individual slide or screen, whether with text or with illustrations. Remember, when you're designing the appearance of your document, you're effectively designing the user interface for the information. And just as with menu items or toolbar buttons in the user interface of a program, your information needs to let your audience know what it points to clearly and without ambiguity. Sometimes, the best way to do that is with text, in the form of clear, descriptive headings.

Complete, Concise Headings: What the User Wants

How many of you have ever been frustrated in coming across a heading titled simply "Overview" in an on-line document? In a paper book or manual, it's almost forgivable because the reader can flip back through the table of contents to see what chapter he or she was reading, and make the assumption that the overview in question is related to the subject of the chapter. It's not optimum, but it's acceptable, because contiguous subjects in a paper document provide a kind of context that makes ambiguous or incomplete headings less confusing.

For on-line documents, however, calling a section "Overview" is eventually going to make some scanner call you up and yell at you. Why? Because you have no way of knowing where that scanner came from when he or she found the link to the section called "Overview." If you call it out as a hypertext jump anywhere except the table of contents, you really have no way of knowing what your reader was looking at before stumbling across this mysterious "Overview." Tell them what the overview covers so that they know whether or not they want to read it.

Similarly, "Introduction," "Tutorial," "Example," "Sample Program," and other ambiguous headings are the beginnings of a disgruntled customer. What are you introducing? What does the tutorial teach? What does the example demonstrate—and is it an example they can look at or an example they can follow?

At the same time, don't put in so much information that the heading becomes unreadable. I've stretched the limits (intentionally) with the heading I chose for this section. It's about as big as a heading should be. How do I know this? I can't make it any smaller: every word matters.

"Complete" and "concise" are important because headings need both characteristics; they need to tell the whole subject, yet they need to do it in no more words than absolutely necessary. "What the User Wants" is shorter than my first pass, which was "What the User's Looking For." In both cases, this added an intentional ambiguity: are complete and concise headings what the user wants, or is there some other connection between headings and user wishes?

And of course, both are true. Users want complete and concise headings, because they're some of the best ways that scanners and browsers have of knowing whether or not that section contains what they want. The heading should tell the user what's in that section, so that users can decide whether or not they want what's in it.

Tutorial: Revealing Hidden Details

For this tutorial, choose the medium with which you're most comfortable: that is, you can work directly with a computer application if you'd like, or you can sketch on a notepad if that comes to hand more readily. The lesson of this tutorial isn't in what keystrokes to push or what menu options to select: the lesson here is on how to think.

As you approach this tutorial, consider a moderately complex subject that you know pretty well. Follow me in the example, then work the tutorial questions for your own subject. For the example, I'll pick something we're all familiar with to one degree or another: going to Grandma's house.

1. **Consider the information in terms of two or three topics.**

   For this example, we might choose the following:

   We're at our house in Sunnyvale.

   We want to go to Grandma's house in Westlake.

2. **At the next level of detail, we might ask another question.**

   How will we get there?

3. **Answer this question in two or three topics.**

   We'll drive.

   We'll take the freeway.

4. **Now, for each topic, add two or three additional topics.**

   For "We'll drive," you might have topics such as "There are four of us," "We'll leave at 8:00 a.m.," "We'll take the four-door," and the like. For "We'll take the freeway," your topics might be "We'll take 85 to 280," "We'll go from 280 to 101," "We'll get off at Lindero Canyon Road," and the like.

5. **Continue until you have a thorough description of your subject.**

You may never actually use all the levels you describe in this tutorial; they may not apply, they may not solve your audience's needs, or you may reorganize your document around a completely different structural metaphor. But analysis like this will help you see how each step in the process contains more details. Essentially, what you've done in these four steps is map out the levels of detail for your subject matter.

Now consider that certain levels of detail will be enough for some users, while other users will require deeper or shallower levels. If you're telling someone in your office how to get from work to a restaurant, you can probably assume that your colleague knows how to get from the office to the freeway, railroad station, or other major thoroughfare involved in the travel. However, you will probably need to provide more detail at the other end, such as the cross-street to look for, landmarks that will help identify the right part of the block, and other facts that will help send someone to a place they've never been.

And that's what interactivity does, at a fundamental level: send people to places they've never been, either inside themselves or inside the information, in a way and with a power and speed that wasn't possible before.

Now, continue with the tutorial. Choose a subject from your own life—in fact, if you've got a possible topic for a multimedia document, choose just part of it. Approach this subject as I approached going to Grandma's house in five steps above, remembering that Step 5 actually repeats Step 4. Keep at it until you reach the stage at which there are no more hidden details: street names, street numbers, turning right or left, and all the other details that are at the very bottom of the process. But as you work with your own subject, consider which part of your audience is going to be interested in the level that you're working in, which part will want more detail, and which part will want less. When you know this, and more important when you know how they're connected one to another, you'll be ready to dive into your document.

Review: Structure, Design, and Content

Until now, we've been doing exercises either on paper or with the computer that have been designed to teach you concepts about packaging, analyzing, and presenting your information. I've done that because it's the single most important part of multimedia design, more important than what platform you choose for development and more important than what software package you choose for your authoring environment. Remember, you're not writing for the Mac or for the PC: you're writing for people, who all work in basically the same way.

In Chapter 3, we discussed the structure of on-line information and how on-line reading, short-term memory and modular design came together in the storyboard. In Chapter 4, you built a prototype of your document. If you ran the on-line examples, you got to see both linear and interactive varieties of some typical multimedia documents. Chapter 5 delved farther into the concepts of navigation, links, and user interface design.

In Chapter 6, we returned to the theoretical with examples designed to keep you connected with your customer—not your software or hardware package but with the people who will be interacting with your CD-ROM when it's published. You've learned about the different audience types you'll be working with, and you've done a tutorial that helped you visualize the internal structure of details within higher-level blocks of information.

Now it's time to restart the computer, load some of the sample files from the CD-ROM, and see the capability of the media. The next three chapters look at video, animation, and their synthesis into the new art form of multimedia. Chapter 7 talks about the whole process of digital video, from camera to disk; Chapter 8 shows you how to do simple animation in a couple of easy-to-use multimedia packages. Chapter 9 then combines them with lessons on how to integrate the navigation, design, and interface skills you worked on in the first half of the book with the technical and media-management skills you worked on in Chapters 7 and 8.

Since this is about the halfway point, I'll add that Chapters 10 and 11 are more concerned with the nuts and bolts of the electronic publishing process, of how to make sure things work and how to build the master CD-ROM with the fewest problems. But from this point in the book, we're still a hundred pages or so away from being able to make copies of your information. Before that, we have to collect or create the media that match the vision you've been articulating up to this point. So get your camera ready, install the capture card, and let's put on a show!

Chapter 7
Motion

Getting Your Money's Worth from Video

More than any other element we've discussed, video brings new technical challenges, requires more advanced technology, and—at a fundamental level—requires more specific jargon if you want to understand it and improve its appearance. So far we've concentrated on the aesthetic aspects of your title, focusing just enough on some of the technical elements of making the components work together. From this point on we're going to get into the details of frame rate, digital compression, data transfer, image size, color models, and other concepts that have a direct effect on how good your multimedia title looks.

For those of you who may view this with apprehension, don't; it's really not much more complicated than desktop publishing, where you have to consider what font you use, what size you want, how much space to leave between the lines and what margins to use. For those of you who have been looking forward to a little more hard-core technical content, this is where it starts. Either way, you may want to turn on your calculator and follow my math in the upcoming examples, as we'll be taking a detailed look at how much video you can store and how fast you can play it back. But first, let's take a look at the basics of shooting your own video for use specifically in a digital multimedia presentation.

Shooting Video for Digital Display

There's an art to shooting good video, and a subset of that art is dedicated to shooting good video that's meant to be digitized. You can check the bibliography for a few sources of good information on the aesthetics of taking good movies. Just because you're planning to shoot video for CD-ROM, you can't ignore composition, placement, focus, and all the other pieces that separate a good movie from something that puts your in-laws to sleep watching pictures of their own grandchildren. Those of you who are developing training materials in particular should do what you can to use pacing, lighting, camera angles, and other aesthetic "tricks of the trade" to make your footage as visually interesting as possible.

You can benefit from a few tips, without turning this into a book on how to make great movies (which anyone who sees my own video segments on the CD-ROM would realize I'm not qualified to write!).

- Whenever you can afford it, hire a professional. If you don't think it's worth the money, take some pictures yourself, then play them next to a well-produced TV show or motion picture. Even if you hire someone to train you in a few basic techniques of lighting, composition, and editing, it'll be worth the money.
- Pay attention to how smoothly you move the camera in tracking shots. Sometimes you may want a shaky, bouncy, jittery camera for a particular effect—say, if you're shooting video that's going into a late-1940s style film-noir interactive murder mystery and you're doing a point-of-view shot of the victim trying to outrun the killer. However, if you're training new employees in how to use the company database, such a frenetic look might not fit with the corporate image. (It may very well be entertaining, and you may even think it appropriate for your workplace, but you will almost certainly have trouble getting it past management.)
- Don't forget sound. Most modern digitizers convert sound along with motion, but if you've got a long lens on the camera (such as a 12:1 zoom), you may not get all the audio you want. Look into remote microphones that connect to your video camera. These will also eliminate the mechanical noise of the camcorder's motor (which you can hear on a number of the clips included on the CD-ROM—we spare no embarrassment to show you how not to do things!)
- Look for the composition of each image, where possible, in a moving scene. If you can control the motion from one side of the frame to another, do so; rehearse your sequences with the actors (or participants) if you can. In some scenes, such as action shots (the various racing car clips demonstrate this), you can't control the action, but you can control the camera: do what you can to keep the action in the frame. Look at the overall flow, motion, and balance of the scene as you block it out and as you record it.

In addition to all the other concerns for shooting video that looks good, you'll also need to add a concern or two about video that digitizes well. Some of these concerns vary depending on the kind of images you plan to display at your end-user's site. Not surprisingly, this can be a bigger issue for Windows than for the Macintosh, because Windows handles color differently. You may occasionally find that after playing a video clip on your Windows computer, no other images look right until you close and reopen them. (During the development of the CD-ROM for this book, we noticed that Windows AVI files and QuickTime for Windows files tend to have competing color maps.)

Sometimes, in extreme cases, you may even find that closing and reopening a video or even a still image doesn't fix it. This is because some other application has loaded the color palette in such a way that images on the screen are adversely affected. You may wish to tell users of PC-based CD-ROMs to close other applications, if possible, before running your video clips to make sure that they have the right color palette for your clip. (And note that if you are running the CD-ROM from this book on a Windows machine, be sure to close other applications—especially Microsoft Word, we've noticed—when you view the video clips.)

The most important concern when shooting video for digitization is light, and in particular the lack of it. Because of the way color values are digitized from the analog signals coming from the camera, as shown in Figure 7-1, the digitizer sometimes adds noise to dark pixels in the source image. ("Noise," in this sense, means unwanted or unfocused information that changes the perceived value of the object being digitized.) For thin lines, hard-edged shadows, or small dark areas such as the centers of people's eyes or other small features, this usually isn't a problem. But if you're taking pictures in dim light, or if you're taking pictures of large areas of a dark color, the resulting images can look noisy when digitized.

There are two reasons for this. One of them has to do with the process of digitization itself, in which a smooth quantity—colors in a dark area—is converted into discrete units, each one distinct from the next. In dark areas in particular, a color that the eye perceives as smooth and continuous may, for various reasons, be right at the borderline that separates two different digital values in the computer. When there isn't much light reflected from a surface, the video camera itself stores values that fluctuate in such a way, and the process of digitizing these fluctuating values accentuates it.

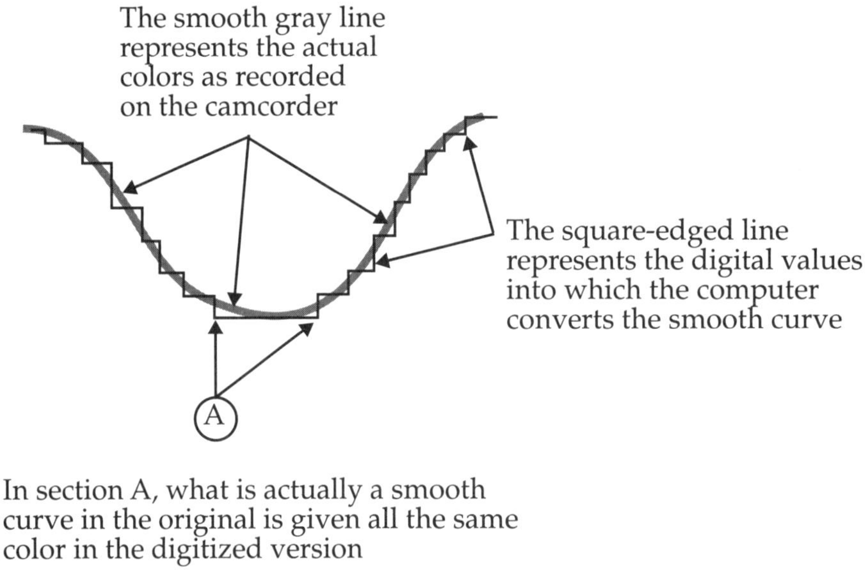

Figure 7-1. What digitizing really means

The other effect that makes dark areas look blotchy involves video compression (covered in more detail later in this chapter). To speed playback and reduce storage, most digital video systems compress the amount of data required to define each frame of the video clip. Most common video compression schemes use pixel averaging. In such schemes, the software samples (that is, reads from) the video image in blocks larger than a single pixel. If a number of adjacent pixels are similar in color, the compression software stores the average of all the pixels instead of each individual pixel's color. The result is an image that loads faster and takes less disk space, but is composed of larger blocks of color. Again, this is most noticeable on dark-colored areas, so light your videos well.

To see an example of what "noisy" means in this context, look at the background (or for that matter, the fenders) on some of the CD-ROM pictures of the British Racing Green MGB on the mountain tour. If you look closely at the shadows under the trees, you can see individual pixels that are red, blue, or other colors besides dark green. These are all cases where the source for the image—that is, the actual trees themselves—were so dark that the video camera's electronics copied them with very low intensities. When the digitizer copied them to numeric format in turn, it assigned numeric values that may only have been one digit off from the adjacent pixel—but which, when taken in the context of the color maps in use on the computer, translated as a completely different color than the one directly next to them. (If this doesn't make sense, just remember to light your images well.)

Other concerns include shaking the camera and doing panning or tracking shots. A pan shot is short for "panorama," and occurs when you turn while holding the camera so that you get a sweeping view of an image too large to fit in a single scene. For example, you might stand at the edge of the Grand Canyon and turn through 90 or even 180 degrees so that you can take in the entire sweep of the canyon, instead of shooting just what your camera can encompass in one frame. In a tracking shot you move the camera, either by walking (if you're very steady) or by rolling it on some kind of stand. In-car camera shots from auto racing events are a very, very sophisticated and specialized kind of tracking shot (which sometimes, as when the car spins completely around, include pan shots as well).

In either case, the process of digitizing can make badly planned or executed shots look worse. The simplest advice is: don't move too fast. When you digitize a video clip, you're taking samples from the video stream at 15 or fewer frames per second. If you move the camera too quickly, the jumps between images look larger than the eye is expecting because the objects on screen have moved in bigger jumps than broadcast video would have shown. The result is jerky, bouncy, or just plain bad video.

Again, there may be times when you will have to track an object at its own speed—a conveyor belt on a production line for a factory-training CD-ROM, for instance, or a runner at a scholastic athletic event for an educational title. For these, be sure to digitize the resulting video at the highest possible frame rate. (Fortunately, the way technology prices keep dropping, frame rates should be higher and prices lower by the time this book sees print.) If possible, use a smaller video image so that the object itself moves a smaller amount on the screen between frames; this also makes the resulting movie look smoother.

Capturing Video from Other Sources

Do you have to stand on one foot and whistle "Dixie" backwards while inhaling to make good video for use in a digital presentation? Can you use ordinary video from an existing VHS cassette without having to reinvent the motion picture industry? Can you really make decent video from VHS machines? You can! Here's how.

The biggest difference that professionally shot video has over home movies is simply that a professional shot it in the first place. Professional cinematographers automatically do all the right things; that's part of their job. They consider lighting, tracking, panning, focus, composition, and the rest of the elements that make up a good video image, to such a degree that the elements that make an image digitize well are probably minuscule components of their overall concern. (If you're digitizing from a professionally produced motion picture, and you haven't been employed by the production company to do so, you may very well be violating copyrights. Don't do that. If you violate copyrights by using the techniques described in this book to digitize video for which you do not have permission, neither the author nor the publisher can take responsibility for your actions. In short, don't do it.)

But let's assume for now that you've been given a VHS cassette of a company training videotape and you've been assigned the job of digitizing it for use in a CD-ROM. Let's further assume that your company hired a professional video production company to shoot, edit, and produce the video, and as a final assumption, let's give the video production company the benefit of the doubt and assume that they knew what they were doing. You may still want to run a few test shots of the sequences you want to use, and modify the brightness and color settings for your video capture card to find out which one works best with the video you've got. The reason lies in the color models used by broadcast video and by computer monitors, meaning the numerical values assigned to different components of the light captured and broadcast (in video) or digitized and displayed (on the computer).

The very short version of this problem is that video splits light into two components, luminance (brightness) and chrominance (color). This was done so that black-and-white television sets could display black-and-white images from color broadcasts, back when the majority of the installed base of TV sets were black-and-white only. Such sets simply displayed the luminance and ignored the chrominance. For computer monitors, however, no such installed base existed. As a result, computer color models are linked much more closely to the mechanisms for generating colors in a cathode-ray tube (CRT), which are electron guns inside your monitor that display varying intensities of red, green, and blue (or RGB) light.

The net result, for those of us more interested in the way it looks than in the physics of light, is that your graphics may look very different on a television monitor than they do on a computer screen. Be sure you test your displays on a television monitor (and this means a PAL or SECAM monitor for international markets, as well as an NTSC monitor for U.S. markets) if the color is of critical importance to your project. The colors will look different on an NTSC monitor than they do on your RGB monitor. (PAL, short for Phase Alternating Lines, is the video standard in the United Kingdom. SECAM is the French video standard, also used in other countries, and stands for Systeme Electronique Couleur Avec Memoire—though some wags like to say that it stands for Supreme Effort to Counter American Methods. By the same token, NTSC either stands for National Television Standards Committee or Never Twice the Same Color.)

Having thus discussed how you might get video, it's time to consider where you are going to put it once you digitize it. While CD-ROM may be your ultimate publishing medium, it's not suited for editing, manipulating, or modifying video files during the production process. For that you'll need either fast, high-capacity hard disk drives, magneto-optical storage systems, or possibly even a high-speed digital tape drive that can store large quantities of data. What's best? How much do you need? And how much will it cost?

Storage Requirements

Storage device prices are dropping so rapidly that any price I quote will almost literally be out of date by the time I send this book to the publisher, let alone by the time it reaches the stores. How fast are prices falling? In June of 1994 I started pricing 1-gigabyte hard drives to use for storing the video used on the enclosed CD-ROM. I found a number of providers who would sell 1.05 GB drives for about $1000 (U.S. dollars). By October, 1.05 GB drives were selling for $750 or so. In November of that year, I quoted this price at a seminar on computers and multimedia in the publishing world. That day I opened my local paper and found that a discounter was selling 1.05 GB drives for $545. The best price I've seen since then is $890 for a 2.1 GB drive.

So the good news is that by the time this book reaches your desk, you'll be able to afford enough storage for nearly any video product you can undertake, remembering that the CD-ROM is only going to have 660 megabytes (about 2/3 of a gigabyte) on it. And if you're going cross-platform, you'll only have 330 megabytes for QuickTime movies for the Mac, and a like amount for your QuickTime for Windows or AVI files to play on the PC.

What does this mean in practice? How many minutes of compressed video can you contain in a CD-ROM (or half a CD-ROM)? The answer depends on your compression scheme, the size of your images, and a number of other concerns. With the ongoing improvements to packages such as QuickTime and Intel's Smart Video Recorder Pro, it's almost as risky to come up with a hard and fast megabytes-per-second figure as it is to put a price on storage devices. But there are some general rules of thumb that will help you plan, design, and shoot the video portion of your documents.

There are three elements that you can control, and which affect video file size, when planning the video components of your documents:

- window size;
- frame rate; and
- clip length.

Window size determines how many bits are in each frame of video. Simply, bigger windows require more pixels—and remember that doubling the window size uses four times as many pixels, because you double the width as well as the height. So larger windows typically require slower frame rates, for the simple reason that the frames take longer to load from disk or from CD-ROM.

Frame rate determines how many frames you need to store (as well as how many you need to display). Full-motion video runs at 30 frames per second (or fps); motion pictures run at 24. Most animated cartoons run effectively at 12 frames per second, which they achieve by shooting the same image twice for two successive frames of a 24-fps movie camera. (Animators call this "shooting on twos.") So when we talk about 15-fps movies, you're actually getting smoother motion than even a justly beloved classic such as *How the Grinch Stole Christmas*, which was shot on twos. (There are other concerns for playback, however, which we'll cover in a few pages.)

Clip length is the final link in the equation (and your cue to get out the calculator). Obviously, if you have a 30-second clip playing at 15 fps, you've got 450 frames. To determine how long your file is going to be, it makes sense to multiply this by the size of your window. So for a 160-by-120 pixel video window, which calculates to 19,200 pixels per frame, you would need to store (and also fetch and play back) 8,640,000 pixels. That, by the way, is more than six floppies full of pixels.

You would need to do this if you were storing raw video. Fortunately, most video digitizer systems not only convert video from the analog signal that comes from the camera into a sequence of digital values that can be stored on the hard drive but also compress the image, sometimes significantly. For example, a recent video project that I digitized to QuickTime for a World Wide Web project began with a video clip that ran 1 minute 15 seconds and took up 5 megabytes of file space—including the audio track. Yet this piece is two and a half times as long as our hypothetical clip in the preceding paragraph; it should have been almost 22 megabytes, not a mere 5 (as large as that file was).

What's the secret? A technology called image compression. There are a number of compression technologies; one you have probably heard of is JPEG. The JPEG compression standard takes squares of several pixels and averages their color, then stores the average in the file. For example, let's return to our 160-by-120 pixel image, a total of 19,200 dots of color. Now divide that image into larger squares, two pixels on a side, and the frame needs to store only 4800 separate pixels. Because the pixels are so small (72 dots per inch on the Macintosh screen, for example), the eye will perceive much the same effect with the larger pixels—as long as the color value in the larger pixels are averaged from the contents.

Tuning Your System for Smooth Capture

The most cost-effective solution for video capture on the Macintosh is the Apple Video System. With a suggested retail of about $250, this provides a board that not only lets you watch a video source on your Macintosh, but also lets you capture images from a video camera, a VCR, or even from television. It supports three preset window sizes that are fractions of the standard NTSC window of 640 x 480 pixels, but you can also resize the window to any dimensions you like. If you choose this option, the image quality will not be as high simply because some sections of the image will require duplicated pixels in order to fill in the image size.

The limit of this board, inherent in its low price, is that frame rate is tied explicitly to the image size you select. That is, the smallest image (160 by 120 pixels) has the highest frame rate (up to 15 fps), while the larger image (320 by 240 pixels) has a much lower frame rate (up to 7 fps). With this board, then, you can have smooth motion or large, detailed images—not both. Of course, single-speed CD-ROM drives can typically only read back enough bits per second to support these window sizes. But if you're specifying a multispeed CD-ROM drive for your delivery platform (and you can control whether or not your end users actually have such products), you can get better performance if you spend a little more money.

On any system, however, there are steps you can take to get smoother capture, which is why the frame rates are preceded by "up to" in the preceding paragraph. If you just start digitizing video without setting up your computer in the first place, you can end up with jerky, patchy clips; I've included a few such clips on the CD-ROM for reference. Compressing video frames takes a lot of calculation, a lot of processing time, and requires the CPU's full attention, so anything you can do to reduce the workload on your processor will result in better-looking pictures. The following suggestions will have a dramatic effect on the smoothness of the video you capture:

- If you are running a screen saver, turn it off. For After Dark on the Macintosh, for example, pull down the Apple menu, go to the After Dark panel, and click the On/Off button in the upper right corner of the panel. Screen savers check the mouse and keyboard 60 times per second to see whether or not you've typed a character or moved the mouse; this is a huge amount of overhead for video capture to contend with.
- Turn virtual memory off. Go to the Memory control panel, look for the Virtual Memory portion of that panel, and click the radio button to turn it off. The extra time required to page in and out of the disk will result in dropping frames during the capture.
- Set your memory cache to 32 KB. This is the optimum size for storing often-used instructions during the capture phase without using too much of your system's RAM as a cache. (Note that the more RAM you can install in your system, the better the quality and the performance of your video capture; 24 MB is a good size for a production video capture system, though you can squeak by with 8 MB if you must.)
- Put a CD-ROM (or an audio CD) into your CD-ROM drive, and put a floppy diskette into the slot. On the Macintosh, the system stops checking the peripherals once there is media in them; as with the screen saver, the processing required to check for disks or CDs reduces the amount of time that the CPU can spend digitizing your movie.
- Close all directory and program windows. Each directory window uses a surprisingly large amount of memory, and requires a certain amount of processing time to keep it active.
- Don't leave other programs running in the MultiFinder; the more video you can squeeze into RAM, the smoother your captured movies will be.

Tutorial 1: From Camcorder to Macintosh

This tutorial describes how to connect the Apple video capture card to a camcorder or VCR through the three color-coded RCA jacks on each piece of equipment. Alternatively, you can use the 50-ohm coaxial cable. The kind of output plug on your camcorder or VCR will determine which method you use. To install the card in your computer, you'll need to consult the documentation that came with it. If your capture card is already installed, you can begin immediately. Figure 7-2 shows the location and type of connectors at the rear of the Macintosh Quadra 630.

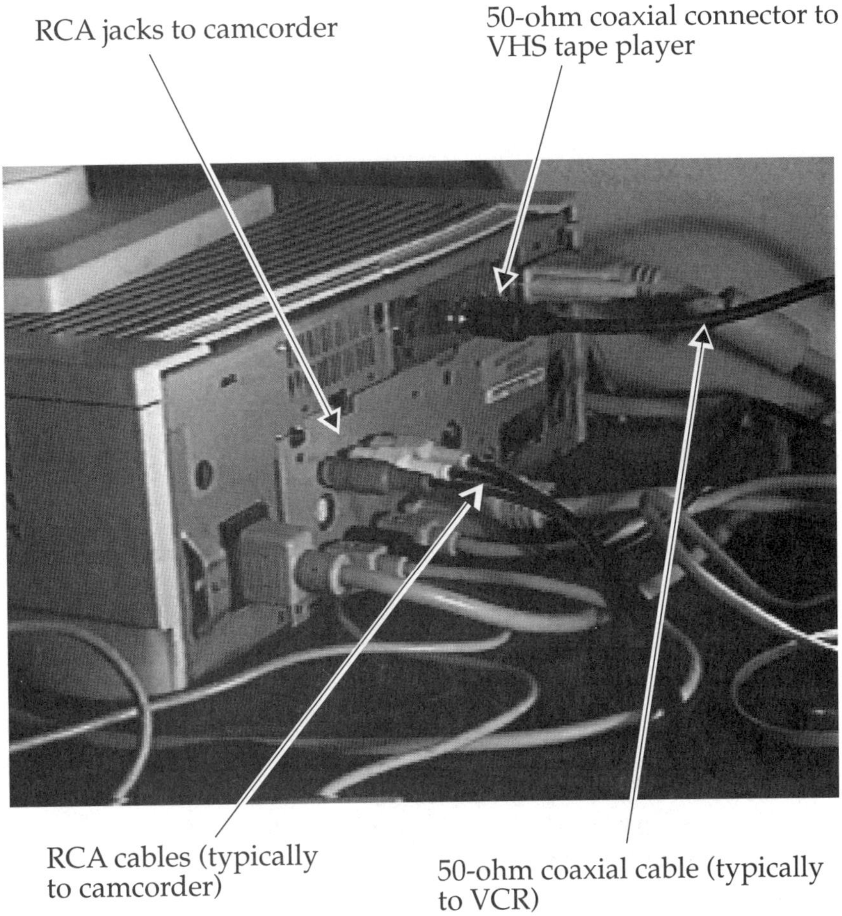

Figure 7-2. Video-in cables and connectors on the Macintosh Quadra 630

To perform this tutorial, you'll need the following equipment:

- A video camcorder with RCA jacks; optionally, you may have a 50-ohm coaxial connector (such as that used on cable TV connections). Figure 7-2 illustrates the two connector types as they are found on the back of the Macintosh.
- An RCA cable with three color-coded leads. Optionally, you may need to connect with a 50-ohm coaxial cable such as the one that goes from your VCR to your television set. Figure 7-2 shows the two types of cable.
- An Apple Macintosh with the Apple Video Capture hardware and Apple Video Player software installed.
- A few seconds of video on the camcorder's internal cassette (or optionally, you can digitize images directly from the camera without recording them first).

In this tutorial, note that older camcorders may only support two RCA jacks: a yellow socket for the video signal, and a white socket for the audio. Newer or stereo-capable camcorders have three jacks: a yellow socket for the video signal, a white socket that either supports monaural sound or the left audio channel for stereo recording, and a red socket that supports the right audio channel for stereo. If you have a stereo camcorder, you can digitize in stereo on your Macintosh with the Apple Video System.

1. **Locate the yellow, white, and (optionally) red RCA jacks on your camcorder.**

   If your camcorder or video camera does not have all three, you can still connect to the Macintosh using only the white and the yellow cables, but you will not be able to digitize the sound track in stereo.

   If your camcorder or video camera has only the 50-ohm coaxial connector you identified in Figure 7-2, see Tutorial 2, "Digitizing from a VCR", but use your camcorder as the video source.

2. **Connect the cable between your Macintosh and your camcorder or video camera,**

   Note: be sure you match the colors on the camcorder jacks with the colors on the Macintosh capture card jacks. These colors may or may not match the color of the cable plugs themselves. (I mention this because I bought one cheapie cable on which there is one white plug, labelled "Video," and two red plugs, labeled "Audio L" and "Audio R." The labels were very, very small and very, very annoying.)

3. **Find the Apple Video Player icon and double-click to start it.**

   If you installed your software from CD-ROM, the Video Player is probably in the Apple menu. If it's not there, use the Find command from the Finder's File menu and look for Apple Video Player.

4. **From the Window menu, select Show Controls Window.**

   This pops up the Controls window, shown below:

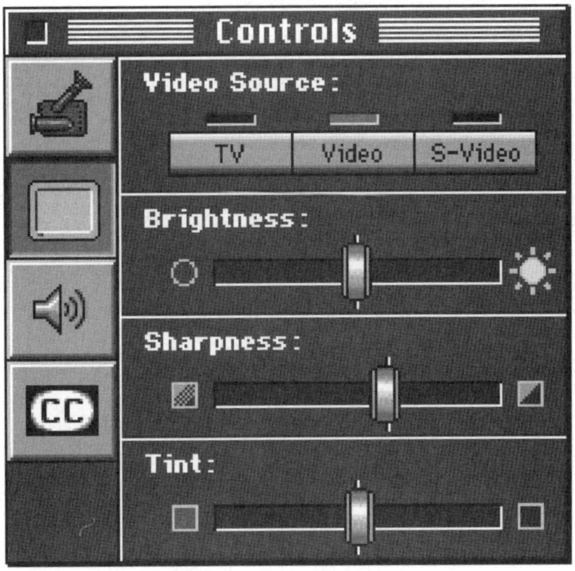

5. Select the second button from the toolbar on the left (the display screen).

This displays the following window:

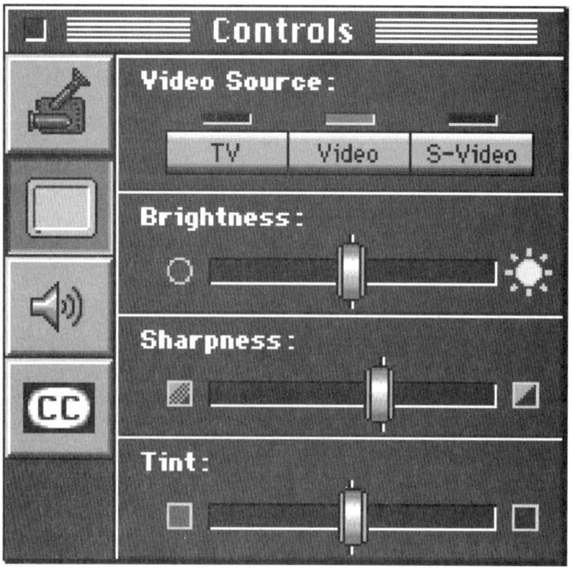

Click the Video button in the Video Source pane to select the RCA jacks as the source of the video signal.

6. Click the topmost button from the toolbar on the left (the camcorder icon).

This displays the following window:

This window controls the capture of movies and still images from your camcorder.

7. **Set up your camcorder to play back video from its internal cassette according to the manufacturer's instructions, then press the Play button.**

   For example, on the Sony Handycam line of camcorders, you'll need to slide the button at the top of the camcorder to the VCR position, not the Camera position, before you can play recorded video from your camcorder.

   If you wish, you can also use the camcorder as a camera and display its images directly on the Macintosh screen. (If you point the camera's microphone at the Macintosh's speaker, you'll also get a free bonus tutorial, "Identifying Audio Feedback". Hint: it's the ear-piercing squeal that you get whenever you point a microphone at the speaker to which it's connected.)

8. **When you come to a portion of the tape that you want to digitize, press the Record button in the Capture Movie pane of the Controls window.**

The Record button changes to read Stop; this means that the video signal from your camcorder is being captured, and the red light above the button indicates that the Macintosh is recording your movie.

Tip: It takes a fraction of a second—which means several video frames—for the video capture hardware to begin storing the incoming signal. This means that you may miss parts of words, actions, or moving shots if you wait until the section you want to capture is already displayed before you click Record.

For best results, click the Record button in the Capture Movie pane a short while before the sequence you want to capture. If you end up with extra frames in the movie, you can remove them individually later with an editing program such as MoviePlayer.

9. **When the scene you want to capture is finished, click the Stop button.**

   The Apple Video Player now compresses your movie, which takes a few seconds.

   For best quality during compression, press Stop on your camcorder so that the Macintosh does not have to display incoming video while compressing your movie.

   Tip: You can control how much compression the Video Player does on your movie by following the steps below.

   From the Setup menu, choose Preferences. Video Player displays the following dialog box:

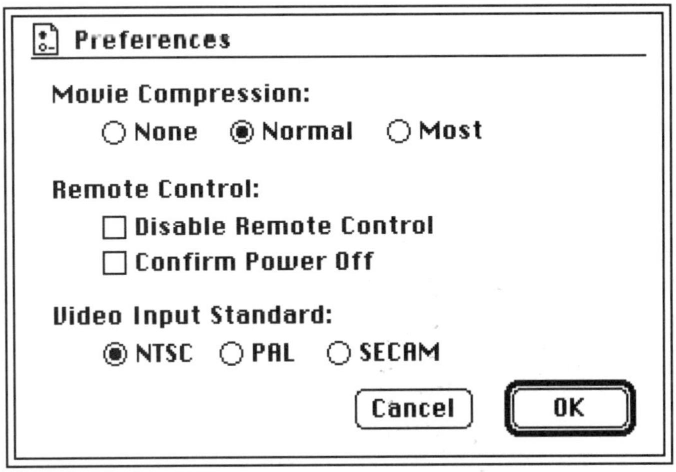

For most applications, Normal compression provides acceptable results, with good image clarity and fast playback speed. If image clarity is more important than file size (and if playback speed is not an issue, such as when you are planning to specify a double-speed or quad-speed CD-ROM drive), you may wish to select None. If you are digitizing long clips that do not require too much image detail, select Most; this can reduce your image size significantly, but at a loss of visual quality.

You need to select the compression you desire before capturing the movie; now that you know how to capture a movie, change the compression and recapture the same image. Compare the playback rates of three versions of the same sequence of frames, one with each of the three compression options. Which looks sharpest and smoothest? How much disk space do you save with compression set to Most? (If you don't have a video capture card yet, look on the CD-ROM under Examples: Compression, and play with some of the video clips you find there.)

Tutorial 2: From VCR to Macintosh

The procedure for hooking your VCR up to your Macintosh is almost identical to that previously described for the camcorder. There are only a few small differences in the cabling and in the selections you make from the Apple Video Player menu.

First, you need to connect your cables as shown in Figure 7-2.

To record from the VCR, follow this procedure.

1. **Start the Apple Video Player program.**

   When it is on the screen, make sure the Controls Window is visible.

2. **Select the second icon from the top, from the control bar running down the left side of the screen.**

   This displays the following window:

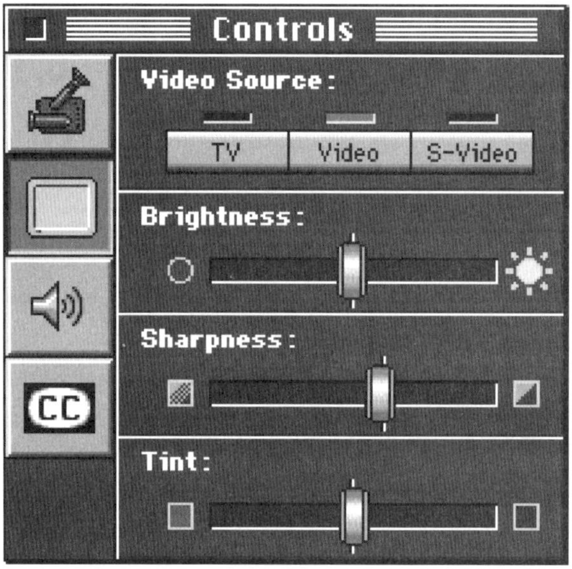

3. **Select the TV button on the left of the Video Source pane.**
4. **Click the topmost button from the toolbar on the left (the camcorder icon).**

This displays the following window:

This window controls capturing movies and still images from your VCR (as well as your camcorder).

5. **Insert the videocassette from which you wish to digitize a clip, then press the Play button.**
6. **When you come to a portion of the tape that you want to digitize, press the Record button in the Capture Movie pane of the Controls window.**

   The Record button changes to read Stop; this means that the video signal from your VCR is being captured, and the red light above the button indicates that the Macintosh is recording your movie.

   Tip: It takes a fraction of a second—which means several video frames—for the video capture hardware to begin storing the incoming signal. This means that you may miss parts of words, actions, or moving shots if you wait until the section you want to capture is already displayed before you click Record.

For best results, click the Record button in the Capture Movie pane a short while before the sequence you want to capture. If you end up with extra frames in the movie, you can remove them individually later with an editing program such as MoviePlayer.

7. **When the scene you want to capture is finished, click the Stop button.**

   The Apple Video Player now compresses your movie, which takes a few seconds.

   For best quality during compression, press Stop on your VCR so that the Macintosh does not have to display incoming video while compressing your movie.

Tutorial 3: From Camcorder to PC

The Intel Smart Video Recorder Pro capture board is an easy-to-install option that gives you essentially the same power as the Apple Video System, with a few differences. To see what it looks like installed in a system, check the example file ISVRPRO.AVI on the Windows portion of the CD-ROM (or the QuickTime movie entitled "iSVR Pro" on the Macintosh side). The primary difference is that if your processing speed permits, you can capture at a full 30 fps, at a couple of window sizes. You'll need a Pentium to get 30 fps, but with a 486 you can get 15 fps video at a decent window size. Remember, however, that fast frame rates and big windows won't work on CD-ROM anyway, because the data rate from the CD-ROM isn't high enough to support anything more than 160 by 120 at 15 fps.

One nice feature about the Intel Smart Video Recorder Pro (which my friends at Intel all call the iSVR Pro, a shorthand form that I'll adopt) is that it comes bundled with Asymetrix Digital Video Producer, a nice digital AB-roll editing system. That is, you can merge two video clips into one, copy sound tracks underneath the video, and even provide room for an overlay channel if you have created text or other effects that you want to make fly onto your screen.

Using the iSVR Pro is about as easy as using the Apple Video System, if you know one or two tricks in advance. The most significant is that the iSVR Pro only captures video—if you want to capture audio as well, you'll need to run it through your sound card. So doing this from the camcorder means you'll need the right cables to connect from the RCA jacks on your camcorder to the jack on your sound card.

The example files on the CD-ROM all use the Creative Labs SoundBlaster CD-16 that came bundled with my Compaq 860. However, I digitized them at 8 bits to ensure compatibility with older PCs, unless otherwise noted in the README.TXT files in the CD-ROM. This capture procedure assumes that you have already installed the iSVR Pro, and that you have a sound card in your PC. The examples I give here are for the SoundBlaster CD-16 from Creative Labs, which is probably the most common and compatible type of sound card in the PC market.

1. **Connect the video cable (the yellow RCA jack) from the camcorder to the RCA jack on the iSVR Pro.**

   You can also connect an S-Video cable if your camcorder has this kind of port; the S-Video connector on the iSVR Pro is located closer to the edge of the card that goes into the motherboard.

2. **Connect the RCA-to-stereo jack between the camcorder and the input plug of your sound card.**

   Remember that red is right! That is, connect the red plug on your cable to the right-hand RCA jack on your camcorder.

3. **Start the Asymetrix Digital Video Producer Capture Tool.**

   This program lets you capture incoming video and gives you control over the file to which you're saving your video, the frame rate, and other options. The Digital Video Producer Capture Tool looks like this:

4. **From the File menu, select Save Video As...**

   On Digital Video Producer, you must first specify the capture file. It's very depressing to get a great shot timed perfectly and have it disappear after the error message, "You must specify a capture file before recording!"

5. **Press Play on your camcorder to watch the video clip on the Digital Video Producer window.**

   Use the Digital Video Producer window to cue the camcorder to the location on your cassette that you want to record. When you have found the section you want to digitize, rewind the cassette and get ready for the next step.

6. **Just before the video reaches the portion of the cassette at which you wish to begin recording, begin capturing video.**

   There are three ways to begin capturing video. You can select Video from the Capture menu; you can press Alt+C, then Alt+V, or you can click the second button from the right-hand edge of the toolbar, shown here:

The iSVR Pro begins capturing video when you do one of these three things. Watch the Digital Video Producer window till you see the end of the section you want to capture.

7. **Click the right mouse button to end capture.**

   You can configure Digital Video Producer to accept other keys to end capture, but the right mouse button is the default.

Once you save your file, you can view it with the Asymetrix Media Player, or you can double-click the file from the Windows File Manager.

Of course, there are many things you can do with digital video once you're captured it. Chapter 9 covers these in detail, with tutorials and references to the on-line examples. Before we get there, however, I want to discuss some other ways of putting moving images into your CD-ROM presentations: graphics, dissolves, and several kinds of animation.

Video across Platforms

Those of you who have both Macintosh and PC systems with CD-ROM drives will notice an interesting fact about the video clips. For most of the QuickTime movies I've included on the Mac, I have corresponding QuickTime movies on the Windows portion of the CD-ROM. Yet for the AVI files on the PC, I don't have corresponding files on the Mac.

That's the state of the art in cross-platform development today. It's easy to do cross-platform video development on the Mac; the QuickTime Developer's Kit, version 2.0 ($199.00 from Apple) includes a CD-ROM full of examples and all the software you'll need to convert your QuickTime movies to QuickTime for Windows. The key piece is MoviePlayer 2.0, which does the conversion.

How difficult is it? You load a QuickTime movie on your Macintosh, then click Save As from MoviePlayer. The dialog box shown in Figure 7-3 pops up.

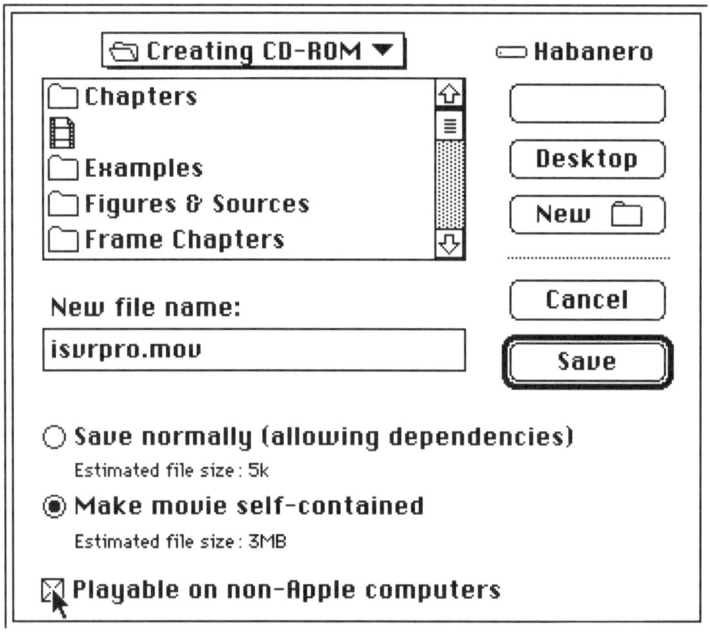

Figure 7-3. The MoviePlayer 2.0 Save As dialog box

The keys to this dialog box are at the bottom. You want to make the movie self-contained, and you want to make it playable on non-Apple computers. By the way, this format is supported on SGI workstations running their version of the Unix operating system, and it's expected that additional Unix/Motif platforms will support the QuickTime extension in the future, so "non-Apple" is not just a way of avoiding saying "Windows" in an Apple product.

You'll notice one other significant feature on the screen in Figure 7-3—the file name. If you're planning to put this file on a PC, it'll need a file name with eight characters, a period, and an extension of MOV. DOS still only takes file names of this format (sometimes abbreviated as 8.3 file names), and the QuickTime for Windows player in Windows expects a file name ending in MOV for movie files.

What this means is that if you use MoviePlayer to save your QuickTime movies on the Macintosh (which you should—it's also an effective frame editor, as we'll see in the next chapter), and if you save them with the bottom check-box set as shown in Figure 7-3, you can use the same files for Macintosh and PC multimedia projects.

Unfortunately, at the time of this writing, there is no way to convert from Microsoft AVI files (the Windows native video format) to run on the Macintosh. If you've got a Mac, you can build Windows applications as well as Mac applications; if you've got a Windows machine, you can't go the other way. This is probably acceptable for a number of professional or game-oriented CD-ROM products, but if you're interested in the roughly 35% of the multimedia market that has Apple systems, or if you're planning to release into the education markets, Macintosh is the way to go.

Review: Issues for Digitizing Video

There's a great quantity of information in this chapter, and much more left out. You may want to look at some books in the bibliography that are specifically dedicated to desktop video; it's a complex and powerful technique that has remarkable subtlety. However, the tutorials you've worked through here will give you the basics you need to shoot good video for use on CD-ROM, and will take you through the steps involved in creating your own digital video files.

To recap the high points, remember the following tips at various stages of the digital video production process:

Light your scenes well. You can play with the brightness controls on both the Macintosh and the PC capture cards, but it's best to have enough light in the scene to begin with. One 60-watt bulb, even in a reflector, just isn't enough; you will want to use several floodlights from several angles to avoid shadows.

Use only scenes that really require motion. Video takes up a great deal of space, so use it wisely. (Chapter 8 talks about some alternatives for where you'd really like motion but you don't want to take up the space required for video.) In the next chapter we'll talk about some ways of adding a soundtrack to sequenced still figures, which can give much of the effect of video at a fraction of the storage hit.

Remember the playback limitations of a CD-ROM. You can only get 150 kbps from single-speed and 300 kbps from double-speed, so keeping to 15 fps and 160 by 120 pixels will ensure that you're safely within the performance of most of the CD-ROM drives out there. Fortunately, this frame rate is supported by a number of inexpensive video capture mechanisms on both platforms, so you won't have to spend extravagantly to get this performance.

Play with your machine's configuration to determine the smoothest settings for capture. In particular, be sure you have virtual memory turned off (and then restart your machine for it to take effect) if you're capturing on the Macintosh. I've included a couple of QuickTime movies captured with virtual memory left on to show you why you don't want to do that.

Putting video into your computer presentations is an incredible way of giving them power, authenticity, and impact. It's worth the trouble and time and now fairly minimal expense to get a capture card and use it. Besides, if nothing else, think how annoying you'll be when you show your co-workers QuickTime movies of your kids, your cat, your spouse and anything else you can think of!

In the next chapter, we'll take a look at animation, both as a medium in its own right and also as a less storage-intensive way than video to convey changes over time. And I'll introduce a completely new technique in computer graphics: a powerful and exciting effect that I call Toymation™.

Chapter 8
Animation

Drawing in the Imagination

The first time I went to an exposition claiming to feature "multimedia," I wondered what all the fuss was about. Most of what was being hawked as a new advancement in personal computing was little more than a few extensions to the field in which I'd been working for years, under the name "computer animation." The first multimedia expos of 1990 or thereabouts looked like little more than a watered-down, hyped-up version of the computer graphics community's biggest annual event, SIGGRAPH—the conference for the Special Interest Group on Graphics of the Association for Computing Machinery. What was the big deal?

Of course, since then the big deal has become clearer, both to me and to the world at large. It's not so much that computers can do animation—it's that they can deliver the power to do animation into the hands of anyone with a couple of hundred dollars for the program, plus a burning desire to figure out how to make it work. If desktop publishing made everyone with a LaserWriter into a potential Gutenberg, then desktop multimedia could make everyone with an SVGA card or a high-end Macintosh into a potential Walt Disney.

Today, multimedia also adds interactivity, a way for users to control the flow and delivery of information in ways that neither Gutenberg nor Disney could have dreamed possible. Multimedia plugs video and audio into the equation, in addition to sharp, to-the-point animation that makes possible training and educational presentations as well as visually stunning games. The ability to copy sections from video frames and animate them, combined with the ability to paste any illustration into a QuickTime movie on the Macintosh, allows you to use the computer to devise your own video-based stop-motion or time-lapse animation. We'll look at a few examples of this, and I'll tell you how to duplicate the effects included on the CD-ROM.

Before jumping into the details and getting out the "Draw Blinky" advertisements, let's talk a little about the basics of computer animation and its foundations in geometry, in art, and to some extent in human physiology. If you are using more powerful 3D modeling or simulation programs, rather than painting individual electronic "cels" and running them in a sequential presentation as a kind of computerized version of traditional animation, you'll need to pay more attention to the geometric part than if you're just doing flat fly-on animation. And if you decide to move on to write your own programs for handling animation rather than using the graphical tools I talk about in this book, you'll encounter some of these terms again then.

Two or Three Dimensions?

First, let's consider the dimensions we use to describe the world we see. Rod Serling used to introduce "The Twilight Zone" by saying that there was a fifth dimension, but he went on without listing the four that we all live in—three of which we can move in relatively freely, and the fourth of which we're more or less stuck with. The three commonly talked about are the dimensions of space:

- depth or length—an object's dimensions from front to back;
- breadth or width—an object's dimensions from side to side; and
- height—an object's dimensions from top to bottom.

Length, breadth, and height are how we define an object in three dimensions. When we draw a picture of it, whether on a computer screen or on a Strathmore drawing pad, we create a two-dimensional (2D) representation of the way we perceive the object's three-dimensional (3D) reality. In terms of computer graphics, this change from three-dimensional space to two-dimensional space is called a *transformation*; you've transformed an object from a world of three dimensions (length, breadth, and height) to a representation of that object in a world of two dimensions (length and breadth).

There are various tricks you can use to convey the illusion of depth, the third dimension, in a two-dimensional medium such as drawing. The most notable is perspective, the technique of measuring the degree to which objects appear smaller as they move farther away from the viewer. Vanishing points, perspective lines, and other techniques for painting can all be handled automatically by the computer, assuming the programmer has encoded the mathematical laws for calculating the relative appearance of the objects in a scene. Alternatively, you can use your own sense of perspective to manipulate the appearance of your drawing on the screen.

But the question posed in the subject heading for this section is a bit of a red herring in the context of this chapter, because animation by its nature manipulates items in the fourth dimension regardless of how many dimensions you've used for representing your pictures. The fourth dimension, of course, is time. To put it in measurable terms comparable to length, breadth, and height, it is duration: how long an object exists. Just as any object that lacks one or more of the dimensions of space will be hard to perceive—imagine an object with no height, and you'll imagine it as a straight horizontal line no matter how much variety of breadth or depth the object had in its original form—so will any object that exists for an immeasurably (or at least imperceptibly) short period of time. An object that vanishes before you see it can no more be perceived than an object that has no height.

Now let's compound the issue by realizing that a computer screen has no depth beyond the thickness of the phosphors (or of the polarizing layers of the LCD panel if you're using a flat-screen laptop). So even drawings of objects that give the illusion of depth are representations of a three-dimensional form, persistent in the fourth dimension, into a two-dimensional drawing space. This means that every perception you have involves some kind of graphical transformation; when you look at a perspective drawing, whether on the page or on the computer, you are transforming a 2D representation into an understanding, in 3D, of where the elements of the drawing are located in the scene.

In effect, the reverse of this is what a camera does—or for that matter what the eye does. Light reflects off an object, carrying with it the wave signature peculiar to that object's surface. This light passes through a lens, the rays are focused on a flat surface at the back of the dark chamber, and the sensitive material on that flat surface converts the light into some form that human beings can recognize. Figure 8-1 represents this transformation from 3D to 2D space.

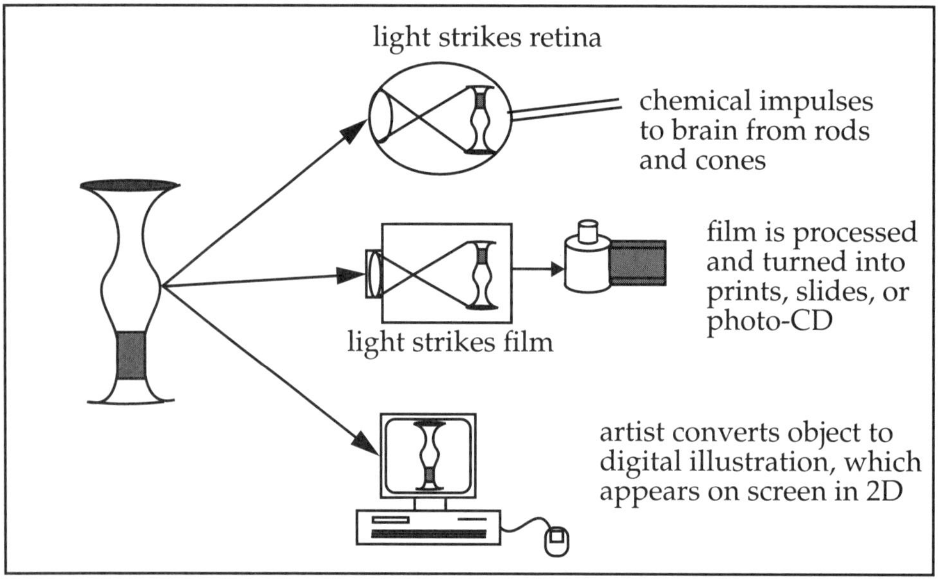

Figure 8-1. 3D to 2D transformations in the camera, the eye, and the computer

Everything we know visually about the world around us comes from one or another of these transformations. The object, which we can measure in four dimensions, is transformed into a two-dimensional representation, with the fourth dimension given a fixed value. That is, every image that we have of an object is the way that it existed at a given moment in time. It could be the exact moment at which we snapped the shutter on the camera; it could be the moment at which the cells in the retina sent their electrochemical impulses down the optic nerve to the brain; it could be the aggregate of the moments during which we drew a picture of that object on our computers and created a digital representation that turns into colors on a computer screen.

There's a reason that I've put the eye at the top of Figure 8-1. No matter what visual medium you choose to employ—camera, video, acrylic, or scratching in wet sand with a pointed stick—if the end result is something you want people to see, you're fundamentally dealing with the human eye; its transformations are the basis for everything you do. So you need to take a look at how the eye works to understand a little about how animation, in particular computer animation, works.

The Eye's Mind

Much of our visual processing depends either on the physiology of the eye or on the eye's specialized support mechanisms in and along the optic nerve. Surprisingly, what we perceive as a rich, unbroken, seamless presentation of reality is at some level every bit as broken, as disconnected, and as jumpy as the individual frames of a movie. In fact, that's why we can watch movies—and multimedia.

The cells at the back of the eye convert light into electrochemical signals that are called nerve impulses. The retina contains millions of cells called rods and cones that react to light in different ways, but with one basic similarity: when light hits them, a chemical reaction inside the cell has an effect on the optic nerve, which is the nerve that sends impulses from the eye to the brain. Some of these cells send out nerve impulses that vary depending on the light's intensity; some vary these signals depending on the light's color. The exact chemistry of this reaction isn't necessary to this discussion, though it does require one of the forms of vitamin A for the eye's cells to turn light into nerve impulses (which is why your mom used to tell you to eat your carrots). Fundamentally, the energy of a ray of light causes a chemical reaction in one or more of the cells on the retina. The result is an impulse (in the form of a chemical ion that causes a chain reaction from nerve cell to nerve cell, changing the cell's electrical potential inside and outside the cell wall) that travels from the eye to the brain at about 240 miles per hour (390 km/h).

But whatever the cells do, they're only human cells, and just like muscle cells between sets of a workout, the rods and cones in your eyes have to rest between cycles. The chemical compounds in the cells of the eye have to regenerate every time they are used, before another ray of light can cause another nerve impulse. It takes a variable amount of time for this to happen—longer when you're tired, for instance. But the rough average for this period of time is typically somewhere between 12 and 20 times per second.

What this means is that anything that happens more quickly than about 1/15 of a second is, for all practical purposes, invisible—not because it hasn't got a visual representation in length, breadth, and height, but because it simply doesn't exist in the fourth dimension, time, as far as our eyes are concerned. Yes, we may see it, but we'll probably see it as a blur—for example, the wings of a hummingbird, or the moving propeller of an airplane. Or we may ignore it altogether, especially if it occurs within a context where we're expecting something different.

It's this latter case that make movies, video, animation, flip books, and QuickTime possible. Because the eye takes somewhere between 1/12 and 1/20 of a second to register an event as having reality in the fourth dimension, any sequence of events that occurs continuously at that rate or faster will be perceived by the eye as a continuous stream, a single event—so long as the 2D representation that actually lands on the retina has some superficial persistence. The visual processing that happens in the optical complex at the back of the brain, our eye's "mind," expects things to stay more or less the same, to move in predictable ways, and to retain various characteristics in the three dimensions we think about consciously: length, breadth, and height. The fourth dimension is taken so much for granted that a simple trick can fool us into thinking that a series of still images is a continuous, unbroken stream of motion.

That simple trick is this: if you show the eye two pictures in which an object's position in length and breadth have changed slightly, the eye will swear on the proverbial stack of whatever book your faith holds sacred that it saw the object move from one position to the other.

There's another trick. Because of the way the laws of perspective work, big objects seem closer and small objects seem farther away. So if you show the eye two pictures of the same object, the second being smaller than the first, the eye will tell your brain that the object is moving away. If the pictures themselves are flat representations of a 3D object, you've used changes in two dimensions to trick the eye into thinking that the object is moving in all four dimensions: length, breadth, height, and time.

Now, your job as animator is to manage the changes in an object's position or size on the computer screen so that the eye fools the brain into thinking that things are moving around on the screen: coming closer, moving farther, moving seamlessly from corner to corner, or walking along a path. You do this in a number of ways by changing from image to image in small increments that the eye can believe, given the context.

To understand the difference that frame rate makes to your perception of smoothness, consider three classic pieces of animation: the original *King Kong*, Chuck Jones' classic interpretation of the Dr. Seuss story *How the Grinch Stole Christmas*, and one of the original Disney classic films, *Pinocchio*. O'Brien shot Kong and the dinosaurs on fours—meaning he printed the same picture of his models on four successive frames of the finished film. Because film is shot at 24 fps, the frame rate is 6 fps for the giant ape's motion scenes. This is why you see him flicker in places.

Jones shot the *Grinch* on twos, meaning that he printed two copies of the same drawing on successive frames of film. This yields a frame rate of 12 fps—actually a little slower than what you'll be using for video if you work with either the Apple Video System or the Intel Smart Video Recorder Pro discussed in Chapter 7. But watching the Grinch steal everything from the unsuspecting Whos, you're not aware of flicker.

Then there's *Pinocchio*, about which I agree with fellow animation fans that it's technically the best animated picture ever made. Just watch the opening scene sometime, where you get the shot from the cricket's point of view as he hops down the street. Notice that the interior of Gepetto's workshop changes as the camera moves up and down: when Jiminy jumps up, you see more of what's on the floor, and when he lands, you see objects nearer to the ceiling. And while most of that film's technical excellence comes from the brilliance of animators like Frank Thomas, Ollie Johnston, Vladimir Tytla, and the rest of the crew of visual geniuses that Disney in his prime was able to attract, a good deal of its power comes from the fact that it's shot on ones: there's a separate piece of artwork every 1/24 of a second. That's 1440 paintings for every minute of the movie, which my videocassette says is 88 minutes long, for a total of 126,720 individual cels.

Having invoked such beloved classics, what can you do with your desktop computer and some of the programs we've been looking at in this book? Well, you can't get 24 fps animation with a presentation program, but you can begin using some of the physiological techniques I've discussed already to create the illusion of motion, even at fairly simple levels. We'll start there, and then build into more detailed presentations that carry your messages in more powerful ways.

Animation within Presentation Programs

For our first examples and exercises, let's take a look at one of the presentation management programs we've examined in the past hundred or so pages. I've used these techniques in both PowerPoint and Persuasion; I'll use Persuasion for this example, for reasons we'll discover in more detail in Chapter 9.

Persuasion provides several built-in ways to do fly-on or fly-off animation of objects within a scene. In the general sense, computer graphics packages call this *path-based animation*, because you give the object a path and the package makes the object follow it.

You can also animate text this way, and the heritage of presentation packages such as PowerPoint and Persuasion as slide presentation tools means that they have some special features for handling this kind of animation easily. It's limited, but you can use it for dramatic effect if not necessarily for simulation or storytelling. It's great, however, for pacing the visual side of your presentation to synchronize with a sound track.

In Persuasion, you can animate the various elements—text and graphics—on your slide. This means you can make them fly on or off the screen in a straight line in any direction. You're restricted in a couple of ways that aren't a real problem if you're just doing a simple presentation, but that will definitely cramp your style if you don't know about them in advance.

One thing, for instance, that gave me fits for about 45 minutes during the development of the tutorial that accompanies this chapter is that if you export to the Player, which I'll explain in the next paragraph, Persuasion only shows the portion of your image that's visible on the screen when you animate it. I originally wanted a picture a car to come onto the screen from the left, roar across the screen in a single unbroken sweep while the sound track played the appropriate noise, and then disappear off the right-hand edge of the screen. I could make Persuasion do this if I did a slide show directly from Persuasion itself—but when I exported to the Persuasion Player, the car never showed up. The end result actually came out better than my first attempts, and you can see it by running the example Ferrari 250 on the CD-ROM.

Persuasion's Player is a royalty-free playback program that lets you distribute your presentations in condensed form and show them to people (or let them play with them on their own) without requiring that they have Persuasion. PowerPoint has a similar setup, as does MediaWrangler. For example, I've distributed the PowerPoint and Persuasion players on the CD-ROM so you can look at the multimedia documents I've developed for this book. I've also distributed the editable files; this way, if you also have your own copies of PowerPoint and Persuasion, you can open the files yourself and see in greater detail how I created each slide.

Persuasion's Player requires that you export your presentation to Player format, with a nice option called Package Movies. This way, if you have QuickTime movies, sounds, or animation files that are part of your presentation, you can package them all in one single file that the Player can find. Then you distribute your presentation, the movies associated with it, and the royalty-free copy of the Persuasion Player. Marketing departments are beginning to send Persuasion files this way as interactive brochures, replacing printed paper copies as a way of promoting the company's products or services.

In Persuasion, you can select individual text elements and have them fly on or off the screen; you can apply these same autoanimation techniques to pictures, either those that you draw or photographs that you import (as I did with the picture of the Ferrari).

Another trick about animating in both of these slide presentation tools involves how they deal with cut and paste. When you copy an element from one screen (by pressing Command-C on the Apple and Control-C on the PC), pasting it onto another puts it into the same location from which you moved it. You can use this to make visual elements (whether text or graphics) appear in the same location in several consecutive screens. For example, in the Ferrari slide that I ended up with, I pasted the photograph of the race car in the same location on both slides, but used different animation on each. The effect is that the car appears to drive onto the screen in one slide, then drives off in the other. It's actually two separate pictures, each with its own animation, but because of the persistence of vision it looks as though I've made the car drive onto the screen, pause for a second, then drive off.

You can do similar effects with words, with drawings, or with pieces of a drawing, making them fly into location or fly off the screen. Many of the other presentations on the CD-ROM demonstrate these other features. For now, it's time to see exactly how this works, so follow along with me and I'll take you through the steps involved in using Persuasion's animation techniques and in building the text elements of a presentation.

Tutorial 1: Animating on a Slide

This tutorial explains how I created the Persuasion document Ferrari 250 on the Macintosh portion of the CD-ROM. If you're near your computer, take a look now at the file and read along with the presentation to see how I built it.

The presentation includes two media elements captured on video: the sight and sound of a Ferrari 250 GTO in action, accelerating out of Turn 11 at Laguna Seca International Raceway in California. After digitizing the video, I used MoviePlayer 2.0 to save only the frame I wanted as a picture, and then to save the sound track of the film clip as an AIFF file (the standard Macintosh sound file format).

With the single frame stored as a PICT file, I brought it into Adobe Photoshop to extract just the Ferrari and not the background. I outlined the car, pasted it into a new document with borders just the size of the image, then painted the backdrop to match (well, to be close to) the background of the slide. (I could stand to do more work in that area, but you'll get the idea from what I've done.) By the way, if you'd like to play with the individual media elements yourself to see what you can do with Persuasion or with some other package, here are the file names:

Cobra Vs Ferrari	A QuickTime movie (playable with SimpleText on Macintoshes with System 7.1 or greater).
ferrari.mov	A QuickTime for Windows version of the raw file.
Cobra-Ferrari Wars	The AIFF file (Macintosh sound track) from Cobra Vs Ferrari. Created by MovieWorks 2.0's "Export to Sound" feature.
250GTO	A SimpleText picture (PICT format) of the single frame I wanted to use. Created by MovieWorks 2.0's "Export to Picture" feature.
Better Gray	The Ferrari itself, clipped out of the picture and put on a gray background. Created using Adobe Photoshop.

Once I had these elements, I was ready to start in Persuasion. We'll pick up the step-by-step action there.

1. **Create the first slide.**

   For this, I selected a background, chose colors for the text, and added the words "Ferrari 250 GTO" to the Title field.

2. **Import the graphic to this slide.**

   For this, select Import... from Persuasion's File menu, then choose Graphic from the pop-up menu. I imported the file called Better Gray (I'd worked on an improved background color for the red Ferrari). When it was imported, I put it in the location on the screen at which I wanted it to stop after its animation.

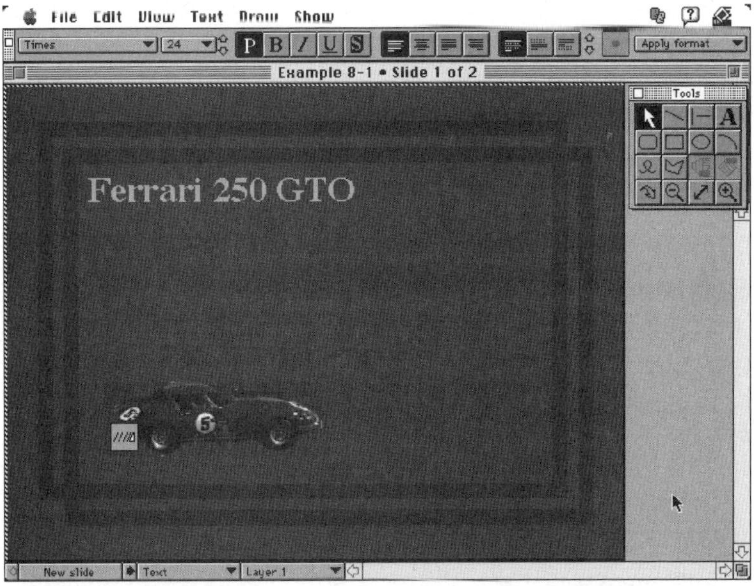

3. **Select an Autoanimate action for this graphical element.**

   To do this, first click on the picture of the car to select it, then pull down the Draw menu and select Autoanimate. Persuasion displays the following dialog box:

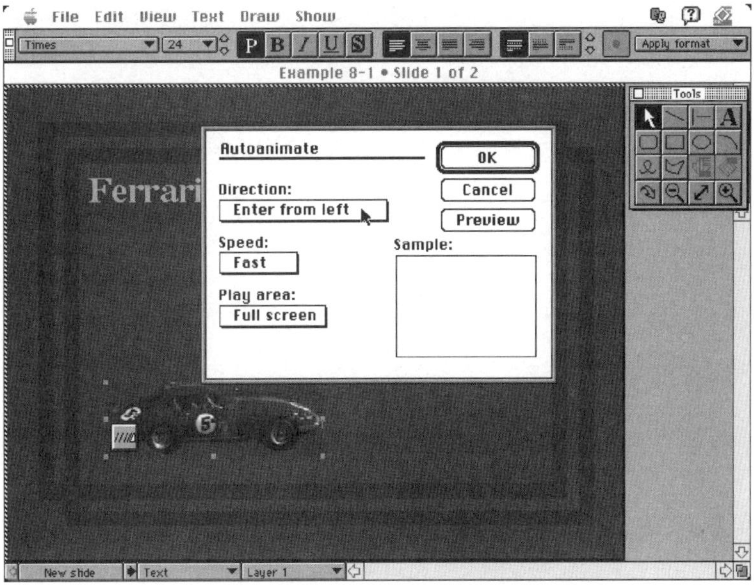

From this dialog box, select Enter from left from the Direction pulldown, Fast from the Speed pulldown, and Full screen from the Play area pulldown. If you wish, you can see an example of the direction and speed of your animation by clicking the Preview button from the Autoanimate dialog.

This will make the car drive onto the screen quickly, coming in from the left.

4. **With the image of the car still selected, press Command-C to copy it to the Clipboard.**

   This copies not only the picture of the Ferrari, but also copies its location so that you will be able to paste it into the same location on the next slide.

5. **Create the second slide and copy in the visual elements.**

   Click the New Slide button in the lower left corner of the Persuasion screen. Persuasion automatically puts the background, text format, and colors that you selected into the next slide.

6. **Paste the Ferrari picture into the second slide.**

   By default, Persuasion pastes the picture into the same location on the screen as that of the previous slide.

7. **Add the subtitle text.**

   Click on the yellow area and type the subtitle text, "One of the last great road/race cars."

8. **Animate the subtitle text.**

   While the subtitle text is still selected, pull down the Draw menu and select Autoanimate. Persuasion shows the following screen:

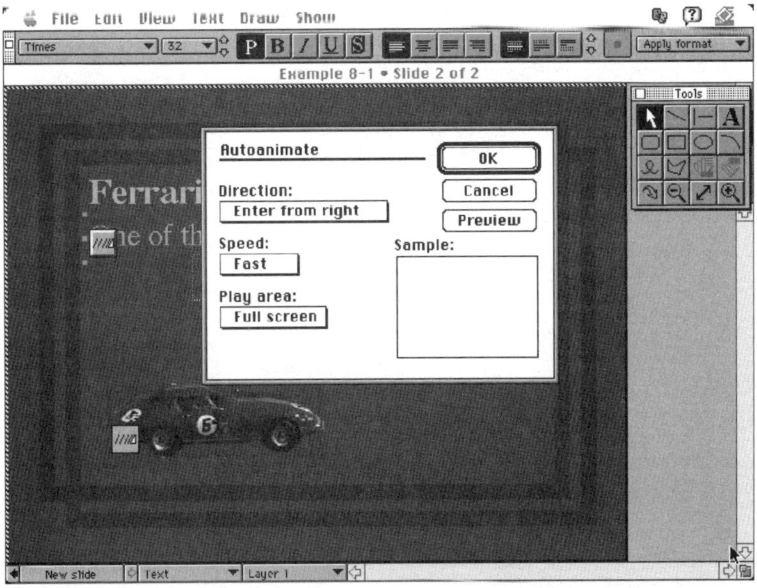

Change Direction to read Enter from right. This makes the text of the subtitle fly onto the screen from the right-hand edge.

9. **Change the Ferrari's animation so that it exits to the right.**

   In the first slide, the car drives into the picture and stops where you see it here. On this slide, you want the Ferrari to drive off to the right (since that's the direction it's pointed). To do this, put the cursor over the badge just behind the Ferrari's rear wheel and hold down the mouse button. Select Direction... from the pop-up menu that appears, then choose Exit to right. This makes the Ferrari "drive" off screen to your right.

10. **Play your slide show.**

    Pull down the View menu and select Slide Show. From the pop-up menu that appears, select Show All Slides. Persuasion displays the following dialog box:

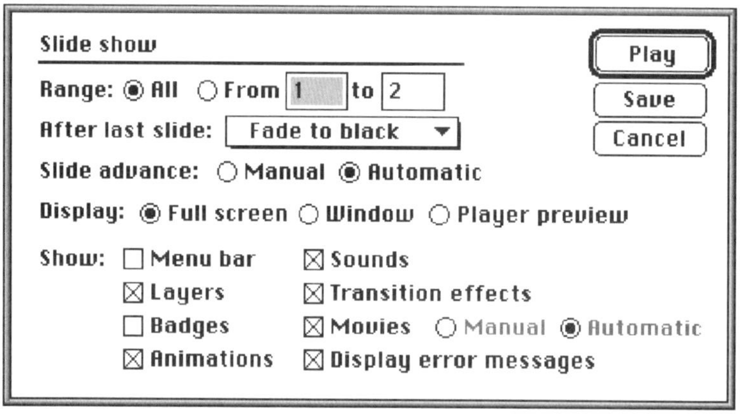

Set the values shown here, then click Play to view your slide show. The important parts of the dialog box are the Automatic slide advance button and the Animations check box; this will play both of your slides in sequence.

There will be more in Chapter 9 about sound, but it's worth noting a few points about it now while we're looking at Persuasion using the Ferrari clip.

Persuasion treats sounds as effects timed by the transitions between slides. Basically, you can choose one of two behaviors when you add a sound to a Persuasion slide: you can have it continue while the slides change, or you can have the slide on the screen hold and make further slides wait until the sound finishes playing. For the Ferrari show, I played the sound track in slide 1, set it up to continue playing (rather than wait), and then played with the timings of each slide so that the car appears to drive off from the second slide at about the time in the sound track that the Ferrari begins accelerating out of the corner.

Again, we'll cover when and why you'd use the two different effects in Chapter 9, when we really bring sound into the equation—whether it's as part of a video clip or in this case, as a sound file in its own right. However, I can't stress enough that sound files plus animation gives a significant reduction in storage. How significant? The Player files for the Ferrari clip are 44K for the presentation, and 105K for the sound track. The video clip from which I took the sound is 2.6 megabytes. What this means, among other things, is that you could distribute something the size of the Ferrari presentation in its Player form on a single floppy; at 149K for the presentation file and 611K for the Persuasion Player, you'd have a lot of room left over. And while it's true that the primary focus of this book is

CD-ROM development, it's always good to know ways to save a little disk space. If you work much in multimedia or digital video, you'll eventually come across a project for which you'll run out of space. Additionally, animation of this kind—where the program moves a graphic around on an unchanging background—gives much smoother motion than typical digital video playback rates, especially from single-speed CD-ROM drives.

So one way to add motion to your titles without incorporating video directly is by using features in your program to make elements of the presentation move by themselves. But you can also use many of the presentation packages I've demonstrated here for simple frame-by-frame animation, where you draw each of the images and then let the program reveal them in turn. This is similar to the technique of traditional animation; let's look at both in turn.

Frame-by-Frame Animation

Traditional animation consists of hand-drawn cels assembled into an animated cartoon or feature by photographing a series of images, then running them back on a motion picture projector. Some computer animation techniques rely on the same kind of animation, replacing the cel-and-ink technique with a mouse (or more likely, an electronic pen and tablet; a good friend of mine, who now does character design for a game company, commented when she first began illustrating with a computer that "doing graphics with a mouse is like drawing with a bar of soap"). The difference of course is that the processor becomes the projector, putting the next slide in the sequence on top of the last one.

There are a number of ways that you can use the same principles, but with different techniques, for creating your own animation. One of the simplest is to draw portions of screens in a presentation package on a succession of slides, then display the slides in a prepared sequence. This chapter's second tutorial will walk you through this technique.

One nice side effect of frame-by-frame animation with a slide program is that you can use the special-effects transitions between slides to reveal the next slide in some interesting way. I've used this in some of the examples on the CD-ROM to make the first frame of a video screen show up in a checkerboard pattern; you've probably seen that already if you've been playing with the CD-ROM. Depending on the package you use and on how you lay out your screens, you can take advantage of built-in transitional effects to heighten the sense of motion from one slide to the next.

The trick to slide-by-slide transitions is this: anything that is in the same place on both slides will appear to persist in the image while the rest of the elements change around it. So you can build a slide with a number of pictures incrementally, by copying each previous slide's content to the next one and then adding the changed element.

We saw in the last tutorial how pasting a picture from one slide into the next makes it look, in the presentation, as though the picture stays on screen. You can get interesting effects by choosing unusual transitions—checkerboards, dissolves, etc.—and leaving common elements on display while you change from one slide to the next. It looks as though you have applied the transition only to the elements of the screen that are changing, while the unchanging elements of the screen keep their location and condition intact.

In the next tutorial, we'll make things appear, move, and disappear while other portions of the screen remain the same.

Tutorial 2: Exploding Diagrams

An exploded diagram is when you show all the parts lying on the table before you've assembled the thing you're building. In multimedia, you can have exploding diagrams in which you actually see the parts peel off one at a time to reveal the components underneath.

For this tutorial, take a look at the file called PC Tour on your CD-ROM. You'll recognize some animation of the type used in the last tutorial in the first couple of slides, but the fourth and fifth slides demonstrate simple versions of what I'm talking about here.

Here's how you do this kind of simple animation in Persuasion (though I've done the same kind of animation in PowerPoint and in HyperCard as well):

1. **Put all the common elements into your slide.**

   For this slide, you'll want to add the title, "The Processor," plus a yellow rectangle representing the processor graphically.

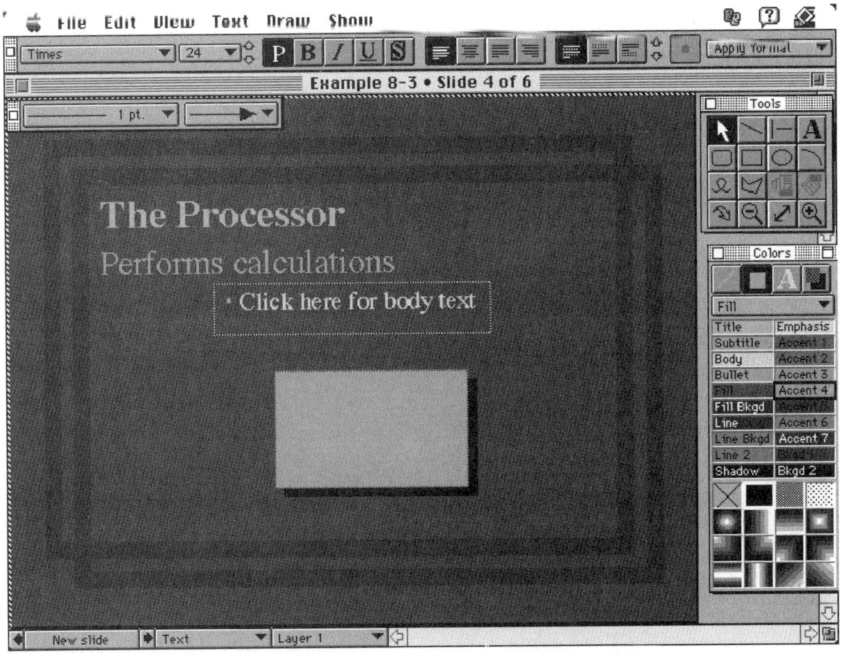

2. **Copy the common elements from this slide.**

   You'll want the title ("The Processor") to be the same, and the yellow square will be in the same location; to get it there, just select it on the first slide and press Command-C to copy it.

3. **Paste the common elements into the next slide.**

   Select the next slide and press Command-V to paste the yellow rectangle into the same location it had occupied on the previous slide.

4. **Add the new elements to the current slide.**

   For this slide, you want to add an arrow pointing into the yellow rectangle for the processor, indicating data coming from system memory. You should now have a slide that looks like this:

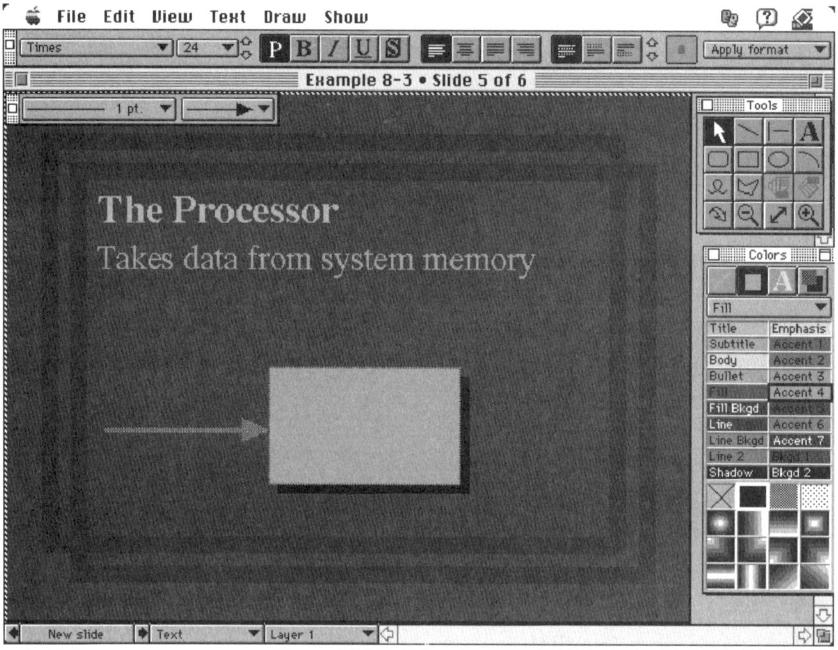

5. Decide on your transitions.

Transitions in Persuasion apply at the beginning of the slide for which you select them. To select a transition, pull down the View menu and select Transitions... Persuasion displays the following dialog box:

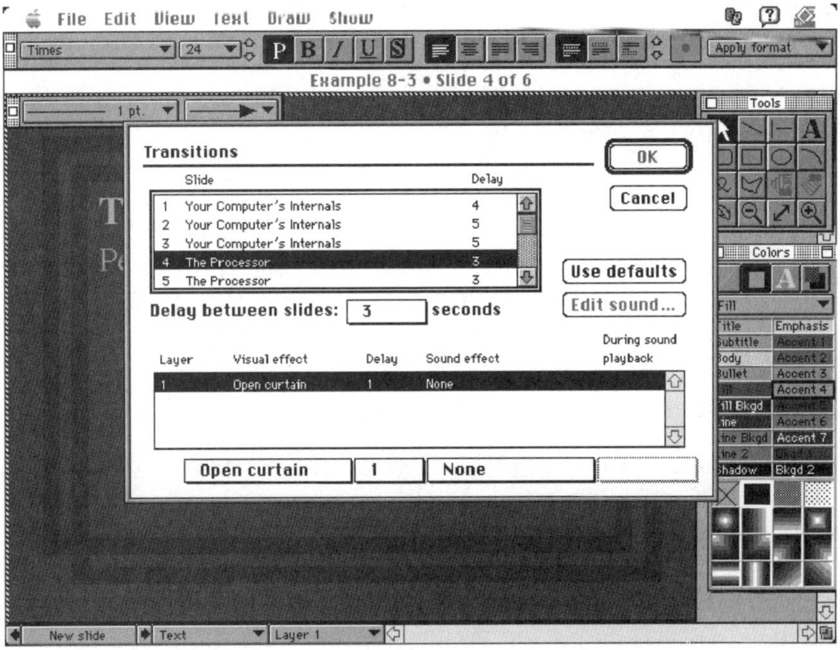

Tip: Transitions look best when the direction of the screen's motion resembles the motion you want your viewers to perceive on the screen.

For example, Slides 5 and 6 from this sequence use Wipe Right as the transition. The effect that this has is that the arrow that you added in Step 4 appears first at the left edge of the screen, then is revealed in the direction in which the arrow ends up pointing. Because the yellow rectangle remains the same in both slides, you notice no change to it, but the arrow appears to move toward the yellow rectangle.

In the presentation on the CD-ROM, I also added another slide in which a second arrow points out of the yellow rectangle, to indicate the results of the processor's operations as output. Additionally, you can see how the technique of revealing graphical elements by transitions applies to photographs in the opening slides.

This is a very simple example of a technique that you can use with great power, especially in combination with the on-frame animation described in the previous tutorial. With these two techniques, you can use Persuasion or PowerPoint to make subtle, incremental changes that give the appearance of smooth motion, lending an understanding of the dynamics of a moving medium to your presentation.

Of course, there's much more you can do with the computer if you're willing to put in the hours. The next section talks about something I somewhat jokingly call "Toymation," a technique that uses a traditional film-animation technique but which can be done with inexpensive home video equipment and Apple Computer's MoviePlayer 2.0 or with the Asymetrix Digital Video Producer on the PC. To understand how it works, let's take a look at the historical background of this kind of animation, in particular a special effect called stop-motion.

Stop-motion Animation on Computer

Willis O'Brien was one of Hollywood's first great special effects geniuses. He created the terrifying (for the time) illusions in the original motion picture version of *King Kong* by building miniatures of Kong, the dinosaurs, and the sets in which they have their epic battles, then composited these animation scenes with live action to make a blend of traditional animation and live action. Later, Ray Harryhausen took the same principles and applied them to creatures from outer space, monsters from myth and legend, and other fantastic visions that could only exist in the imagination. Most recently, Tim Burton's *The Nightmare Before Christmas* combines model animation with computer image manipulation to tell a story impossible to tell in any other way, at least with the richness and visual detail of film.

The technique that winds between all these different elements is called stop-motion animation. The basic premise of stop-motion animation is that instead of drawing cels 1/15 of a second apart and putting hand-painted images together to make up the illusion of motion, you use a camera to shoot pictures of a model in a particular pose. You then move the model to the next pose and take the next picture. Eventually, you'll have enough pictures to run them through a projector and your audience will see a giant ape climbing the Empire State Building, or a gorgon with snakes writhing in place of her hair, or the Pumpkin King soliloquizing before a full moon in a nightmare landscape.

One of the simplest ways you can achieve this effect in live video is by shooting from a tripod, using the remote to turn recording on and off, and then moving or repositioning elements of the scene while the camera is off. The movie clip "Presto" (or the QuickTime for Windows file presto.mov) demonstrates how you can make the PC look as though it has magically closed itself up. Achieving this effect was very simple:

1. Set up the first image, with the camera on a tripod.
2. Use the remote control for the camera. This avoids jiggling the image when you turn the camera on and off.
3. Shoot the "before" video (in this example, video of the PC with its cover still removed), then press the red button on the Remote to put the camcorder in "Standby" mode.
4. Being careful not to jiggle the PC or the camcorder, replace the side cover.
5. Press the red button again to begin recording, and add a suitable narration.

This is a useful way to get certain kinds of special effects in a video. You can make people and things magically pop in and out of the scene, or turn an annoying little sister into a frog, with just a press of a button. As a technical note, if you are using actors in your scenes, especially amateur or young actors (such as elementary students), it's impossible to get them to hold still long enough to register in the same location exactly from frame to frame. One way around this is to have them start a "jump" reaction just as you roll the camera, so that they appear to be moving naturally when the recording resumes. Fortunately, a slight jump looks plausible if, for instance, you'd tapped your little sister on the head with a magic wand and had her turn into a plastic frog. And you can always edit individual frames in either MoviePlayer or Asymetrix Digital Video Producer.

You can do stop-motion animation with a video camera through a similar technique, if somewhat laboriously. The movie "Terrorsaurus Rex" (or the file terrorex.mov on the PC) uses Toymation. You'll enjoy the film, I hope, but I also hope you may have some ideas for doing the same kind of work in your own multimedia presentations. You may not necessarily want to make a movie with plastic dinosaurs, lucky wishing trolls, and ceramic penguins, but consider using the same techniques for showing the assembly or disassembly of your company's products. As an alternative, you can use time-lapse photography by waiting minutes or hours between shots instead of seconds. Consider the impact a science presentation would have for an elementary school class if the students could record a seed sprouting, sending out its root and its leaves, and then replay the video to watch the whole process in seconds instead of hours. Here are some suggestions on ways to do the best looking stop-motion or time-lapse animation with your video camera and a frame editor.

Making Toys Come to Life

We've all wished that our toys could move by themselves. With a video camera, a digitizing board, a lot of patience, and a video editor such as MoviePlayer or Digital Video Producer, you can make movies in which your toys (or your products, or models of some mathematical or scientific process) come to life and move around.

Traditional stop-motion animation uses flexible figures built on armatures, which are essentially metal skeletons with joints that allow them to be posed from one frame to the next. Not having any such armatures lying around the house, but wanting to demonstrate how to do stop-motion animation with a video camera, I decided to find toys that could tell a story (with two little girls in the house, we have lots of toys; the hard part was getting them not to move the props between shots).

My first experiments with Toymation involved two toy cars and a pair of small houses to serve as background. The cars simply drove up to one another, swerved to avoid a head-on crash (though I admit to having considered making a horrific wreck with flames and the works), and sped out of the scene. But you can use anything in stop-motion animation: a romance between a salt shaker and a coffee cup might be fun, with Tchaikovsky's *Romeo and Juliet* as the sound track, for example.

Before getting into the step-by-step technique, it's worth noting that the hardest part of stop-motion animation isn't the digitizing, isn't editing the clip, and isn't redubbing a sound track. The hardest part of Toymation for me was getting the feel of how far to move my characters between each frame—too far and the movement looks jerky; not far enough and the action slows down.

So one exercise that you might want to undertake is to block out how long you want your characters to take doing whatever they're doing. ("Block out" sounds so much more professional-theatrical than "play with your toys," doesn't it?) If you're really concerned with smooth motion, you can calculate that if the tyrannosaurus has to cover 15 inches in one second, and you'll be shooting at 15 fps, you need to move the monster one inch per frame. As with so many other things, the rule applies here that every unit of time you spend thinking before you start working saves you four units of time you would have spent working before you started thinking.

Here are some suggestions for smooth motion and good-looking results.

Have some kind of marks on the surface so you can measure your actors' progress. In the dinosaur clips, you'll notice that I shot them on a butcher block table. Originally I did this because it was convenient, but I noticed that it became much easier for me to gauge the tyrannosaurus' "steps" against the strips of wood on the tabletop. You might want to use a very, very faint grid on the surface, with indistinct colors so that the camera won't pick them up.

Add natural-looking motions to give your video more lifelike appearance. As you watch the dinosaur stalk past the village in "Smooth Walker," notice that about a third of the way through his tail starts to move from side to side. After that point, the motion looks much more natural, even though his legs still aren't articulated. Animation is all about illusion; anything you can do to add to the illusion will improve the end product.

Shoot somewhere that you won't be disturbed. I was worried throughout shooting that someone would bump into the table and I'd be unable to position all the characters in my "crowd scene" after they'd fallen down. It didn't happen, but it would have been a nightmare if it did. You probably will want to do your shooting in a studio where cats, dogs, and children fear to tread.

Think about all your effects before you start them. When the tyrannosaurus has to reach down to eat the teddy bear (okay, mark this page so you can find it again after rushing out to watch the video clip!), I didn't have a clue as to how I could hold the dinosaur up. In the initial video, you can see one or two frames in which my hand appears holding the monster's tail up so that his head can reach down to grab for the teddy bear. If I were going to do this again, I'd construct some kind of brace behind the tyrannosaurus, out of the camera's view, that would let me pose him at any angle. Of course, if I were going to that much trouble, I should probably just build a poseable tyrannosaurus model.

Use more, smaller increments of motion rather than fewer, larger ones. In the "Smooth Walker" clip, I move the tyrannosaurus about 1/4" between shots, then leave three frames (effectively shooting on threes at 15 fps, for 5 fps of animation—not that far from O'Brien's majestic ape) for each pose. Because of decompression and playback restrictions, I found that shooting on ones occasionally produced jerky results: the computer simply drops a frame now and again, and if it drops the only frame that has a particular pose, the jump from the two frames that it does display is too great.

Remember that the digitization is itself a sampling effect from the video: you shoot video images at 30 fps, then digitize them at some slower rate (15 fps for the samples in the small window) that extracts samples from the clip. The fastest I was able to get the start/stop cycle down to was about 6 or 7 frames of QuickTime per pose, or about half a second.

To get smooth motion at the right speed, I went into MoviePlayer and deleted unwanted frames from each pose, leaving two or three frames in each position. When you start to edit your movie, you'll get into a rhythm (at least in MoviePlayer) whereby you advance a frame or two, look for the change in pose, then start removing extra frames. Being consistent with the record/standby button helps production go smoothly.

You'll also note that this is where you'll wish you had a bigger disk drive. The natural tendency is to leave the original digitized video untouched, and to use Save As from MoviePlayer to store your edited copies. This is a good, safe, and prudent way to proceed, but it consumes disk space at an alarming rate. I went from 70 megabytes remaining to 8.4 just during the first few tests developing the "Terrorsaurus Rex" clip. Video is really appallingly disk-intensive, and particularly so for production where you may create multiple copies of the same scene in order to try out different effects.

Using Animation Packages

One of the advantages to Toymation is that it captures images that originate in three dimensions. That is, when the trolls are escaping from the tyrannosaurus, you can't see the teddy bear till the middle of the clip because they're in front of him, and when the tyrannosaurus takes a bite out of the bear and shakes it, you see the tail wiggle because it's actually a 3D object.

But you can also use the computer's mathematical capabilities to simulate 3D objects inside the computer. The kinds of digital tools that used to be available only to movie and television studios are rapidly coming down to desktop prices, so you can add flying chrome robots to your QuickTime presentations. One of the least expensive packages is Logomotion from Specular Software. Retailing for about $80, this package is designed for simple animation of 3D logos, words, and other text-based objects.

Logomotion makes it easy to type in text or import drawings from other packages. Once in the program, you can determine the color and the surface characteristics, and you can assign motions to text or other elements of your scene. Then you render the animation, which on the Macintosh takes the form of QuickTime movies. Logomotion lets you specify the frame rate. (Remember, however, that too fast a frame rate in too slow a system will actually lead to jerkier, uglier video; 15 fps and small windows results in the smoothest appearing video across both platforms and the various processors and CD-ROM drives you're likely to encounter.)

There are a few words and concepts that you'll need to understand as you approach completely synthetic, computer-generated animation:

- *Surface*. 3D objects have surfaces that reflect light; in the computer, you assign surface characteristics (shininess, bumps, color, and the like) to the objects you're drawing, and the computer renders them by simulating what would happen when light reflects off a real surface with those characteristics.
- *Light*. Computer graphics systems use lighting models that simulate the way light works in the real world. The simulation isn't exact, and you can sometimes achieve a better looking result by playing with the way that your drawing package simulates light. One note: objects and lights can each have color. If you shine a blue light on a white object, you'll get a blue object; if you shine a blue light on a red object, you'll get a purple object. It doesn't matter when you start a scene whether you make the light or the object the color you want it to be, but if your designer or art director decides to add another object later on in the same scene, it'll reflect the color of the light you choose.
- *Reflectance*. The classic lighting model for computer graphics says that light comprises three separate components, which make up the object's total reflectance (as opposed to reflections, since that word implies mirrors). These are the ambient, diffuse, and specular components of an object's lighting characteristics.
- The ambient component represents the light that, in the real world, reflects off of elements in the scene—for example, you can probably still see under your table even though it's in shadow, because of the ambient light in your house. Similarly, the ambient component of an object in a computer simulation imitates the way this works in the real world, and gives what some people call its "dark color."
- The diffuse component represents the object's basic appearance without taking into account sharp highlights or other features. However, the diffuse component represents the part of the object that is in direct line with the light source—that part of

the object that's away from the light source is modeled by the ambient component.

- Finally, the specular component of an object defines its sharp highlights. The specular component has an effect on how we see an object's surface, as smooth and shiny or matte and dull. You can change the appearance of a surface, making it look like unglazed porcelain or shiny white china, simply by changing the specular component of that surface.

The way that each of these characteristics affects your operation of the program varies from package to package.

I've included a short sample that demonstrates what you can do with Logomotion. To create this clip, I typed in the text, assigned a color to the surface of the text object, placed lights of particular colors at specific locations in the screen, and then made the text fly up and to the left. It's simple and doesn't do anything particularly exciting, but it shows you what Logomotion can do.

The advantage to this kind of animation, at least on the Macintosh, is that the resulting series of moving images are a QuickTime movie, meaning it is possible to use the animation you generate in any other document that lets you include QuickTime. Furthermore, you can save the QuickTime movie as playable on non-Apple systems, using MoviePlayer as described at the end of Chapter 7.

Now that you've had some practice making various kinds of animations with some of the simple packages I've talked about here, it's time to put them all together. In the early chapters, we talked about designing interactive documents, building your prototype, and planning your navigation model. In the last two chapters, we've talked about capturing and generating the media components for your presentation. In Chapter 9, we'll put them all together and use some of the clips we've made (or that you've been looking at) to create some presentations that integrate audio, video, animation, and interactivity—in short, you'll put it all together.

Chapter 9 Multimedia

Lights, Camera, Interaction!

Now that you've been practicing visual thinking, video capture, animation, and other ways of putting together moving images in whatever subject you follow, it's time to start building applications. You've got all the components; how can you put together all these elements into a single presentation?

To some extent, the answer is in two additional technologies that you may have heard about: OpenDoc on the Macintosh, and OLE (Object Link Embedding) on Windows. These two technologies are moving toward a different way of dealing with information on computers, a way that you'll understand a lot better at the end of this chapter—so I'll save that discussion for the last section. For now, we'll look at how you can support the organization that you planned in the early chapters with the media you've been collecting and creating in the middle chapters.

Chapter 3 included a tutorial on making storyboards; Chapter 4 turned that into a prototype. In this chapter, you're going to add some media elements to prototype documents like those you created at the end of Chapter 4. If you don't have a digitizing card of your own, you can use some of the video clips included on the CD-ROM to begin adding different media to your documents.

The tutorials in this chapter, of course, are all designed to use topics based on the media I've included on the CD-ROM. While the video clips and illustrations I've provided are, I hope, interesting, you'll almost certainly have your own interests, your own subject matter, and your own area of expertise for the multimedia projects you wish to undertake. So as you follow the tutorials in this chapter and learn the skills and techniques, keep thinking in terms of the projects and subjects you want to pursue.

The examples that I've developed for this chapter use a number of playback tools, some of which are included on the CD-ROM. You're familiar by now with PowerPoint and Persuasion players, and you'll see some more sample documents built using those tools. I've also included some documents that I created using popular, though by no means universal, products, incorporating video into word-processing documents. You'll find files built using FrameMaker and Microsoft Word 6.0 for Windows on the CD-ROM. To view them requires the program in which they were created, but this should be little or no problem for the Word documents, and only slightly more difficult for the Frame files. You won't really be missing any essentials of this chapter if you can't find a copy of Frame with which to read the files I've included; the basic principles are covered in the tutorials in this chapter, and in the Persuasion and MediaWrangler examples that are available to everyone.

Hypertext Organization for Video

At this stage of the computer industry, if you're reading this book you probably know what hypertext is. You may, however, not know the term itself. Simply put, hypertext is the ability to click on a word when it appears on the screen, and have the computer display information that's connected somehow to that word. If you use any on-line help files with your Windows applications, you have used hypertext.

What makes hypertext so powerful is that it lets you skip over sections of information that don't pertain to you, so that you can instead focus on the information you want to see, read, or learn. While you could always do this with books, by looking for items of interest in the index or the table of contents, it's only with the advent of digital multimedia that you could apply hypertext concepts to video, animation, and other time-based media. Imagine if you could see the introduction to a television show, then select which individual items you wanted to see and jump to them directly instead of waiting until the program's director chose to show you the clip. (This addresses one of my personal peeves, when the trailer for a news broadcast teases my interest on a story that doesn't run until 27 minutes into the program, thereby ensuring my exposure to television's real purpose: advertisement.)

With Persuasion, HyperCard, MediaWrangler, and some of the other programs we've talked about here, you can do just that. You can define an introductory section that may have narration, navigation, information overviews, and all the other content we discussed in the first chapters of the book, and you can branch from there to the topics themselves. And if you're willing to invest in a more expensive, powerful program like FrameMaker, you can develop sophisticated hypertext navigational tools that link to audio, video, and animation clips as well as to the full text of a book.

Let's review a distinction I introduced in Chapter 4: the distinction of linear versus interactive multimedia. At one level, the distinction is meaningless; when it comes time to import media into your document, it doesn't matter whether your viewers will be clicking on links or watching a movie. At the design level, however, you'll need to develop some kind of user interface for your interactivity, following the navigation models discussed in Chapter 5.

How do you make video interactive, though? It's relatively easy with text, because the text persists until the user turns the "page," moving to the next electronic section of the document. With video, you can't do this the same way: each "page" lasts for 1/15 or 1/30 of a second, far too short a time for the user to see a button, much less move the mouse to it and click. You need to make sure that there are natural starting points in the video, places at which your viewers will be able to pick up a thread without requiring too much background information to be able to understand what's being said.

The trick to designing interactive video is to plan it in advance, when you are deciding what to shoot. It's possible to go into existing video and give yourself markers that represent individual modules, but your production looks better if you think of these as stand-alone modules when you plan them, design them, and write scripts for them (if any). Here are some suggestions for organizing your video shots for best use in the hypertext model of interactive multimedia:

Be complete but concise. Put into every scene that you shoot enough information for the viewer to get the point, but no more. Rambling, disconnected video scenes don't make it easy to navigate.

Think about information boundaries. This means take separate shots for setting up, performing, and completing an action. You may be able to reuse the same video clips in several places, if you're creating a training CD-ROM about how to perform a task, but only if that clip is a stand-alone scene. For example, if the video shows how to repair the brakes on a car, you should include how to remove the wheel on a separate video clip, because removing the wheel applies to many different tasks on the car.

Consider other ways in which your audience might want to get to a clip. This is the flip side of information boundaries: making sure that people can get to the start of your video clip from another subject that interests them. For example, a multimedia presentation on animal habitats should have separate modules for each of the animals in a habitat. A student might be doing a report on reptiles and would therefore want to look for reptiles in the desert, in the rain forest, and in the mountains.

Keep track of your modules. There are a number of ways to do this; Aldus Fetch is a promising software technique, but I know people who simply keep a matrix of the clips on a whiteboard, with columns for the file name (and the disk drive if you're in a multi-drive environment), the subject, and any other relevant information.

Remember that you can always link up video scenes in your control structure. This means that if you have a sequence that's made up of three or four separate clips, you can embed each clip into a separate slide in Persuasion and then play each slide in succession. The video clips will play in order, but you'll be able to start any of the subsequent slides independently, as shown in Figure 9-1.

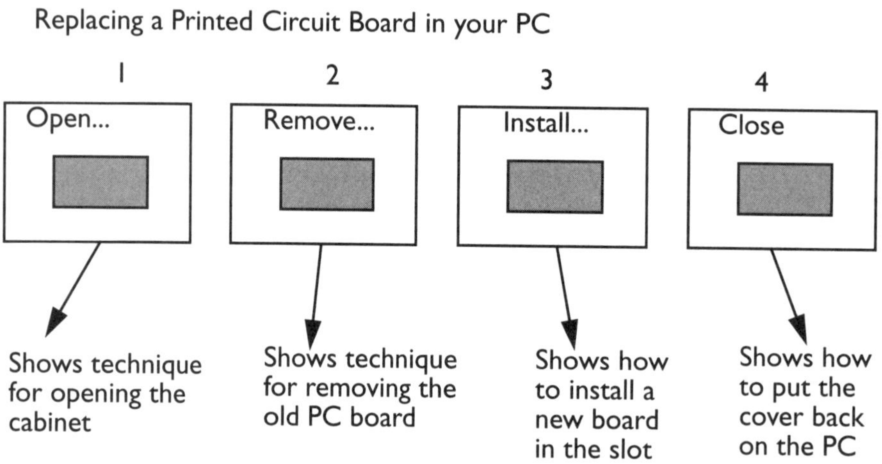

Figure 9-1. A series of independent video clips running in sequence

In the example shown here, each slide (numbered 1 through 4) contains video (represented by the grey rectangle) that shows what the words below the picture describe: Slide 1 shows how to open the PC cabinet, Slide 2 how to remove the old PC board from the motherboard, and so forth. Where a linear videotape on repairing PCs might include all four steps in the process as a single take, our hypothetical modular CD-ROM includes four separate, short video clips. This way any of the video clips can be reused in other procedures (for instance, you will need to open the PC board to replace disk drives, to install modems, or even to get rid of the dust that seems to settle all over the circuits). Additionally, you can direct users to slide 3 if they already know how to open the PC.

So that's how you enable hypertext organization in video: by designing your video in the same modular fashion in which you design text for a hypertext reference document. Now, what are some techniques for putting buttons into a moving picture? There are several ways of incorporating into video the kinds of links, jumps, and branches that make hypertext so hyper. But doing this efficiently requires well-done video clips.

Tutorial 1: Branching while in Motion

If you've been following along closely, especially if you've got a copy of one of these authoring tools, you've probably figured out that the reason you designed your video in stand-alone modules is so that you can have convenient, accessible, and discrete starting points for your video procedures. That's the key to branching while in motion: you have to tell the computer where to start playing.

By contrast, putting buttons into the scene is fairly simple. In Persuasion, for instance, you simply put a button on each of the slides that needs it. That way, from every slide you have the ability to jump forward, backward, or to any slide you define. To put jump buttons into a slide in Persuasion, follow this procedure:

1. **From the Tools palette, select the Jump tool (shown here highlighted in black,):**

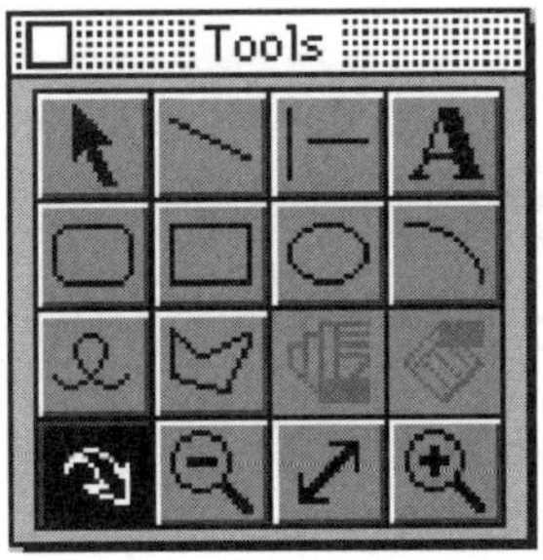

You can now draw a rectangular region on the screen, indicating the location that you wish to make sensitive. When you release the mouse button after drawing this region, Persuasion adds the Jump icon (the same as the Jump tool in the Tools palette, above) to the region you drew.

Note: Don't worry that the Jump icon appears on the top layer of your slide. When you run the Persuasion slide show, the Jump icon disappears.

2. Double-click the Jump icon to bring up the Autojump menu:

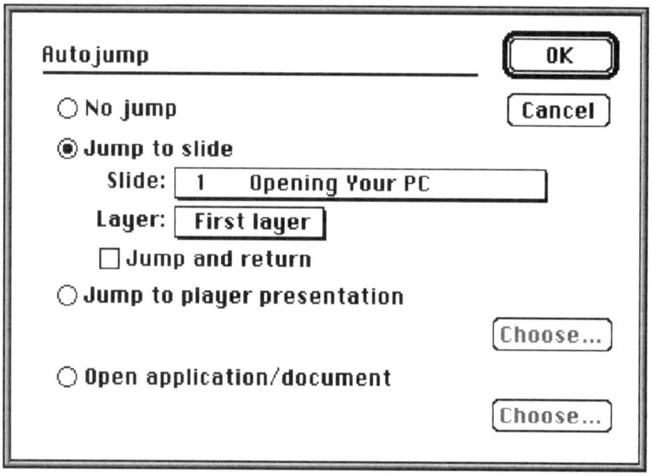

The Autojump menu lets you determine a slide and a layer to which you wish the presentation to jump when you click on it. In the snapshot shown here, I've specified that the presentation should jump to the first slide, "Opening Your PC," when the user clicks this jump.

3. When you have selected the slide to which you wish the presentation to jump, click OK.

You can also jump to player presentations and open other applications. This is discussed in more detail in a later section of this chapter.

Now that you have seen how to put a jump into a slide in Persuasion, you can learn how to branch while your presentation is in motion. By making the buttons unique to the slide, you can specify different locations for each slide if necessary, and because the video is tied to each slide, the buttons automatically track the video clips. If your users never click a button, the presentation proceeds to the end (or runs as an autoloop, if you have set it up to repeat when it reaches the last slide).

This is the way we set up the Winter Animal presentation for our back-to-school night presentation at Cherry Chase Elementary School. The program could run uninterrupted, in which case it gave a slide show with embedded art and video. However, when the kids wanted to show someone a specific slide (one that contained their work, for example), they could get to the Navigation screen and track down the section of interest.

Here's how it works (and of course you can see this on the CD-ROM for an example of the usability):

1. Set up the transition for each slide to delay several seconds after the movie finishes playing:

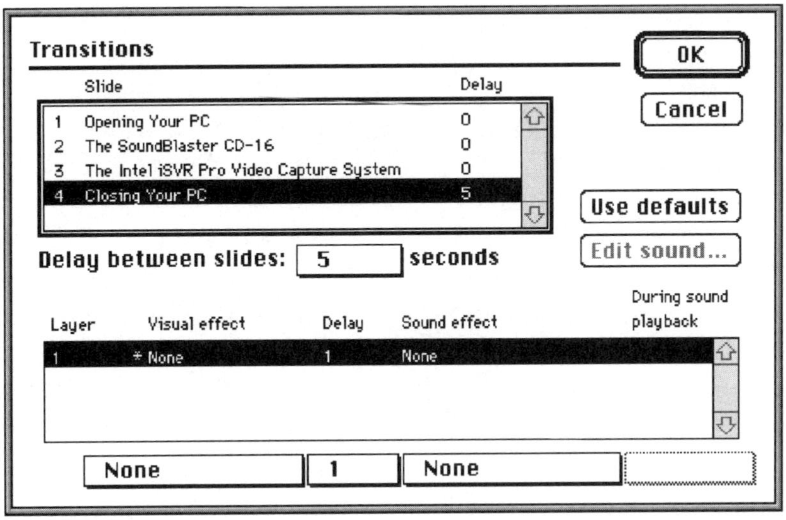

This will give your users time to select the button before the next slide appears. Some people think of this as a "timeout" value—that is, if (as shown here) you delay five seconds after the movie finishes, Persuasion waits that long before it "times out" and plays the next screen. (You can also use the delay transition feature to determine how long a text slide stays visible, if you are using Persuasion to support a spoken presentation.)

2. **When Slide 1's movie finishes, Persuasion exposes Slide 2 and plays its movie.**

   This also shows the buttons (if any) that you designed into Slide 2; if you have several possible jumps that are logically connected to the video showing in Slide 2, their buttons are exposed now, but not before Slide 2 appears.

3. **When Slide 2 finishes, Slide 3 starts and its buttons appear.**

   This process repeats until the end of the presentation. You can of course tell Persuasion to run as a loop, continually playing the presentation, and yet your audience can select the buttons from the screens that appear for any of the video clips.

Real Power: Macromedia Director

As useful as Persuasion can be for making even simple interactive documents, it doesn't give you split-second timing capabilities. If you really want a seamless presentation of information, Macromedia Director provides a much finer level of control over the time at which objects appear. Director is a powerful, complex, and expensive multimedia authoring package, but it gives you unsurpassed detail over the placement of visual elements on a screen at times that you can control down to 1/120 of a second.

Director uses four elements to control the elements of your multimedia presentation: the Stage, the Score, the Cast, and the Controller. Figure 9-2 shows where these appear on the screen when you start Director (the Windows version is shown here, but the Macintosh version looks identical).

In addition to the precise control over time, Director gives you very detailed control over interactivity. You can pause, jump, select parts of the presentation, and do almost anything else you can imagine by using the Lingo scripting language.

Scripting is basically what multimedia developers call programming when they want to let nonprogrammers know they're going to have to do some coding. If you consider yourself a nonprogrammer—and my vision of the typical reader of this book is as a trained professional in a specific field such as education, training, or marketing, with little or no programming experience—you needn't be too concerned with scripting in Lingo. After the next tutorial there'll be a section on how to set up a button that jumps to another video clip. But first, let's take a look at the elements that make up Macromedia Director.

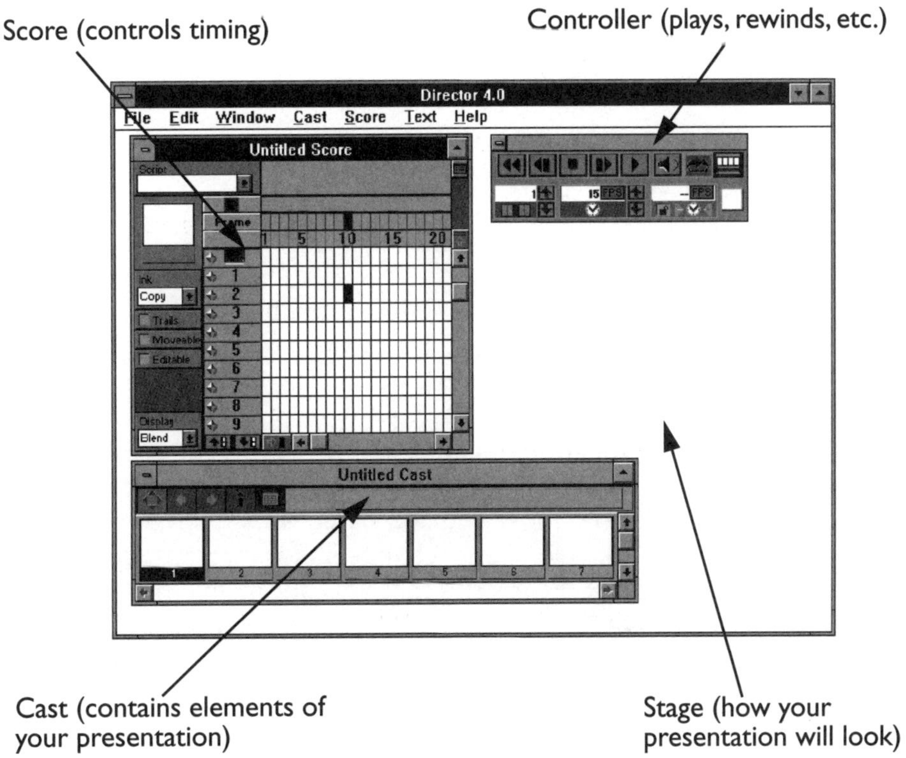

Figure 9-2. Macromedia Director main window

Tutorial 2: Making a Button Stay Up

In Director, you can make a button appear on the screen and remain there for a specified time by performing these steps:

1. **Create the button either by drawing it with Director's own drawing tools, or by importing it from another program.**

   The Tools window of Director has a special tool for creating buttons, but you can also use any graphic for your button. For example, you can draw the button in Freehand, Adobe Illustrator, or (on the PC) the Draw utility. Director supports importation of any visual element you can create on your system (including digitized video or photographs cut from video frames).

If you want the button to show two positions—to make it look as though it stays in when pushed, for example—you need to draw two views of the button. For now, to keep it simple, let's talk about only one piece of artwork.

2. **Put the button art into the Cast.**

   To do this, select one of the frames in the Cast window, pull down the File menu and select Import, then choose the file containing the art you wish to import.

Now you have the button image ready to display in your presentation. But where, and for our purposes when, do you want it to appear? Look back at Figure 9-2 and notice that in the Score window, there is a grid section that looks like graph paper. Across the top of the grid are numbers counting by fives; those numbers represent the frames of the presentation. Down the left-hand edge of the grid are numbers counting by ones; those are the channels, which is how Director puts elements into the presentation. The images that you put in channels closer to the bottom of the screen appear in front of the images that you put in channels closer to the top of the screen. Director supports 48 of these channels in any single Score.

Where you put the button art determines when it appears; the button will not appear until the frame in which you place it (represented by the column in the Score), and it will appear in front of any images that are in channels closer to the top of the screen. So if you know that you don't want a button to appear until frame 72 of a movie, you simply drag the button's representation to frame 72 and that's when it becomes visible.

There are several ways to make it stay visible. The easiest way is this:

1. **Select the frame at which you wish the button to appear, and drag the Cast member into it.**

   Following the example so far, this would be frame 72. Drag the Cast member for the button art into frame 72 of a channel closer to the bottom of the screen than any background images or characters, so that it appears on top of all other images in your scene.

2. **Select the last frame in which you wish the button to appear, and shift-click.**

   This highlights the intermediate frames of the channel you selected for the button.

3. **From the Score menu, select In-between Linear.**

   This fills all the in-between frames with the art associated with this cast member. Director automatically writes in the number associated with the Cast member you have selected, and you will see that number in every frame between the first and last frames you selected.

   Tip: In addition to pulling down the Score menu and selecting In-between Linear, you can also type Command-B. This is a quick way to fill the intermediate frames with copies of the Cast member you have selected. For example, this (using channel 1 or 2) is a quick and easy way to make a background image display throughout your presentation: just select the beginning and ending frames of the sequence during which you want to see the background image, then Command-B to make the selected cast member visible.

You can also make video clips appear in the same way as the button, by dragging them into individual frames in the Score to establish when they begin and by placing them on the Stage at the location you want them to play.

Tutorial 3: Making a Button Respond

To make the button respond to your clicks and perform some action requires a different kind of script, one written in Macromedia's Lingo programming language. While learning to program in Lingo is beyond the scope of this book, you can follow along with this tutorial to learn how to control the flow of your Director documents with a few simple Lingo scripts.

For the record, all the Lingo you really need to know in order to add basic interactivity to a Director document is the command "go to frame." That, plus an identifier for the specific frame to which you want to go, redirects the user to the point in your document they have selected.

Here's how you add interactivity to a button in Director:

1. **Select the Cast member that corresponds to the button.**

   To do this, make the Cast window active, then click on the thumbnail that corresponds to the art you're using for this button.

2. **Click the Script button at the top of the Cast window.**

   This pops up a window in which you can type the script that you wish to associate with the button. Figure 9-3 shows these parts of the Director screen.

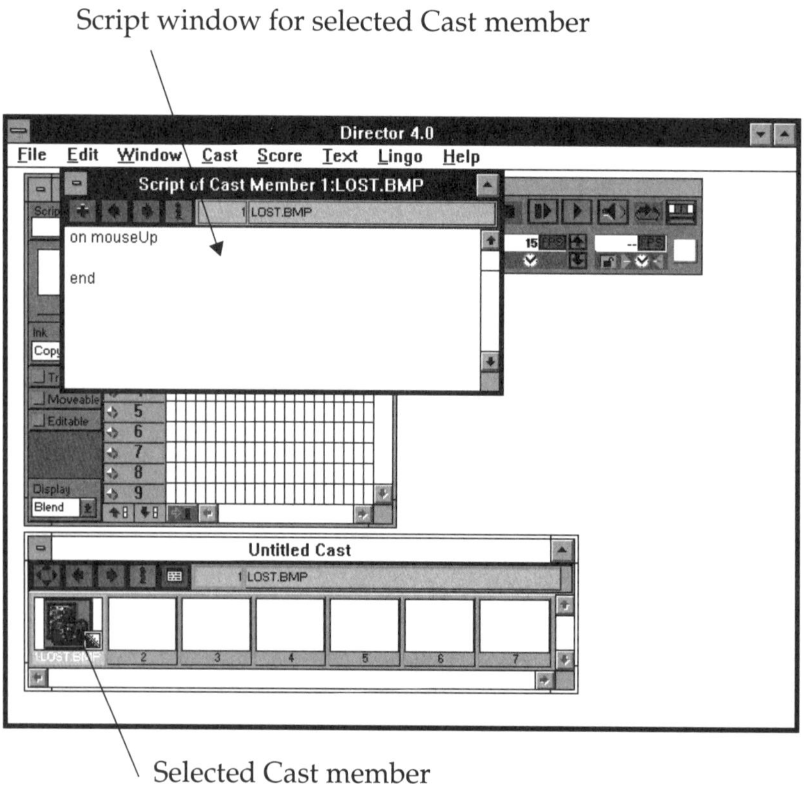

Figure 9.3. Director window with Cast member and Script window

3. **Add the following line to the middle of the script:**

```
go to frame 64
```

   This script performs the following actions when your document is running:

   Director checks to see whether the mouse is clicked (that is, the action is performed when you release the mouse, not when you press it).

When the mouse button is released, Director begins playing the scene at frame 64.

The word "end" signifies to Director that there is no more information in the script.

Basically, that's all there is to interactivity with Lingo—well, in the sense that you can assign similar scripts to a wealth of buttons in your Director document and have just about as much functionality as you have in the Persuasion examples presented in this chapter. In reality, of course, Lingo gives you much more power, which we don't really have time to discuss in this book. Director's manual set, however, is very clear, and if you have the opportunity and the interest you should work through the exercises in "Learning Director" that come with version 4.0.

Additionally, note that using frame numbers is a bad idea. If you add frames before the specific number used in this script, the script will no longer point to the right part of your presentation. Director permits you to name key frames in your movie, so you can include lines like "go to frame GreenFlag," where GreenFlag is the name you've associated with a particular event in the movie.

So we've seen how in Director, you can create buttons that appear for a specified length of time—a number of frames that you control. Likewise, you can use these buttons to redirect the movie's flow to any frame in the entire presentation, at a degree of accuracy greater than 0.01 second. In short, you can use Director to create a dynamic, interactive index into the content of your movie, letting your users find the key segments (using some navigation technique such as those discussed in Chapter 5) or presenting information overviews of different kinds for different users (such as the browsers, scanners, and students talked about in Chapter 6). Director really is the top-of-the-line authoring tool, and because it runs on both platforms (as well as making Windows run-time movies out of content developed on the Macintosh), it's really the premiere way of creating interactive CD-ROM for Windows and Macintosh.

The manuals for programs like Director, Persuasion, and FrameMaker are designed to teach you how to put together interactive presentations on your CD-ROM. What no manual tells you, however, is how to make a good presentation, one that people will learn from, enjoy using, and go back to time and again for the value of its content and its usability. Good presentations are those that are easy to navigate, in which users know where they are and what's happening, and in which the information is clear and distinct. So it's crucial that one of the buttons you put up at appropriate moments in the document should display or take the user to a screen that reviews the information that is available.

Information Content Review

Books have had such an information content review for centuries, in the form of the table of contents. Books also have topic-based information reviews, in the form of the index. The reason these parts of a book are at the front and the back, respectively, is to make it as easy as possible to find them, and also to find your way around in the book.

The best way to provide a review (or an overview) of the information content is to provide an illustration that resembles the object you're describing. If your multimedia title describes an actual object, it's easy to develop the interface: draw the object and add hot spots, either directly to the illustration or in the form of text callouts. If your multimedia title describes something like a process, you may wish to have smaller illustrations of various stages of the process that act as the hot spots, with some indication of flow (either left-to-right across the screen, or top-to-bottom). And if your multimedia title is more abstract, your solution will have to be more creative.

If you're using your multimedia presentation for training, documentation, or some other instructional use, make sure that your users can get to this information overview from any screen in the title. In the PC repair title represented in Figure 9-1, for example, you might have a series of illustrations showing the process of replacing a board inside the PC, each of which was in turn a hot spot for jumping to that section of the title. Then, from within the section that deals with the individual steps of the process, pick a consistent place on the screen where your users can click to get back to the overview. Figure 9-4 illustrates such a screen.

The concept of "home" has become something of a standard in multimedia design. The home screen is an adaptation of a HyperCard concept, the home card, which was the original or fundamental card in the stack. Additionally, HyperCard had a "home stack," which was the stack (multimedia title, in today's terminology) that was used to guide the user to the remote branches.

Most powerful multimedia authoring systems permit a similar way of linking not only screens within a single title, but also separate titles (stacks, presentations, slide shows—or whatever metaphor rules your

Figure 9-4. Part of a video tutorial on PC repair, with a "Home" button

authoring system's design). In Persuasion, as mentioned previously, you can insert a jump to another file, which does not even have to be another Persuasion document: you can run external applications.

In the general sense, this is known as an *application programming interface*, or API. An authoring system's API provides you with enormous power, because it can essentially put the entire capability of your system under the control of the tool. For example, developers of programming manuals might link the on-line documentation directly to the examples that the on-line manual talks about, so that rather than seeing listings on paper the students could click on a line of code and watch it execute. In the days when processing power was cheaper than storage space, it used to be common to include a small example program that drew images rather than including movies or digitized video clips, because the programs took up far less space than 40 or 50 picture files.

In Persuasion, you can link to additional Persuasion presentations or to external applications and documents. For example, you can run a Director file, open a FrameMaker document, edit an animation, or run any program you can reach from within your presentation.

The interface to this capability is through Persuasion's Jump menu, the same menu you used to select the destination slide from your links. To choose a different player, select the Jump To Player radio button from the Autojump dialog box. Persuasion displays the following dialog box:

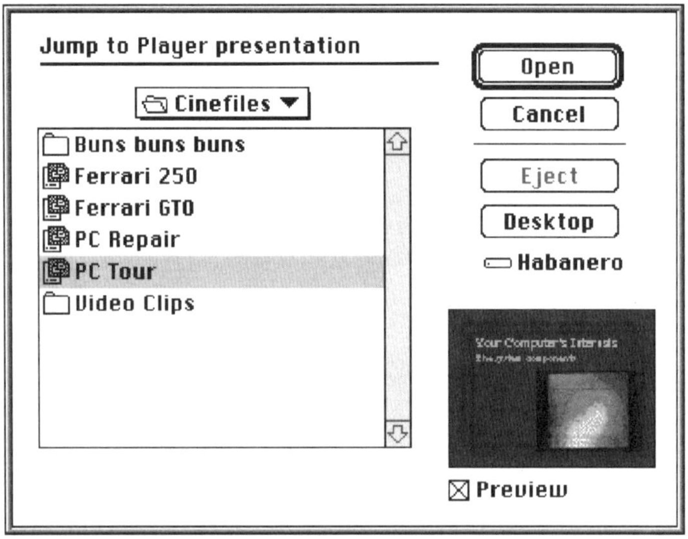

A similar dialog box appears if you select the radio button to Open application/document:

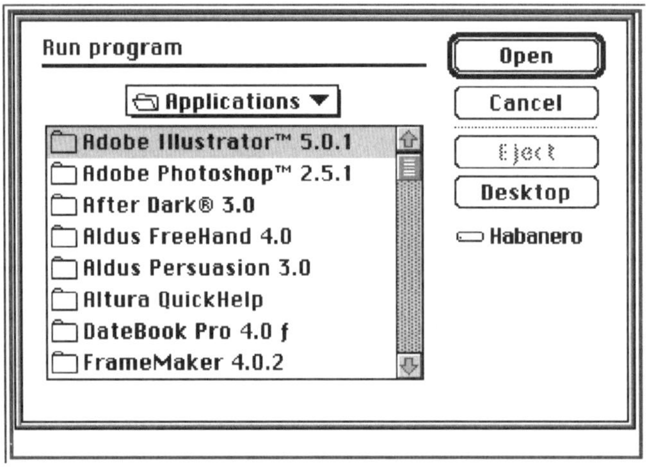

With this power, you can use Persuasion (or some other program that has an equivalent API) as the basis for a multimedia tutorial or training document for your organization's computerized procedures. You can essentially use the presentation program to show, guide, and teach your own users—first by demonstration, then by example.

But don't lose sight of the fact that such APIs, document links, and other ways of navigating the entire surface of a CD-ROM only compound the issue of information interface. Unless you have a consistent, understandable way of getting your user back to someplace they recognize (with the obvious exception of adventure games), the power of such APIs will simply get your users into worse and worse trouble.

Still, this is all covered with great detail elsewhere in this book, and this is only meant as a review. It's time to try it out: fire up one of your applications, load the CD-ROM into your system, and let's put on a show!

Using Your Movies: QuickTime and AVI

Now that you've captured and digitized movies, let's work on putting them into the structure of your multimedia document as you've been planning it since Chapter 3.

If you don't have a capture board and you want to try putting together your own multimedia presentations, you can import QuickTime movies from the CD-ROM into most newer Macintosh applications, and you can use AVI and QuickTime for Windows files in many Windows programs that are compatible with Microsoft's Object Link Embedding (OLE) software. This is particularly useful for education; many teachers have CD-ROMs that contain digitized movies that they wish to use for developing their own classroom materials. Furthermore, many educational CD-ROMs include a license to copy such movies into student presentations; not all do, so be careful what you copy and be sure to read the license.

And while I not only expect but actually hope that you're all taking the video clips off the CD-ROM in the back of this book and learning to build multimedia applications with them, you should be sure to read the fine print on the license, carefully. I'm of the opinion that teachers have the advantage of the moral high ground in potential copyright infringement as long as the use is clearly for the benefit of students and the furthering of their education, and not for making money on the side; but not all copyright holders have the same respect for educators that I do.

Before proceeding, let's talk a bit about cross-platform development. If you are really planning to produce a document that runs on both Windows and Macintosh, you can save yourself time and trouble by developing it on the Mac. Once you digitize your movies, you can convert them to QuickTime for Windows with Apple's MoviePlayer. MoviePlayer version 2.0 lets you save QuickTime movies in a form suitable for playing on Windows platforms as well as Macintosh platforms. The only catch (and it's only a catch for Macintosh users who are just beginning to work in DOS and Windows) is that you need to give your movies a file name suitable for DOS, meaning eight characters, a period, and the letters MOV. That extension is how DOS and Windows know that the file is a QuickTime for Windows movie.

If you're planning to publish exclusively on the Windows platform, you will most likely be working solely with AVI files, as this is Microsoft's native Windows video format. All the examples that I digitized for the CD-ROM using the iSVR Pro, for example, are in AVI form. With Video for Windows and Microsoft OLE, you can then import your AVI files directly into another document. We've focused on presentation software and multimedia development tools so far because they're easy to come up to speed on, but with OLE and OpenDoc, you can put video into almost any application that calls for it.

Tutorial 4: Using QuickTime Video on the Macintosh

Importing a QuickTime movie into a Macintosh application is as simple as importing any still graphic. If you're using Persuasion, PowerPoint, or another presentation tool, everything you've been learning so far applies to the design, timing, layout, and interactivity of your document. But the addition of digital video means you can insert time-based media into the document you're working on.

You can probably import QuickTime movies into any application program you choose. For example, here's how to import QuickTime movies into FrameMaker:

1. **Pull down the File menu and select Import.**
2. **Choose File.... Frame displays the following dialog box:**

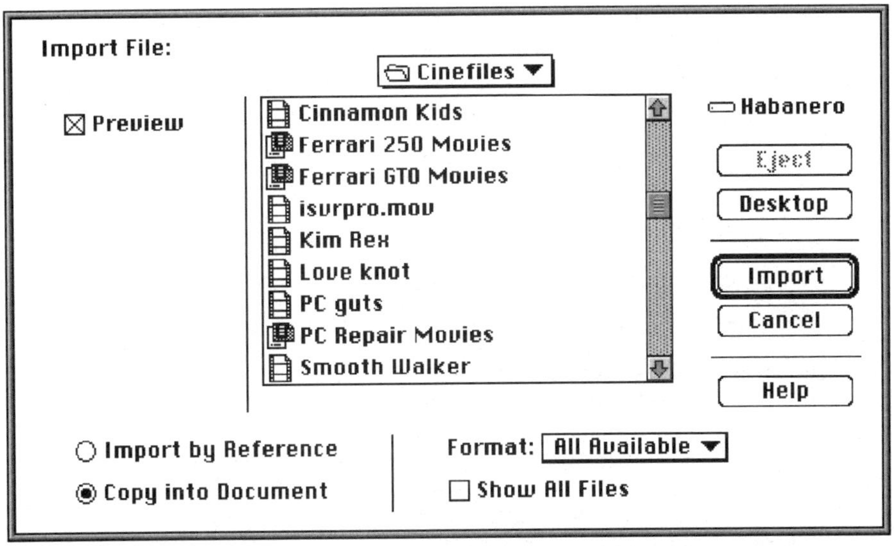

3. **Select the QuickTime movie you wish to add to your Frame document and click Import.**

   When you do this, Frame adds an anchored frame containing the QuickTime movie:

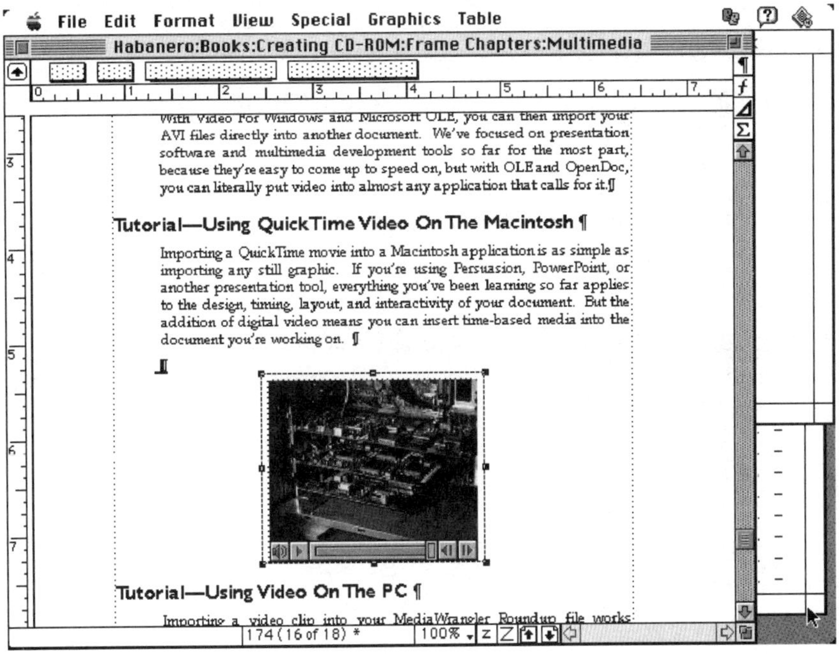

When Frame first imports the video clip into your document, a movie badge appears in the lower left-hand corner. To make the movie playable, click on the player badge once; this opens the QuickTime control bar from which you can play, step forward or backward, and control the volume of the audio playback.

The basic procedure is the same for all other Macintosh applications that support video. For Persuasion, it's only slightly different, as follows:

1. **Pull down the File menu and pull right to select Import, then choose Movies.**

   Persuasion displays the following dialog box:

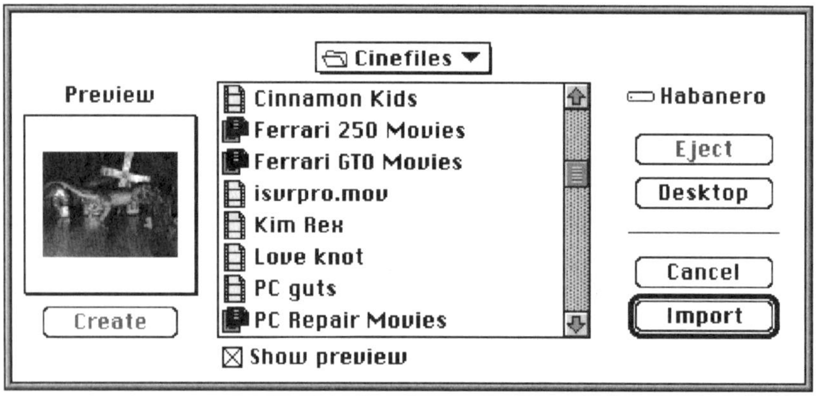

2. **Choose the QuickTime movie you wish to import.**

   Persuasion adds the movie to your presentation. By default it adds it to the center of your screen, but it gives you handles so that you can drag the movie to different screen locations.

PowerPoint, Macromedia Director, and even Microsoft Word work in much the same way. For an extra exercise, start thinking about how you could use video as an element in the software package you are currently using most often, whether that's a word processor, a graphics package, or anything else on the computer.

Tutorial 5: Using Video on the PC

The mechanics of importing video into a PC application are slightly different. Windows uses a technology called Object Link Embedding (OLE) to incorporate links to other objects into the body of documents and files on the PC. Additionally, there are certain applications that have their own means of incorporating video into their applications; one that you've been using already is MediaWrangler.

Importing a video clip into your MediaWrangler Roundup file works the same as with any other media element: you draw the Media Area Pointer (MAP) that you want people to click on, select it, then use the Import/ Browse Video button from the Toolbar to select the video clip.

You can also import video clips into the Hitching Post, which acts much like the Cast window in Macromedia Director. From the Hitching Post you can drag media elements into any of the MAPs you create in your roundup file. However, note that all video clips use the same icon in MediaWrangler—the video camera. You'll need to give your video clips descriptive names when you digitize them. Alternatively, you can use something like MediaWrangler as a kind of visual indexing tool for a library of video clips. You might store individual frames from the movie, then set them up so that the entire surface is a "hot spot" that plays the video clip when you click on it.

The following tutorial takes you through the steps of loading a video clip into a Hitching Post, then associating that clip with a MAP.

1. **Run MediaWrangler, either by clicking on its icon or by running the file MWRANGLE.EXE.**

2. **Create a new Roundup file.**

   From the File menu, select New and choose Roundup File from the pop-up menu.The Roundup file, you may remember, is MediaWrangler's mechanism for controlling and organizing other media types.

3. **For the root image, select the file GOO.GIF**

   You can find the file GOO.GIF, a photograph of a yellow-green fish, in the directory C:\MWRANGLE\IMAGES (where C: is the name of the disk on which you installed MediaWrangler).

4. **Create a new Hitching Post file.**

   From the File menu, pull down New and select Hitching Post File from the pop-up menu. When the file is created, the window that it occupies will automatically have input focus. Call the Hitching Post file VIDEO.HPF.

5. **Click on the Video button in the toolbar and select the file SUGRPLUM.AVI.**

   This loads the indicated file into the new Hitching Post.

At this point, your screen should look something like this:

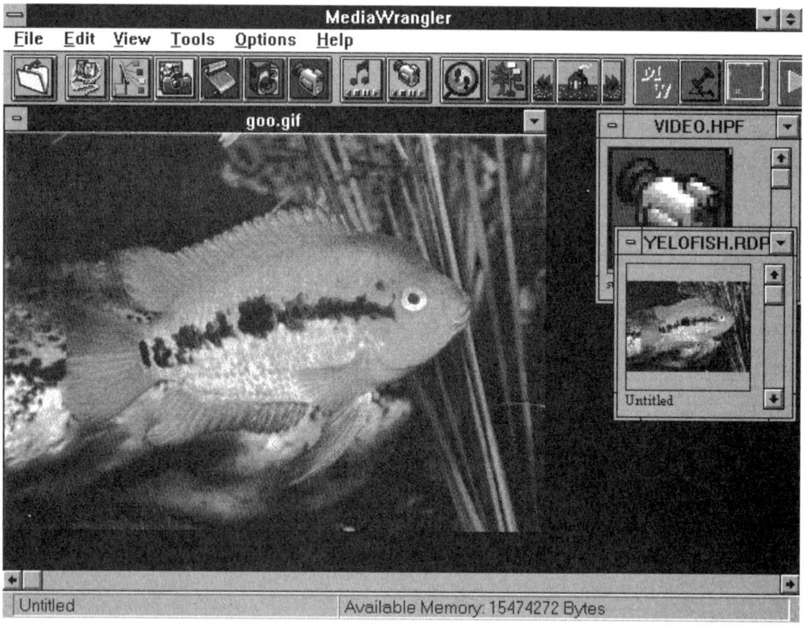

6. **Draw a MAP around the fish's eye and mouth.**

   Remember, one of the nice features about MediaWrangler is that you can draw links of any shape. Make it cover most of the fish's face.

   To draw a MAP, first click the right mouse button, then draw the MAP by clicking the left mouse button at every corner of the MAP. Then click once with the left mouse button to select it.

7. **Select the video clip from the Hitching Post and drag it into the MAP.**

   To do this, click the video icon once with the left mouse, then drag the clip into the MAP. As you drag, you'll notice that the cursor changes to the icon of a movie camera. When the cursor is inside the MAP, let go of the mouse button.

You can now test your new link by double-clicking (with the left button) inside the MAP. You should see the video clip of two little girls sleeping in front of the Christmas tree while "The Dance of the Sugarplum Fairies" plays softly in the background.

Tutorial 6: Pasting Video into a Document

You can also use OLE directly to import media elements into a document created by a program that supports OLE. For example, you can include an AVI or a QuickTime for Windows file in a FrameMaker document on the PC by first copying the object in the player appropriate to the file type (that is, the MediaPlayer for AVI files, or the QuickTime for Windows Movie Player for QuickTime for Windows files), then using the Paste Special option of the Edit menu. Here, for instance, is how you would import a Video for Windows movie to Frame on the PC:

1. **Open the movie in one of its native players.**

   For example, this screen snapshot shows the Asymetrix Digital Video Producer's Media Player main window:

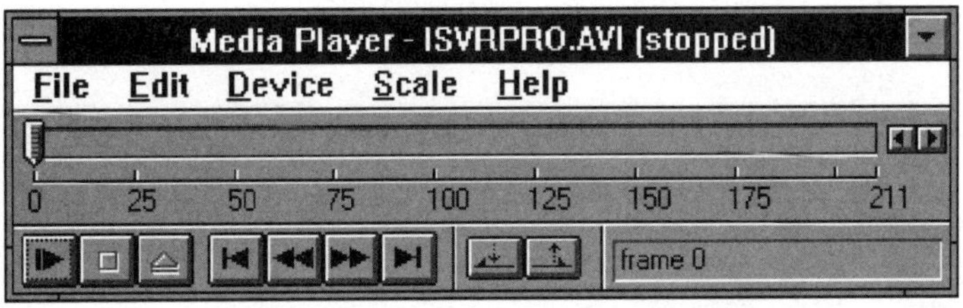

2. **When the movie is exposed, pull down the Edit menu of the Media Player and select Copy Object.**

   This copies the entire video onto the clipboard.

3. **Open (or maximize) Frame and find the location in the document at which you wish to insert the video clip.**

4. **From the Edit menu, select Paste Special.**

   Frame displays the following dialog box:

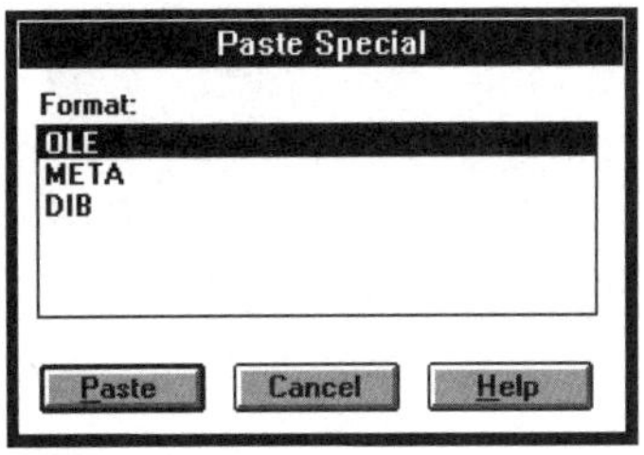

5. **Choose OLE, then click Paste.**

   Frame then inserts the video clip into your document:

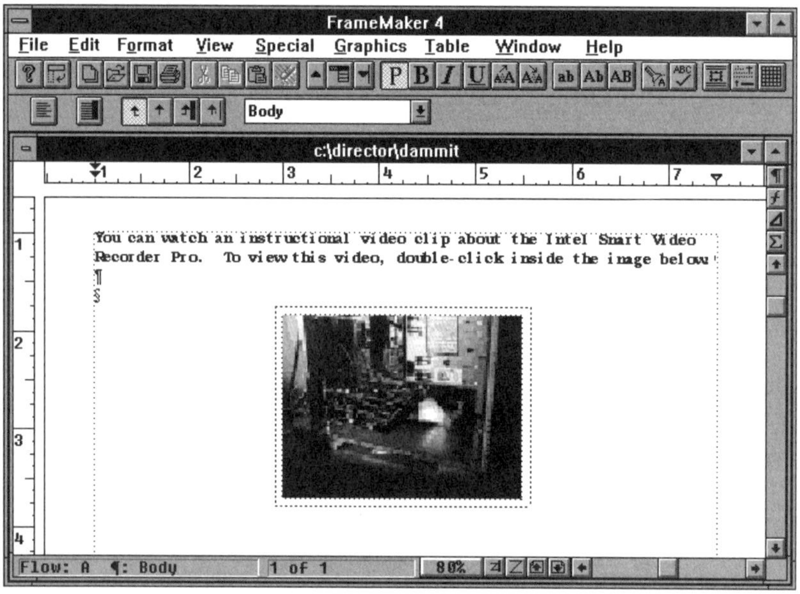

That's it. If you have Frame, a video compression card, and a local area network at your site, you can use Frame to create interactive FrameViewer documents with Frame's powerful hypertext capabilities, but you can also incorporate video clips in the same way that you can incorporate screen snapshots, block diagrams, or any other static art.

Review: File-centric, Not Application-centric, Media

At the opening of this chapter, I mentioned that OLE and OpenDoc herald a new way of dealing with information on the computer. You've had a taste of this now, following some of the tutorials and examples. The change deals with the most fundamental way that information has heretofore been grouped on the computer: the file system.

In the past, computer files (or documents) stored data that had been created by a particular application. The file was formatted, contained special characters, and otherwise managed all its information in particular ways that were special to the application that created it. In spite of the fact that all computer files consist of ones and zeroes at the lowest level of detail, you couldn't use the information in the file unless you had the application that had created it, or at the very least one that could convert it.

This is still true today—for example, if you don't have FrameMaker or FrameViewer on your computer, you won't be able to read the Frame examples on the CD-ROM (which is why there are so few of them). But more and more often, documents are becoming compounded by containing information in entirely different media that were not created by the original authoring program. If you've ever incorporated a picture in a word-processing document, you've done the precursor to this.

What we've seen with documents that include video as well as text, graphics, and other forms of information is the forerunner of a new way of managing information. No single application will be able to capture, digitize, transfer, and display a chunk of video or an animated picture. What the OpenDoc and OLE architectures promise is a future in which the individual applications will focus on managing a particular kind of medium or a particular format of information—spreadsheet data, for instance, rather than spreadsheet files. That way if you need to include a spreadsheet in a report, you can use the spreadsheet program directly from within the report you're writing, rather than having to exit Frame or WordPerfect or whatever document authoring system you're using. The document becomes the method of controlling information, not the application program.

The first steps on this road are already incorporated into this book. The basics of making information available in standardized types have already been distributed: QuickTime, AVI, PostScript, GIF, TIFF, JPEG, MPEG and the rest of the acronyms we've discussed are all enabling technologies for this new, document-centric approach to information management. But it's particularly exciting for multimedia developers because as OpenDoc and OLE become more pervasive, appearing in more and more applications on each of their respective platforms, you'll be on the cutting edge of a new aesthetic, a new way of approaching information based on its own needs and its own content, rather than based on the capabilities of the program you happened to use or inherit for your project. You will be able, with increasing ease, to put together presentations, school reports, training documents, even holiday form letters that have the kind of media that your subject calls for.

But as media types become more pervasive, how can you be sure that your message is getting through? In the past, it would have required the services and attentions of an editor, a review staff, or other specialists to determine the style, format, and syntax of whatever the medium was in which you chose to cover your subject. As the media merge on the computer, it becomes necessary—in addition to all that, not instead of—to verify whether or not the media really do dance when you call the tune. The industry calls this testing, quality assurance, final editing. Whatever you call it, it's the difference between a successful multimedia presentation or title, and one that fails miserably.

In the next chapter, we'll look at some successful testing strategies, both from the standpoint of developers of internal, scholastic, and technical training materials, and from the standpoint of developers of commercial multimedia titles.

Chapter 10
Testing

What Does This Button Do, Anyway?

It's easy to like multimedia. It's showy, fun to play with, and gets your message across easily and effectively. People respond well to seeing video (at least now that the performance is getting better) and animation on their screens instead of columns of unintelligible text.

But all it takes is a single breakdown for all these good feelings to evaporate. Reading "The application 'unknown' has unexpectedly quit with an error of type -255," or even worse, "Error reading Drive A: Abort, Retry, Fail?" may be all it takes to turn a satisfied customer into a technical support call, an irate posting on the Internet, or even an informal word-of-mouth campaign about how your multimedia document fails all the time.

Worse yet, multimedia lends itself to confusion by its very nature as a revolutionary way of organizing and accessing information. Links that go nowhere, buttons that do nothing, mouse clicks followed by an empty silence—all are sure ways to turn off an audience. In some ways, the traditional process of editing and proofreading a document has expanded to also include testing its functional components to ensure that they work as expected.

Cross-platform developers, or developers for the PC, have a slightly rougher time of it than Mac-only developers. In fact, it's becoming something of a truism in the cross-platform world that it can be more work to put a PC version of a product out on a different configuration of PC than it is to put the same product out on Macintosh and PC. In this chapter, we'll look at some ways to minimize this risk, and to develop testing and development strategies that can help you get the best possible product to market. In the worst case, these methods can help you ensure that a breakdown for your customer is handled in a way that will leave your end users with the best possible picture of your organization.

Why Test Your Document?

That's not a bad question. Even if you already think testing is a good idea, what do you hope to achieve from running a battery of tests on your document? Asking yourself this question, and running through the exercises in this section of the chapter, will help you have a more successful testing program, leading to better-quality products by the time version 1.0 hits the stores. So let's discuss some of the answers to the question of why you should test.

A multimedia document is really two completely separate things—a document containing information, and an instance of an application program that lets you navigate through and display that information. Before you know that your multimedia document "works," you need to test both of these components. That is, you need to have someone verify the information (assuming that you're producing a reference, training, or other nonfiction document), or you need to have a story editor check the dramatic components against the original story to make sure that all the elements are present. In other words, you still need an editor, just the way you do with a book, an article, a documentary film, or a major motion picture.

Where multimedia brings a new twist to all this is in the additional need to verify how it all works together. In testing the two separate parts together, a third part—the information interface, as distinct from the user interface—becomes visible. Testing the function of the program is one thing; testing the completeness of each individual piece of information (and the presence of all the required pieces of information) is a second, and out of the two of these comes the synthesis of a third, which is testing how well the first part gives users access to the second.

So with this in mind, you really need to start developing a test plan fairly early and signing up members of your organization to use the product when it approaches completion. What will they look for? How should they test? And how should they report back their findings? To answer these questions fully, let's look at them in terms of when you test the document, what stage it's in, and how you can continually refine both the information and its presentation by stages along the development process. In this light, let's examine testing at the proposal or prototype stage, testing during development, testing a first-draft version of the product, and final pre-release testing. In the software industry, these four phases are often given the names proof of concept, development testing, alpha testing, and beta testing, so I'll use those terms here.

Proof of Concept: Early Testing

In some ways, proof of concept begins as early as the first napkin sketches you made to convince someone you were working on something exciting. It takes on a more formal aspect when you prepare a proposal for the people who will be funding your development. And it becomes fully fleshed out by the time you have a specification, shooting script, or other document that your development team can use. So that's the phase of design we'll focus on for proof of concept: from rough idea through beginning production.

The testing you do at the napkin-sketch stage is obviously far less formal than the testing you do just prior to ordering 10,000 copies of your CD-ROM, but it's the first step on the road to those 10,000 copies. When you start to sell friends, colleagues, and family on a new idea, you're testing it by seeing whether the idea turns anyone else on. If it does, it passes the test; if it doesn't, and where it doesn't, you know you have work to do.

The biggest potential pitfall facing new multimedia developers at the proof of concept stage is getting bogged down in the difference between whether you're testing the concept or testing the way you're expressing the concept. If the idea is still half-formed in your own imagination, you'll have difficulty getting others to visualize it. If, however, you have a more thorough understanding of what you want to create, it'll be easier for people to visualize it themselves. Chapter 2 is about that stage of the process.

Most multimedia developers rely on the software technique of the proof of concept project. In programming terms, this is a small, prototype version of the tool that you plan to build, one that does just enough to demonstrate what you plan to make, yet that is compact enough to be put together in a short period of time. A typical multimedia proof of concept document might have only one working option on the main user interface screen, only a short video clip (and one that may not even have much connection to the eventual subject), and just enough link to give the flavor of the creator's ultimate vision.

As the name indicates, the goal of this part of the project is to prove whether the concept works. If the prototype has flaws beyond those to be expected from the outset (such as incompleteness, use of sketches or wireframe drawings, and the like), it's best to identify and solve them now rather than to spend hundreds of collective hours on a project that has fundamental flaws. At such an early stage, you can easily correct fairly global, vast-reaching portions of the document's basic design (for example, the look of a character or the layout of a building that is crucial to the plot of an interactive murder mystery). Later in the project, when such design issues may affect hundreds of screens or potential plot points that render implausible a number of possible endings, the price to rework story, art, or other media would be too high. If there are fundamental problems, find them and fix them now, before development starts. Then you can begin the task of creating the content with a fairly strong sense of the project's direction.

Development Testing: Running Changes

While you're writing, photographing, drawing or recording the media you want to incorporate into your document, you need some kind of regular "reality check" on the team to make sure they're all working in accordance with the overall design. There are actually two schools of thought on how to proceed with development testing, and I have very strong opinions about which one works best for me, but I'll try to propose both in as even-handed a way as I can. You may well find that the other method is effective for you, your team, and the kinds of documents you're developing.

The approach I prefer to use during development is to make regular, small, incremental checks and changes, tracking what's happening in short, informal meetings every week or so to make sure that everyone on the team is still synchronized with the original concept. There are costs, of course; following this goal sometimes means that individual team members will make changes one week that end up being reversed the following week.

That's the risk of regular assessment; if you're still in the middle of development on a project, you will by definition not have as clear a picture of the overall project as you do when it's nearly finished. On the other hand, the changes required are typically small because the amount of work you have to deal with is incremental rather than total. In my personal experience, for my style of working and for what drives me nuts in a project, this is preferable to the alternative, but I concede that this is a personal opinion.

The alternative to testing, checking, editing, and sharing progress on a weekly basis is to let the team go—let everyone work with an informal understanding of the common project, then after a period of time pull it all together and see how the pieces fit. The downside to this style of development is that you risk having one or more team members go off in directions that are inconsistent with the overall picture. If what you really want is something that looks unified and that gives the appearance of having been the product of a single creative vision, this approach carries a number of risks.

However, it also has some payoffs for certain kinds of productions. If you want a kind of anthology of multimedia—if you're trying to get a free, creative, disjointed, deconstructionist feel to your document—or if you're trying to brainstorm for creative approaches, this is a great way to proceed. (Since deconstructionist isn't a word often used, I'll give you my working definition: deconstructionism is the aesthetic philosophy that says that the original intent or involvement of the author is irrelevant, even indeterminable, in a creative work. The only intent or involvement that we can measure, the only one that matters in some sense, is the involvement of the audience, their own participation in the creative work. If you've been reading this book all the way from the beginning, you'll have an understanding of why deconstructionism should appeal to developers of multimedia, or at least interactive, documents.)

So you have to decide whether your document has a single, unified feel to it, a unity of content and tone that carries across the entire range of the presentation; or whether your document has a jumpy, diverse, multifaceted approach to its aesthetic elements. If you choose the former (and again, developers of training documents and other professional types of multimedia and CD-ROM information will almost certainly produce this kind of document within the structure of the corporate, academic, and professional worlds), then regular weekly "reality checks" are a great way to keep everyone working in sync with one another.

If you're striving for a new kind of aesthetic, and in particular if you have creative people from very different styles working together to make something experimental or groundbreaking, then you may find it easier to let everyone develop for several weeks or a month, or more, before pulling them all together. You'll have to decide based on your team, your subject, and, of course, your audience. However, I will say that the regular-meeting approach isn't anathema to the creative environment; as someone who is often picked as the most creative person in the room, I'll say that the ability to spin off, brainstorm, and develop ideas on a weekly basis can have tremendous benefit to the process of forging a unified creative vision as well as writing a user's manual. In the end, multimedia is about communication, and you may find that regular communication about the document itself is a great way to make sure that the document communicates.

Alpha Testing: Resources Required

In any case, eventually your document will be "done" by some definition. That is, it'll have sufficient mass to be able to show it to an audience without standing over their shoulders telling them what is supposed to come next or why a particular button doesn't work. In the software industry, this stage is called alpha testing.

Alpha testing requires a number of components before it can begin, and a certain amount of understanding before it can become successful. First let's look at the components; we'll get around to understanding the alpha test process later.

The most important part of an alpha test process is a stable, relatively complete product to test. You should have most of the user interface done, most of the media elements completed (even though some may be in rough form, such as wire-frame illustrations instead of fully rendered 3D images), and the majority of the links in place. In many ways, the links are the most important thing to test at this stage, because they're going to be how your audience (in the deconstructionist sense mentioned previously) brings your document to life. Unless you are essentially putting a movie, documentary, or TV show on CD-ROM, the links are what makes it multimedia. They're also how your audience gets to all the neat stuff you've been putting into the document; any "missing links" mean that your users will be unable to get to the information at the other end of that link.

The other critical part of an alpha test process is, of course, a reliable batch of testers, preferably drawn from a community that doesn't have an intimate knowledge of your document. That means the programmers, writers, artists, and developers themselves will probably not be the best crew to do an alpha test, for the simple reason that they will take too much for granted. A programmer who knows that a function isn't working yet will often adapt his work style to take the missing function into account, without even knowing that he or she is doing this. Likewise, an author who knows a subject well can sometimes pass off in one sentence a piece of information that a less well-informed audience will require a page to understand.

Of course, you can still use team members to test the document, and you should: it's a great way to show everyone what the overall product is turning into. Let the artists see how their work looks and sounds when it has music; let the writers see how their characters will look in the visual design; let the interactivity developers (the scripters, we'll call them) see how their sense of the flow through the document translates into different interactions with the information and with the characters in the document. They'll gain a new sense of the overall vision toward which they're all working.

The third, and often overlooked, component of an alpha test is a thorough mechanism for getting tester feedback to the creative, technical, and managerial functions in your organization. When something doesn't work for a tester, find out what and why and who needs to fix it. A close relationship between the testers and the developers is essential, yet you don't want the people doing the testing to call the development staff nineteen times a day to log every problem that comes up.

The best approach is to choose someone to manage the testing process. Software companies typically hire quality assurance (QA) specialists. These people apply methodical approaches to tracking product design, testing all features, and reporting failures in a concise and standardized way.

You may wish to consider consulting a QA specialist, if none already exists in your organization. Barring that, you should choose one person to manage the test, even though you should have as many people as is practical performing it. Centralizing the control this way means there's only one head to look through for answers about issues uncovered during test.

Your QA specialist should consider the following things while testing your CD-ROM:

Completeness. Is there a specification, a table of contents, a production plan, or some other document that lays out what will be on the CD-ROM? If so, let your QA specialist refer to it to see whether or not you included everything that your document called for. If, due to the nature of alpha testing, you know of modules, art, or other components that are incomplete, nonfunctional, or simply missing, be sure you let the tester know. If there are known bugs that the developers are working around, let the testers know the workaround so that they don't stop when they encounter the first bug.

Function. Does everything work? Does it work on more than the development system on which you wrote it? If this is a Windows application, does it work with a different video card, sound card, processor type (386 instead of a 486), memory configuration (4 or 5 megabytes instead of 8 or 16), or with different driver software installed?

Interactivity. Part of this is a subsection of testing for function: do the links all go to the right place? More important, when you get there, is the information useful, usable, concise and complete? If it's not, log it and get it back to the writer, project manager, or whoever else is responsible for the overall information architecture.

Aesthetics. Does it "look good" when the testers run it? If you're developing a game, is it too hard or too easy for the desired age and skill level? If it's educational software, are the images engaging and the presentation attractive? Is there a reasonable balance between modules—not too long in some places, too short in others (discounting content issues—a section on "Mad Emperors Throughout History" will by nature be longer than "Best-Loved War Criminals," even though the two subjects have considerable potential for overlap).

Accuracy. Only an issue for nonfiction titles, accuracy is no less important just because the presentation is showy and high-tech. (Ask the news agency responsible for putting model rocket motors in the gas tanks of vehicles used in on-the-air crash tests some time ago.) If you're doing a medical CD-ROM, be sure that the information is peer-reviewed by specialists in the areas covered on disk. If it's an encyclopedia, make sure that your alpha testers are adept in specific areas of the encyclopedia's content, and be sure that you get the right people looking at the right modules. For instance, if you had famed avian artist Roger Tory Peterson consulting on a wildlife CD-ROM, he'd be a natural to review the technical accuracy of the section on birds, rather than primates; leave that to Jane Goodall, as long as we're fantasizing about a dream team of reviewers.

Fun. Sometimes the hardest to quantify, fun is no less important than accuracy, even in training material or purely educational software. Remember the example of programming a VCR versus telling the story of a favorite soap opera: even the most complex situations become memorable when you engage the emotions. Here, one interesting technique that can bring fun into a document is to reverse the reviewers. Have Jane Goodall look at the birds out of her background in the study of animals' social organization and interaction, and see what new ideas she might provide regarding the way the birds behave in the video clips. Likewise, if Roger Tory Peterson looked at the primate sections from the viewpoint of an artist, illustrator, and visualizer, he might be able to offer suggestions on image composition, color, clarity, and selection of the visual elements. Specialists in one field often bring a fresh perspective to another one. Besides, that's what interactivity is really about: the juxtaposition of information inside the viewer's head, and how this leads not only to knowledge, but also to fun.

How long should alpha testing take, and how do you proceed? Each tester should have the product for at least as long as it would take to go through the entire content at least once, and that only if every tester is taking a different path. Remember that with interactivity you're not simply testing page by page through the document; you need to test every link, every jump, every connection, and this may take a multiple of the amount of time a typical user is expected to take in going through the document once.

As a practical matter, check to see whether your authoring system can automate or simplify this matter at all. Users of FrameMaker for publishing on CD-ROM should check into the ability to make an index of markers with that product. To do this, follow these steps:

1. **Pull down the File menu and select Generate/Book.**

   FrameMaker displays the following dialog box:

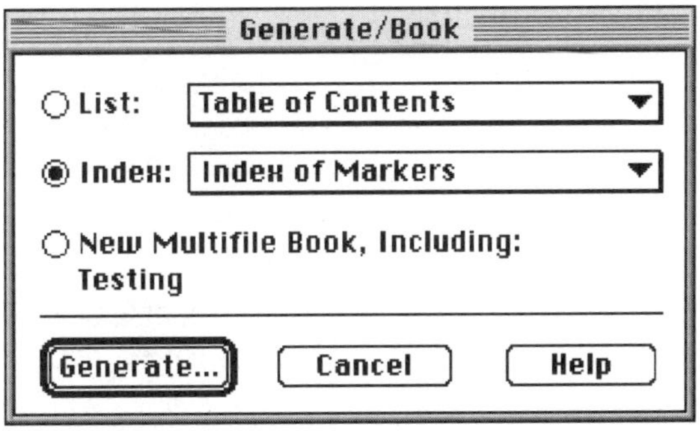

2. **Click on Index and select Index of Markers from the pop-up menu, then click Generate.**

   FrameMaker displays the following dialog box:

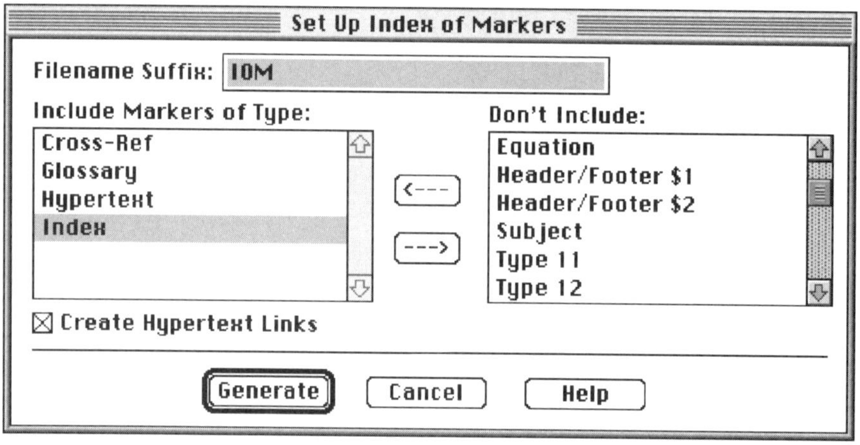

3. **Include the markers of interest to you in the left-hand box.**

   To do this, click on the marker type in the "Don't Include" box, then click the left-pointing arrow between the two boxes.

As a general rule, it's a good idea to click the box marked Create Hypertext Links, as shown here, whether or not you actually plan to distribute the index of markers (or any other index Frame creates for you) as a hypertext document. Your testers will thank you because it will give them a way of tracking all the markers of various types in the document they are testing, as well as an interface to the portions of the document that contain those markers. If your testers simply click on the entry in the index of markers, Frame will take them to the location in the document that the marker references.

As for how to proceed, anyone involved in the production side of an alpha test, or the test side of the same process, fantasizes about having enough time for everything. The developers wish that they could put the product out for six weeks, two months, as long as possible and not hear anything about it till the end of the period. The testers wish that they could go through the product many times, testing things again and again even when they fail so that they can be certain of why it failed before calling the developers. And life would be great if we all had wings, too!

The fact of testing is that it's always done late in the process; the trick of testing is to make sure it isn't too little, too late. Production schedules are a fact of life in every industry that touches CD-ROM, whether that's publishing, education, professional training, or marketing. We all have pressures to get it done faster, so that it can get out the door sooner and start earning revenue at the beginning of the window of opportunity, when prices are typically highest.

A short cautionary tale, then. A close friend, who wishes to remain anonymous and therefore not irritate anyone who might have been associated with the similarly anonymous organization in this anecdote, tells the following story. She worked at a company that was among the first to develop third-party software for a new type of personal computer. The demand for any kind of software for this new computer was so great that the company she worked for began to sell tens of thousands of dollars worth of their product. (This is a phenomenon that I call "market vacuum": a new market often sucks along anything it can get, bad as well as good, until the pressure reaches equilibrium.)

The company grew, and released new products based largely on its ability to be the first into a new market niche for this computer. Yet to keep up with production schedules, products were released before testing was completed or occasionally contrary to the direct recommendation of the testing manager not to ship a product until problems were resolved.

Eventually, word got out that this company's products were often buggy, poorly developed, and sometimes even misrepresented. Eventually no one bought the company's products, and it lost not only the money it had made with their first products, but also an unbelievable opportunity to be a tremendous force in the marketplace today, many years later—an opportunity that would have, could have, should have arisen from its position as an early leader in development for this computer.

The moral of the story: Give your testers enough time to look at everything, and if they tell you something is really broken, get it fixed. Besides, it's still alpha test; you've got weeks to go before beta!

Beta Testing: Are We There Yet?

So the alpha test results are in. Your development staff has a list of things to fix. Your story team has reams of notes about where your audience got lost. Your graphic artists are looking in *Gray's Anatomy* to see how to make bullet-riddled body parts look more authentic. It's back to the production cycle, finishing incomplete items from the original production plan and also fixing problems in the design, interface, and function that the alpha test team discovered.

The next stage in the test cycle is beta test. While the meaning varies from company to company, the general consensus on beta test products is that they have to look, feel, and work as much like the finished product as they possibly can, given the stage in the production process. By the time you go to beta, you should have everything in place, as far into the production cycle as possible, so that your testers will be exercising something that is virtually identical to what customers will get.

In some ways, this is more important for CD-ROM material than it is for other types of software. Because the product has such a visual component, and because the interactivity is such a crucial part of the product's effectiveness, it's necessary to approach beta testing a multimedia title with a high degree of seriousness about the content, function, and other elements that make up the document. With that in mind, here are some suggestions on organizing your beta test in advance of the fact so that you can have the most rewarding experience possible.

For this section, I've relied on my wife and editorial assistant, Kim Fisher, for her expertise in testing and product support. Kim spent several years managing the product testing and technical support department of a mid-sized software company. One of her best tips is hidden in that job description: the product testing and technical support functions were performed by the same department. This led to unparalleled communication between testing and development, for a simple reason. The people responsible for reporting bugs uncovered during the test process were the same people who would have to answer the phone and explain those bugs to unhappy customers if the product didn't get fixed.

A side benefit of this is that the phone support staff were extraordinarily well versed in the product's function and in how to recover from bugs that did slip through. Having the support staff test the product before shipping it not only made them knowledgeable about the product's features, it also gave them a much-needed break from solving customer support problems all day, which is an unbelievably tiring job. Rotating people off the phones for a week or so at a time as a new product became available for testing made going back to the grind a lot more bearable, and made the people doing it a lot more effective, because they had collectively experienced most of the problems that the callers had.

From that background, here are a number of suggestions about ways to improve the effectiveness of the testing process.

Set up clear, regular communication between testing, support, and development. Even if it's not practical in your organization to put testing and support into the same department, consider assigning one person to be the liaison between the two organizations. Make him or her responsible for keeping everyone on both sides of the team up to date on new developments in either area.

Tell your testers to be thorough and unstoppable. "They need to know if all of the other stuff works," Kim says, even if one feature fails. Chances are the developers already know that a feature is broken; the testers need to find other results, expected and unexpected. When something breaks, write down what, and when, and then move on to a different feature.

Try all combinations and all contexts. Sometimes a bug will only surface when certain features are present, either in the program itself or in the system. For example, as I write this I am involved in researching a problem between two applications on the Power Macintosh platform, one of which is a live video feed used for desktop videoconferencing. When a second application displays images in a certain way (and we don't yet know what way that is), the screen blanks out the video image in the conferencing application. As of yesterday we had determined that this only happened if you set the monitor to 256 colors: setting the monitor to "Thousands" or "Millions" cleared the blank screen in the conference window and the problem didn't recur. This points pretty clearly to a problem in the way the second application handles color maps. At the moment, we don't know exactly what this other application is doing to cause this problem, but testing other possible combinations has led us not only to identify where the problem is occurring but also to give it a workaround.

Make charts of the features you need to test, and follow every branch. This is another application for the whiteboard: make a flowchart containing all the features of the document (or use your storyboard drawings), then check off the components as they're tested. This lets you track which ones work, and which ones fail. You also need to track when something fails because, as the previous paragraph indicates, sometimes the context will cause problems that individual elements alone won't experience.

You can't take anything for granted. "You have to be like Sherlock Holmes," Kim says, recalling the detective's constant admonishments to Watson: *Never assume*. Test even irrational combinations—your customers certainly will. "Testers used to tell me, 'Nobody's gonna do this.' And sure enough we'd get a support call from someone who had done just that, and had a good reason for it."

This highlights the crucial difference between alpha and beta testing: alpha testing is normally done by internal test staff, while beta testing involves customers using the product for the purposes you hope millions of people will find essential. No matter how carefully you think about ways you expect your customers to use your product, they will do things you hadn't thought of. Some of these will work, and in fact may turn into a huge new market for your product that you hadn't realized was there. Some of what they try will break the product and you'll have to fix it.

The Care and Feeding of Testers

By their nature, testers are busy people. Internal testers are usually on loan from some other department, where you hope their experience will provide value to your CD-ROM. Beta testers are usually customers, and if you're creating a CD-ROM to help them in some technical aspect of their job, you know they're busy enough to spend the suggested retail price of your title for getting assistance with whatever task your CD-ROM tackles. Even if you're doing a pure entertainment CD-ROM, the people who help you test and review the last version before customer release are giving up their time to help you make the product better.

Two categories exist in which you can make their contributions more effective, and they're right up there in the section head: care and feeding. The care starts when you give your testers a copy of the product, whether alpha or beta. You should take the time to acknowledge them for helping, but you should also give them a clear structure within which you want them to test. Let them know what you want and how you want them to respond. Set up an electronic mail account for their responses. Give them documents that lay out the structure of the product you want them to test, if that's the stage of testing you're in—this is usually more suited to alpha test, both because the staff is internal and because it's more crucial to verify the product's completeness at this stage. It may not be appropriate for you to provide reams of "fill this out in triplicate" forms to a customer, but some kind of notes suggesting methods of testing will make it easier for your customers to focus on the areas for which you want feedback.

Care continues by having someone in your organization responsible for communication with the customer. You may wish to go as formal as designating a beta site administrator at the customer's location, enlisting the aid of that person in keeping communication open from both sides. And every so often, tell the customer testers what a great job they're doing to make your title better. Acknowledgment and appreciation let beta testers know that you understand how important their role is to your title's success.

As for the feeding, that's been one of my secrets for successful meetings for years. If you are having trouble getting everyone to show up on time to a particular meeting, order food. Every organization has its preferences; at one company, the magic word was pizza. If I had several pizzas from a favorite local pizzeria in the meeting room, everyone would be there early and motivated to contribute. Find out what works for you and for the people you're working with, and get it delivered.

Links between Testing, Development, and Documentation

A few pages back I covered the benefits of linking testing with support. Some of those benefits are personal responsibility and a sense of ownership of the issues involved in finding and reporting bugs, because every bug fixed before the product shipped means freedom from several hours of misery on the customer hot-line. Other benefits include having knowledgeable support staff, people who understand the product and who probably have already faced the caller's problem and know the solution. In addition, rotating phone support people off the hot-line for a few days or a week at a time is not only a humane thing to do, it's also a good idea for job effectiveness and reducing employee turnover.

There are similar benefits if you can link your developers and documentation groups to testing in the same ways. First let's talk about the benefits you can realize from these links; then we'll discuss some techniques for keeping such links strong.

Documentation takes on a different slant when the product is an interactive book, but with some of the same issues. Someone needs to write the instructions on installing the CD-ROM into the customer's system; if you have elements that need to be copied onto the system's hard drive, whether manually or by running a SETUP.EXE file on Windows, then someone has to tell the customers what to do. Likewise, if there's on-line help for part of your title, you'll need documentation for the modules in the help files.

Whatever documentation the customers will see belongs in the package you're testing. Whether that's installation notes for the software, on-line help for the user interface, or a "hint book" for complex games, it needs to get into the hands of the people testing the product. The product benefits by having the entire package undergo testing; the documentation benefits by being checked out in its place in the product. What some people don't see at first is that the technical writer can also benefit from getting information earlier out of test, support, and development; this is a great way to break the cycle of documentation-as-afterthought that makes many documentation professionals' lives miserable in the traditional technical world. Like the process of making regular, small tests continuously during the development process, making regular, small edits during the writing process—even at the risk of making and unmaking the same changes from time to time as the product's vision shifts during development—pays off big when the product ships and the documentation is finished at the same time.

Development wins in similar ways. The real advantage to testing early and often is simply that if you make test-related changes while you're building the product initially, you will have fewer test-related changes to make at the last minute. This holds true for budgeting, for promotion, for marketing, for production, and for all other parts of your organization, but it's especially true for the creative staff in your title development groups. Having them linked with the people who will be testing can help the designers visualize their users much more readily, as all creative work is more effective when the creator can visualize his or her work in use.

So how does an organization forge such links? And how do you forge them in a way that fosters creativity, energy, and solutions? The answers differ with the varying dynamics of different organizations, but I'll hold to the care-and-feeding approach. To recap:

- Acknowledge your testers early and often.
- Get everyone involved as soon as you can.
- Show them how early, regular testing can benefit them in their roles in the project.
- Make sure your developers, writers, and other staff can put faces to the people who are doing the testing.
- Enable efficient, centralized communication between testers and internal staff responsible for evaluating recommended changes.
- Order in pizza to make sure everyone shows up and contributes.

Testing for Windows

After having worked in the cross-platform arena for some time now, I have come to the conclusion that there can be more work involved in taking a product from one PC configuration to another PC with a different configuration than there is in taking the product from Macintosh to Windows in the first place. In some ways, there's nothing you can do about it; a 386 and a 486, for example, are quite different at fundamental levels of performance. With the degree of customization permitted by the PC's open architecture and the Babel-like proliferation of options from literally thousands of vendors around the world, it is impossible to come up with a PC application that is guaranteed to run on all PCs in the installed base without some tweaking.

Let's talk about video cards for a moment, by way of example. First, there's VGA versus SVGA. Resolution clouds the picture: 640 by 480? 800 by 600? 1280 by 1024? What about monitors, how much resolution can they manage? What software drivers do they use and are there any conflicts with the video portion of your CD-ROM? (Note that the Macintosh isn't completely immune to this last part; I once installed a piece of software that included a system extension, then discovered that another application that I relied on for my business would no longer run unless I moved the suspect files out of the Extensions folder.)

Some of the PC issues really are the responsibility of the owner, because of the nature of the PC at this stage in its development. The industry talks a lot about "plug and play" as a solution to the mess of conflicting interrupts, driver compatibility problems, WIN.INI and AUTOEXEC.BAT files, and the problems inherent in the open architecture approach that the PC has always made possible.

The answer, at least in the context of this chapter, is testing. Try out your product on as many different machines as you can. If you can't afford to buy 20 or 30 different kinds of systems (and no, I didn't really expect you to), get in touch with a user group or a school and arrange to have your product tested on their systems. If you can't press a sample CD-ROM, SyQuest drives are a great way to carry data from site to site. Load your document onto a cartridge and take it from place to place, letting people with customized machines try to make it work.

And take notes! Every weird configuration you encounter is one less technical support call you'll have to take when the product starts shipping — but only if you remember how you made it work. Automate if possible, and document only if you can't automate it.

Similarly, work on error messages so that they have meaning for the customer as well as for the developer. Most of the time, during the development process, programmers rely (rightly so) on error messages to tell them where the program failed, in what operation, and in what context. However, customers are less interested in the name of the routine that caused a General Protection fault than they are in how to recover or how to keep the error from happening again. Work to make your error messages clear, helpful, and articulate. Remember, as I said at the beginning of the chapter, that it's easy to like a multimedia program until the first error message shows up. Some of them will be unavoidable, but you can change error messages from reasons for the customers to hate your product to reasons for your customers to think of your organization as a talented group of creative professionals.

Testing for the Unexpected

I'll close this chapter with a bit of conjecture based on a matter of public record (and I'll clarify which is which), in the hopes that it will prove educational. The matter in question is the case of the *Lion King* CD-ROM from Disney Interactive. The company suffered quite a bit of bad press in December 1994, which is public record, because of a huge load of support calls about this CD-ROM, released shortly before Christmas. The story as reported in all major newspapers painted the gloomy picture of kids opening the CD-ROM on December 25 to shouts of joy, which turned to tears of frustration when the CD-ROM didn't run on thousands of home PCs. As a parent, I can assure you that the last thing I want to do on Christmas morning is to explain to my daughter why she can't play with the toy she just opened. It's plausible to assume that it was the last thing Disney Interactive wanted, too.

All the published interviews with the technical staff at Disney pointed out that they had been thorough in their testing, that the software worked in the environments on which they tested it, and that the product had not been knowingly released with bugs that could have caused the failures. They had developed and tested the CD-ROM for a particular configuration of Windows system—specifically for 16-bit sound, 5 megabytes of RAM and a 486-class processor. It's a high performance specification, but not prohibitively expensive; by December of that month, such a machine could probably be had for $1200, or even less if you were willing to upgrade from an earlier system, and there were easily millions of such systems in the installed base.

It was a reasonable choice for the delivery platform, a good system to provide the rich sound and complex graphics that the Disney artists had included in the title. The "Minimum Requirements" panel on the packaging clearly described the specifications. On such machines the game was developed, on such machines it was tested, and on such machines the CD-ROMs performed flawlessly. Yet the customer support calls came exclusively from users who had bought the CD-ROM and tried to run it on machines with an 8-bit sound card, 4 megabytes of RAM, a 386-class processor, or some combination of one or more of these features. In spite of this, Disney's technical staff worked long hours over the holidays to produce a patch that would let the program work on the older, lower-performance systems—not with the speed, smoothness, and beauty of the specified delivery platform, but better than trying to explain "Abort, retry, fail?" to a seven-year-old who wants to see baby Simba. Because of Disney's resources, they were able to give their customers solutions instead of excuses. They turned a miserable public relations problem into a case study of a company's responsible behavior in the face of unexpected disaster. For many, the *Lion King* story has become an object lesson in what it means to do the right thing.

Now for the conjecture: Disney really did nothing wrong. They played by the rules, they tested their product thoroughly, they did everything they could think of to make sure that all those kids would be able to play with their new CD-ROM come Christmas morning. They don't need to rush something to market knowing it's going to crash (a strategy sometimes called "renting market share" from the habit it has of swelling sales records for a few weeks, till the word gets out). This wasn't some predatory start-up firm out to make a name for itself in any way possible so that its investors could cash in quick and buy a lot of German cars—this was Walt Disney Interactive.

The only thing they hadn't planned on was that so many people would try to run the CD-ROMs in the wrong kind of machine. They hadn't realized that so many people don't know that on the PC in particular, there's more to a multimedia configuration than whether it's designed for Windows or Macintosh. A product that should have been a dream come true for thousands of children across the United States became a public relations nightmare for one of the largest, most influential, and best-loved entertainment companies in the world. And all because of a problem they hadn't expected—hence the section title for this part of the chapter.

When you're planning your own testing strategy, then, don't limit yourself to thinking only about what kinds of problems you expect. Think about things you don't expect. Ask people who aren't intimately familiar with the subject matter, with CD-ROMs, with computers, with multimedia, with the whole process; get them involved in the test phase. See what other people outside your normal focus expect; it may not be the same things you expect. You can never cover every possible contingency, but you can at least acknowledge that there is a world of contingencies out there that you aren't currently visualizing. Try to step into that world and see your project from their perspective, and test for the unexpected.

Disney bounced back from the blow. They're a multibillion-dollar, multinational corporation with vast resources of talent, goodwill, and sheer creative and technical genius, and they spent the money to do the right thing for their customers. They had the money to spend, and it mattered to them.

But as you get ready to release your product to the marketplace, as you rationalize a few minor problems in compatibility or platform-specific bugs, ask yourself this question: Could your organization bounce back if your technical support department had to give ten thousand parents instructions on how to break the news to their kids that they couldn't play with the CD-ROM that Santa just brought them?

Chapter 11
Publishing

Preparing the CD-ROM Master

For the past 200 pages and more, we've been talking about preparing for publishing the CD-ROM. Now we're getting to it. In a book about creating CD-ROM, why wait until the last chapter to talk about actually creating the CD-ROM?

Because the preparation can take months. Designing the content, developing the media, managing the flow of information to the user, and providing the navigation on the disc surface is much more complicated than hooking up the machines and clicking OK. Before you can have a CD-ROM to publish, you have to have the content for it.

But because the publication of a CD-ROM is the culmination of months of design, development, integration, and testing, it's important to make sure that everything you need is on the CD-ROM. You can't change it once it's in the field. You can't add files to it later. You can't change the data that's on it. You can't even move the files around on the surface once they've been written. That, just in case you've forgotten, is what ROM stands for: read-only memory.

So before we get into how to build the contents of a CD-ROM, it's a good time to review what they are, talk a little about their technical details, and discuss how they work. When you understand that, it's easier to understand the rest of this chapter and why certain things are so important.

Compact Disc, Read-Only Memory

That, of course, is the phrase for which CD-ROM is the acronym, or list of initials. It's one of the latest steps in a string of other kinds of read-only memory. Some of you may have seen other kinds of read-only storage that are hundreds, even thousands of years old. The oldest piece of read-only storage equipment I've seen was the stone on which the Code of

Hammurabi was carved more than 6000 years ago. If it comes to that, the caves in Lascaux were used for graphical read-only storage even earlier, though I've only seen copies of the images from there.

There's a reason that I choose these examples: they point out that the basic principles of publishing something that you can read from but not write to have been with us since before the invention of writing. Read-only effectively means that it's cast in stone: you can't change it. In a way, most human storage media have been read-only; ink on paper, paint on canvas, scratches on stone are all things that you can't easily modify once they're finished. What makes CD-ROM different?

The answer, of course, is the computer. CD-ROM provides the cheapest form of storage, publication, and distribution for computer data. The actual manufacturing cost of the goods is minimal, and the storage space is astronomical by comparison. The cost to produce a single CD-ROM (out of a run of reasonable quantity, at any rate) is roughly the same as the cost to produce two floppy disks. The information you can store on a CD-ROM would fill 471 floppy disks. It's those proportions that make CD-ROM so significant.

How does it work? To understand it, remember that all computer information boils down eventually to binary digits, 1 or 0. There are many ways you can represent the values of 1 or 0: dots and dashes as in Morse code, for instance, or lights blinking on and off. Inside the computer, the ones and zeroes are stored as voltage levels (high and low) in your system RAM or in the CPU. On your hard drive, they're magnetic levels.

On a CD-ROM, the high and low levels are literally that: they're little holes, or pits, in the surface of the CD-ROM. This high-low surface variation shows up as the iridescence you see when you look at the back of a CD-ROM: you see rainbows from the interference patterns caused as rays of light bounce off millions of these tiny pits, which are very smooth and highly reflective. The CD-ROM drive uses laser light reflected off the disc's surface to determine whether the surface of the CD is high (closer to the laser) or low (farther from the laser); the drive's electronics convert this into voltages appropriate to the type of computer, these voltages travel through the cable or the computer's internal bus to get to RAM or the CPU, and the numbers are converted to colors on the screen for human beings to read, look at, and enjoy.

Once these peaks and valleys have been carved into the surface of the CD, however, they can't be reversed. A magnetic disk carries its patterns of ones and zeroes in the way that the oxide lines up on a magnetized region of the disk surface. To write over part of the disk, the computer simply magnetizes the whole area again; new patterns are as easy as waving a magnet over the platter. (Incidentally, this is why you never want to get a magnet close to a floppy disk; it will erase the information in an instant, replacing the legible pattern of ones and zeroes with random areas of magnetization.)

Furthermore, inscribing all these tiny peaks and valleys on the surface of a CD-ROM takes highly specialized equipment. That's why CD-ROM writing machines have traditionally been so expensive, and why in the early days it might cost as much as $2000 to make a single CD-ROM master. As I write this chapter, $2000 will buy a cheap CD-Recordable (CD-R) device, and I've heard rumors in the industry that within a year, CD-R devices will cost under $500. When that happens, CD-ROM will be as practical an output medium as the laser printer—and life in the publishing, software, business, and education fields will change dramatically.

In that light, it's worth talking about what a CD-R is, and how you can benefit from it. As the price comes down, many of you will find that you can master your own CD-ROMs with this comparatively inexpensive tool, using it to store records, data, and even backups of important information as well as using it for publishing information.

Compact Disc, Recordable

A CD recorder actually creates the peaks and valleys that the CD-ROM drive reads. It can only do this once for a given section of the CD-R medium, however, because like regular CDs it's a physical storage medium, not a magnetic one. It's like carving in stone rather than writing with chalk.

But most CD-R devices coming out on the market now are of a variety called multisession. A single-session CD-R device could create a CD-ROM, but it did so by writing to the entire surface of the CD; if you put 1 megabyte of information onto the surface, you wasted the other 600+ megabytes of storage space on that CD. A multisession CD-R device lets you write a few files now, and a few more files later. You still can't write to the same area of the surface, and once the CD-R is filled up you have to put in a new one. But you can keep recording to the CD-R until you run out of room.

One possible application for a multisession CD-R would be to keep a child's academic record on a CD that he or she could take from teacher to teacher, year to year, storing transcripts and even samples of schoolwork on the disc. Because it would be impossible to rewrite the files put there in a previous session, teachers would not have to worry about students tampering with grades or with comments (at least not after the CD-R had been written—there would have to be some way of ensuring that the student hadn't read in the transcripts to a home computer, changed a few C's to a few A's in software, and then remastered his or her own CD-R to make things look better).

From the cross-platform standpoint, CD-R devices that use the standard SCSI connection present the possibility of being used to store both Macintosh and PC files. (In case you have never heard it explained, SCSI, pronounced "scuzzy," stands for Small Computer Systems Interface. It was the standard interface protocol for Macintosh for years; recently, Apple began using the PC device standard, IDE, which permits buying disk drives at lower prices.) Before you rush out and buy the first multisession CD-R you find with the intention of plugging it into one computer, then moving the connection and getting the next one, make sure that there is software for both platforms that will let you use the CD-R in either environment.

But beyond these concerns, CD-R makes creating your own CD-ROMs effectively no more than writing a very, very large floppy. You just pick the files you want, drag them over to the icon for the CD-R device on the desktop or in the File Manager, and let go of the mouse button when the pointer is in the right place. Right?

Well, sort of. Remember, you can't change the contents of the CD-R once you write to it, so this is a one-shot deal. And remember how much attention I've paid to providing a means for the user to navigate through the information? You have to provide a means for the computer to navigate through it as well. And that means making a sample and testing it.

There are also some tips on how you write files to a CD-ROM that make a difference in the performance of your application later. I'll discuss these techniques in a few pages; some of them may surprise you. That, however, is a different issue, so let's focus for now on the concerns of whether your application is going to depend on other media.

Dependency on Imported Media

If all your files can stand by themselves, then it doesn't matter where you include them. By "stand by themselves," I mean that the files do not depend on another file, or more specifically that they are not going to look for another file in a specific location on the disk. If the file is a movie, an application program, or something else that is self-contained in this way, then in some ways it doesn't really matter where you put it. Structure your CD-ROM in such a way that it's easy for people to see where things are in the file system.

If your multimedia presentation uses media elements that you imported from another file when you were developing the title, you need to exercise a little care in how you structure the document during development so that it works most effectively when published. This, by the way, is true whether you are publishing on a CD-ROM, a SyQuest cartridge, or any other medium, including diskette; once again, the real difference about a CD-ROM is that your users can't change the location of files on the CD-ROM. Any time you change the relationship between the files that make up the different elements of your presentation after development begins, you risk making that presentation not work.

Figure 11-1 demonstrates the relationship between elements of a presentation before and after moving the contents of the presentation directory to a new location. Folder Four may even be on the hard drive of a different workstation in your organization's network, for example, as well as on a SyQuest cartridge or a CD-ROM in the office of someone miles away. The issues discussed here are similar for all of those situations.

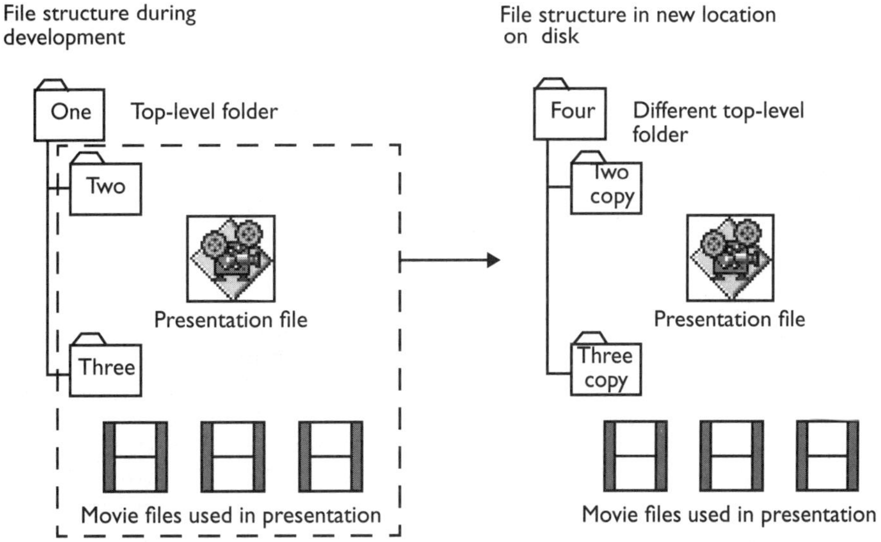

Figure 11-1. Risky model for moving files to a new location

During development, you have a folder (represented by One in the illustration) that contains two additional folders: one containing the presentation file (in Two) and another containing the movie files used in the presentation (in Three). This is a hierarchy of files, with relationships between them on which the smooth playing of your presentation depends. When you publish this hierarchy, you must ensure its integrity in any situation: you must make it possible for the presentation to find the movie files in the new relationship.

Here's the potential problem. If you import your movie files into your presentation following the model shown in Figure 11-1, the application that builds your presentation file probably will not insert the movie file itself into your presentation. What the application will most likely do is insert a reference to the movie file's location on the disk—in this example, in folder Three, which is contained inside folder One. As long as you don't change that relationship during development, you're fine, and your presentation will run as expected.

But things can get sticky over on the right-hand half of Figure 11-1. When you run the presentation file in the copy of folder Two, which is now inside folder Four, one of several things may happen when your presentation runs, depending on how the program was written with respect to looking for movie files. None of them is particularly encouraging to consider:

- **The presentation may simply not run.** It may or may not give an error message about why it's not running. Even if it does, consider your users: do you want them to have to locate the movies for you? And if they could, remember they can't move them on the CD-ROM.
- **The presentation may run, but put up a dialog box asking the user to locate the movies.** This isn't much better for you. It's a good message during development, because it tells you you've made a mistake. But this is not a message you want your users to read, because it tells them you've made a mistake, too.
- **The presentation may run, but be unable to display your movies.** Again, this is probably not the image you want people to have of your vision or your organization. And note that even though I'm specifically using movie files in this example, this holds true for any files that are not included directly in the presentation itself—even for certain kinds of still graphics.

- **The presentation may run, but stops to search the entire CD-ROM for a movie that has the right name.** In some ways this is the best result; in others it's the worst. Consider the scenario of having published a CD-ROM of emergency procedures for air traffic controllers. Clearly, this is not a situation in which you want the presentation to pause for several minutes while it looks through every file in 660 megabytes.

A safer way to proceed is shown in Figure 11-2. If you have other files not illustrated in this example that must reside at the level of folder One (for example, a license file, a Read This First file, or some other information that needs to be present at that level), this technique will copy those files as well.

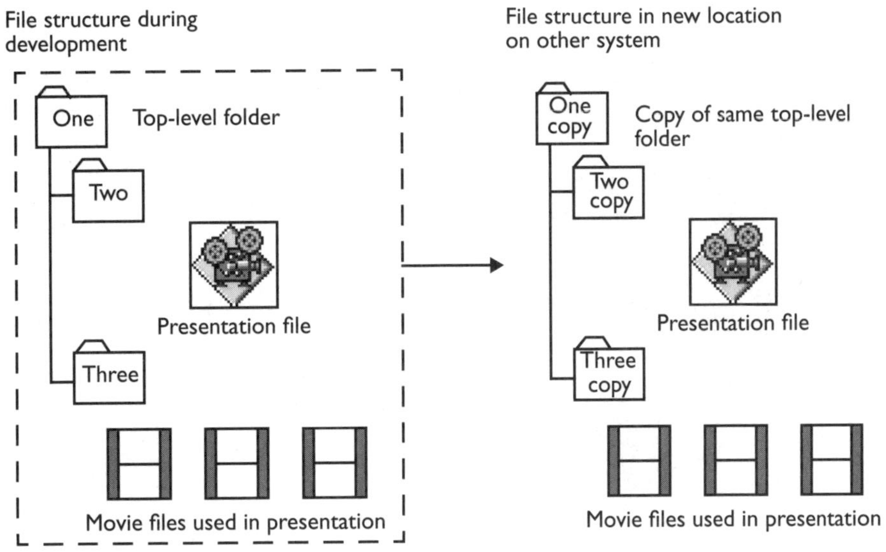

Figure 11-2. Copying an entire directory hierarchy is somewhat safer

This technique is not entirely without risk, however. The chief risk is in the way that your operating system, or your artists, call out the file's location in the hierarchy. Here it has to do with how far up the system's hierarchy your program goes to look for files. The application in Two, your presentation file, expects the movie files to be in a folder called Three; so far, so good. But the next step depends on how your operating system identifies the location of files and folders on the disk. When your application looks for a movie in folder Three, it may simply go up one level (to folder One), then look for a folder called Three, and then look there for the movie file it's supposed to play. This uses an operating system method called relative pathnames. In essence, the application looks for movies using logic like this:

- Go up one level to the folder called One
- Look for a folder called Three
- Look in there for the movie you want

But it's also possible on some systems to use absolute pathnames. An absolute pathname says, start from the highest possible directory level on the system and go down this path through the folders.

If folder One (and its corresponding One Copy folder in the destination system) is actually the top-level folder on that drive, volume, or CD-ROM, you're probably safe. But if you do something like Figure 11-3 and you (or your applications) use absolute pathnames, you can be in trouble.

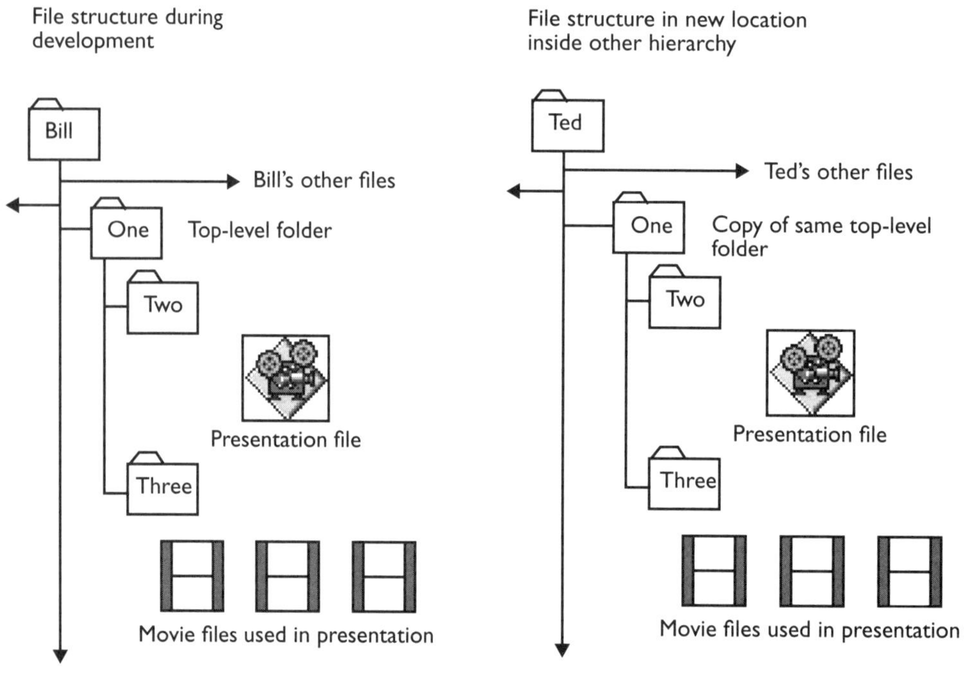

Figure 11-3. Moving part of a hierarchy from Bill to Ted

The reason Figure 11-3 has such potential for trouble is the way the application looks for files. As long as your application looks for files as described on the preceding page, by going up one directory to a known folder, looking in there for another known folder, and then going to that folder for the movie files, you're all right. The problem begins when you come up with an application that starts by looking in Bill for folder One, then going to folder Three and looking for the movie. Once you copy the hierarchy into the folder called Ted, your application won't play its movies because there will be no Bill directory to search through. The farther apart you store your movies and the application that plays them, the more likely this problem is to occur.

The safest way to be positive about finding resources is to put all the necessary files into the same directory during development. Figure 11-4 shows the most secure way of storing your files: all in the same folder.

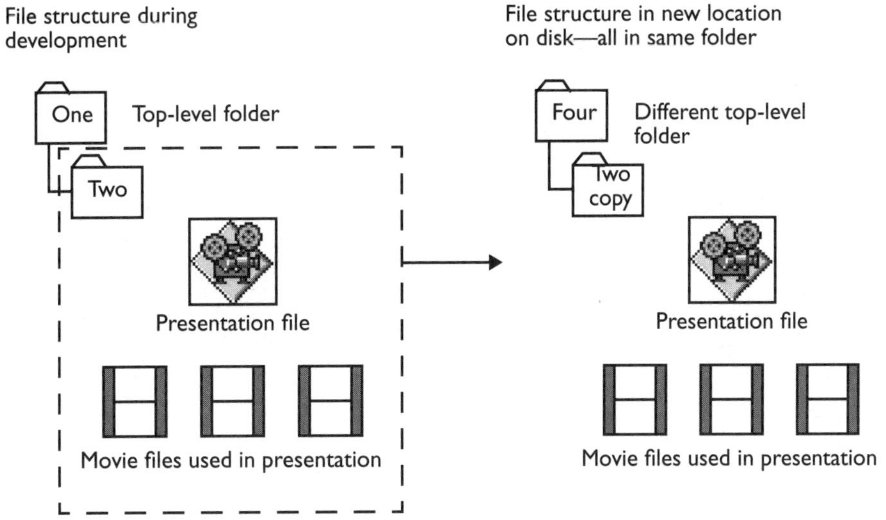

Figure 11-4. Safest way to ensure that the presentation can find the movies

In Figure 11-4, all references to movies used by a presentation file are at the same level in the directory; instead of having to move up or down or across a hierarchy, the application simply goes and gets the desired file. This structure works no matter where you put folder Two, and no matter what you call it. And the issue of what you call it takes on new meaning if you're developing on one platform to publish on another, because different platforms use different naming conventions.

Cross-Platform File Naming Issues

Developers who grew up using the Macintosh are familiar with giving your files names like "Introduction to Computing," "Movies Till Dawn," or "Live, Love, Laugh"—descriptive file names that can include upper and lower case letters, spaces, and even commas. Likewise, developers who grew up using PCs often can't get used to the idea. On the PC, files can have eight letters in their name; then there's a period (called a dot in the interest of saving unnecessary syllables), followed by a three-letter extension that usually indicates the kind of file. Microsoft Word, for instance, uses the file extensions of .DOC; QuickTime for Windows movies all use .MOV as their extension.

The state of the art in cross-platform CD-ROM publishing is such that there are one or two applications in which you can just pick up your files, move them across a network, plunk them down on the opposite platform and have them run. The one with which I'm most familiar is Frame, easily the best choice today for no-hassles cross-platform CD-ROM publishing. Frame's hypertext links copy without a hitch from one platform to the next; you can develop on either one and, as long as you keep the file structure as shown in Figure 11-4, jumps to remote files work flawlessly.

Until, that is, you put in a hypertext jump to a perfectly valid Macintosh file name like "Chapter 3 Structure" and you try to run it on a PC. The PC will not let you copy a file called "Chapter 3 Structure" onto the disk; the old undercarriage of DOS still lurks beneath the glossy facade of Windows. You now have to find every reference you have made to the file called "Chapter 3 Structure" in your entire document set and change it before you publish the CD-ROM. And if you don't, your customers certainly will find them when they click on a hypertext link and the jump doesn't work.

There is no problem with using a file name like CH3STRUC.FMR on the Macintosh, however; it will look odd to people whose only experience is with the Macintosh, but it's a perfectly valid file name on either platform. So if you are dedicated to publishing on CD-ROM to run on either platform, use the DOS file name conventions on both platforms.

This naming convention and hypertext jump issue, by the way, also works if you are creating on-line help for a PC application using WinHelp files through an application like RoboHelp, then converting them to run on the Macintosh with Altura Software's QuickHelp. Altura's product has the additional benefit of using the original PC bitmap files for screen snapshots and other graphical elements. The RoboHelp/QuickHelp combination is one of the only cases I know of where it's easier to develop on the PC and publish on the Macintosh.

Run-time Licensing and Distribution

All the packages included on the CD-ROM at the back of this book have royalty-free players, for which I am very grateful; it removed one potential source of headaches from the production of the CD-ROM, and was important to understanding the process of using these packages to create multimedia. Royalty-free players are the best way I can think of for a multimedia authoring company to gain acceptance, become more popular, and improve its market share. It's a constant source of surprise to me to learn about authoring packages that require authors to pay a run-time license to use the playback features of the system. But a number of packages do this, and you need to look at the license agreement that came with the software when you bought it. (If you didn't buy the software, you have more to worry about than paying the license agreement.)

Just to clarify what a royalty-free player is, and what run-time licensing means, let's talk about the top of the line for multimedia production, Macromedia Director. Director itself is an expensive product, with a suggested retail price of $895, but that's pretty much where the expense ends. When you create a title with Director, you're using this sophisticated, powerful, and expensive program to create something which you can then distribute free of charge. You can't distribute Director, but you can make self-playing files (called projectors) that you can distribute on CD-ROM.

In the case of Director, the projector that you create is all you need to include on the CD-ROM (plus, of course, any other movie files that include required media). You can also use Director to save your title to a QuickTime movie if you aren't using any interactivity, and QuickTime movies are playable on any system that has the QuickTime or QuickTime for Windows extensions loaded. That's one of the reasons Director has been so successful as an authoring package; it produces self-contained output that requires no additional cost to distribute, license, or run. In other packages, you may need to distribute the player file along with the media, so that your customers will be able to see the files you created.

Let's take Aldus Persuasion as an example. Persuasion makes it possible for you to send your presentations to people who don't already have the product. It does this by providing an option for exporting your presentation to the Persuasion Player format. Additionally, you can package the movies that your presentation uses, putting all external media elements into a single file. If you develop your presentation with Persuasion, you thus need to distribute only three things on the CD-ROM:

- the exported Player version of your Persuasion presentation;
- the packaged movies that your presentation uses (if any); and
- the royalty-free Persuasion Player.

You may wish to tell your users to install the Persuasion Player on their own hard disk rather than reading it from the CD-ROM. It's only 611 kilobytes, not even half a floppy drive, and loading the Player on their internal drive will keep the CD-ROM from taking the time to search for it when it is required.

Other authoring systems may require more files, more complexity, or other specific operations to make them work in the CD-ROM. If you have any questions about the application you are using, contact the support line for the product. Your own testing, of course, will help you determine what is necessary; you should test on a system that does not have any of the files, applications, or tools you used to author your package.

About Copyrights

The rights to digital versions of images do not belong to the person who digitizes them, but rather to the person who holds the copyright to the original image. If you digitize some scenes out of *Jurassic Park* and try to sell them on a CD-ROM, don't be surprised when Steven Spielberg's lawyers knock on your door (and don't count on a tyrannosaurus rex to help you with those lawyers, either). The safest bet is to presume that if you didn't shoot the video yourself, you don't have the right to sell it. If you have any doubts on this matter, simply rent a video from your local store and read the FBI warning at the beginning. If it's against the law for you to make a copy of a movie you rented at the video store, it's certainly against the law for you to digitize that movie.

There are agencies that specialize in searching for the owners of various copyrights. If you absolutely must have a particular piece of video in your presentation, you can usually obtain permission to incorporate it. You may have to pay a fee to obtain the rights; if you're using the footage solely for educational purposes, many organizations waive the fee. And there are more and more CD-ROMs coming on the market with royalty-free images, video clips, and other digital content that you can use as moving clip art in your multimedia presentations.

Working with a Service Bureau

At the time of writing, it's probably still the case that you'll use a service bureau rather than write your own CD-ROMs using a recordable device. It's currently a matter of economics: at about $2000 for a CD-R machine versus a few hundred to have the service bureau master the CD for you, it's hard to justify the additional expense. Of course, if you're planning to get into the business of CD-ROM production on a semi-regular or recurring basis, you may wish to invest in a CD-R, in which case you should read the next section.

Service bureaus, however, have a number of advantages if you use them carefully. The primary advantage is that because CD-ROM publishing and preparation is their job, or part of it, they can be a tremendous source of advice when it comes time to prepare your media for publication. They've been through the procedure many times and can offer advice on setting up your presentation or title for the final step.

The most important thing you can do in your relationship with the service bureau is to ask questions. Especially the first time through the process, ask as many questions as possible about preparing your title, about the kind of equipment they use, and about any aspects of the process that concern you. Perhaps the biggest advantage to using a service bureau is the relationship that you have with them: you're the customer. You get to call the shots, within the limitations of the technology; but you can only call them if you know them in advance.

So here is a list of questions you should ask your service bureau when preparing to give them your multimedia title:

- **How would they like to receive the data?** Most service bureaus work with SyQuest cartridges in 5.25" size, which works with 44 Mb, 88 Mb, and 200Mb cartridges. SyQuest also produces a 3.5" drive that can write 100, 200, and 270 Mb cartridges. It's your choice at this point; the 44 Mb, 5.25" drive is in the widest use (and the least expensive, at around $200 at time of writing, with cartridges as low as $50), but the 3.5", 270 Mb drive fits the most information on a single cartridge. Other options may include magneto-optical drives, digital audio tape (DAT), and of course CD-Recordable discs. And many people still simply write all the data to an external hard drive and take it in to the service bureau.

- **What do they charge for?** You may find that you can save a little money by doing some of the preparatory work yourself. Don't, however, pursue the saving of money as the most important part of the project. You probably have months of work invested in your title at this time, perhaps years if you include the collective creative and technical efforts of your entire team. Don't jeopardize that in an effort to save $25 on some simple task. And it may simply not be cost-effective to do some of the work yourself; that, after all, is why you've elected to hire a service bureau instead of buying the CD equipment yourself. It might well end up costing you more in lost time to do the work yourself, time that you could have spent on some aspect of the project that only you could have performed.
- **How long will it take?** If you're working on an external deadline, be sure you find out how long your service bureau requires so that you can build this into your own production and publication schedule. Even though the fastest CD-ROM mastering equipment today takes less than 20 minutes to write a disc, that's from the moment you click OK to the moment you can take the master out of the drive. Preparation, checking, formatting, building files, and other activities involved in creating the first CD-ROM are where the expertise, time (and the money) come into the equation.
- **How much will it cost?** Yes, you probably figured out for yourself that this was a good question, so let's talk about some of the answers you may get. Basically, the CD-ROM publishing industry is in a period of astonishing growth and technological change right now (it's early 1995 as I type these figures). In 1992, I heard a service bureau quote a price of $4000 to make the first master CD-ROM for a client. In 1994, I spoke with a service bureau in the Bay Area that charged $2000 for a master CD-ROM with a one-day turnaround, but they had a sliding schedule that dropped to $500 if you could wait ten days. And at the end of 1994, I saw advertisements for service bureaus offering to make the initial CD-R disc for about $70.
- **How can they optimize the performance of my title?** Several factors affect how rapidly or smoothly your title plays back; while some of these are discussed in more detail in the next section, the service bureau you choose may know a few more tricks that can help you publish the smoothest, most effective title possible.

The biggest advantage that a service bureau has to offer you is their experience at the job of building CD-ROMs. They should already know what to expect, what works and what doesn't. You should learn to rely on your service bureau in the same way that you would rely on the printer for a book project, and you should have the same kind of relationship with the bureau that you would with a printer. Perhaps the most important part of that relationship is to choose someone who knows more about the process than you do. Once, while shopping for a printer, I had to explain to several of them the meaning of the term "perfect-bound" (the way the book you're reading is bound—assuming you're not reading this on CD-ROM). While you may not have had reason to learn the meaning of the phrase, you can well imagine that it did not fill me with confidence in speaking with these printers to learn that they did not know what the phrase meant. As the customer, you have the right to expect that your vendor knows more about the subject than you do, just as you have the right to expect that your doctor, accountant, or lawyer knows more about the subject for which you are hiring them.

Buying Your Own CD Machine

Eventually you may decide that you really need your own CD-R machine. It's an issue of economics versus efficiency, and the economics are getting more convincing all the time. I've heard from several sources that by the end of 1995, CD-R drives will cost about the same as a low-end printer. It makes sense: when the laser printer first arrived on the scene, it cost $5000 and only service bureaus could afford it. Today, laser printers are a tenth the cost and offer vastly more performance, and they have revolutionized the way we produce media on paper. The ability to have your own CD-R device in the shop will revolutionize multimedia as a communication vehicle and CD-ROM as a delivery platform to the same degree.

When this time comes, if it hasn't already for you, the basic equations will stay the same but the numbers will change drastically. Justifying a $2500 piece of equipment is simply more difficult than justifying a $500 machine. But the same basic rules about value for money apply.

One of those rules concerns the way you can use the money you spend on equipment as a way of saving money on other projects. Just to use sample prices (which will probably be amusing when the book hits the stores), assume that it's going to cost $500 to have a CD-ROM mastered, and that it costs $2500 to buy the CD-R device with which you can build your own CD-ROM masters. The math is easy with the numbers I've chosen here: if you're going to press more than five CD-Rs before the machine wears out, you save money.

One suggestion that is often used to justify the purchase of hardware is to share the cost among departments in your organization. You may have several places that could use the storage capacity that CD-ROM provides. Some of the departments that could collectively justify the purchase of a CD-ROM may include the following:

- Marketing—for the publication of interactive brochures, presentations, specification sheets, technical white papers on your company's product, and other information that can help educate your potential customers about your company's products and services.
- Technical publications—for producing on-line documentation, whether in hypertext or multimedia form; a comparatively inexpensive way to incorporate graphics and animation into the user manuals would not only revolutionize the industry, it would also bring some much-needed fun into the lives of the documentation staff.
- Technical support—for publishing an "encyclopedia" of answers to customer questions, either for internal use or for delivery to the customer; of course, it might also increase the number of support calls about how to install it in the computer!
- Information systems (MIS)—for making backup and archival copies of the contents of the organization's file servers; CD-ROM doesn't deteriorate like tape, takes up less room to store, and is faster to access if you have to restore from backup copies.
- Software production—for making the master copy of software to be distributed on CD-ROM, remembering the 2:471 rule (it costs about as much to produce a CD-ROM as to produce two floppies, yet you can fit the information of 471 diskettes on a CD-ROM).
- Training—for producing self-paced teaching guides and for publishing the course notes; an internationalized multimedia training CD-ROM might not only be an exciting thing to have in the organization, but it can also save money in air fare if you can ship the CD-ROM instead of the trainer.

If you're reading this book to learn how to use CD-ROM professionally, you probably knew about at least one of these groups because you're in it. But if you're looking to purchase a CD-R machine for your own organization, talk with the heads of the other departments on this list. Together you may end up with enough justification to buy the machine and share it.

For that matter, use the list itself as a brainstorming tool; before I began, I thought the list would include only technical publications, marketing, and training, and as I looked into it and talked to people in other specialties it became clear that many departments could benefit from having a CD writer in the workplace.

How about having one in the classroom? Here are some of the uses to which you might be able to put your own CD-making equipment:

- Storing students' work. Paper degrades, gets lost, tears easily, and otherwise deteriorates. As you move toward doing more classroom work on the computer, you could use the CD-R as a way of keeping not merely a record of your students' work, but the work itself. Imagine how much more effective a parent conference would be if rather than remembering examples to support the points you wanted to make, you could pull up a copy of the work and discuss it directly with the parents.
- Storing students' academic records and transcripts. Already mentioned briefly, there is much promise for this application as the costs start to fall. The principle is simple: keep files of the student's work, report cards, and other educational information on multisession CD-recordable media. The students will be unable to change the files that are already there, but you will be able to add new information as the child grows.
- Publishing multimedia yearbooks. An interactive yearbook on CD-ROM would be a great way to bring students into the new technology. Have the students videotape and digitize the kinds of activities they would have photographed and printed for the traditional yearbook; teach the students to design an information interface along the lines discussed in the early chapters of this book. Produce the master at school and have copies manufactured for sale to the student body.
- Communicating with multimedia "pen pals" in other cities and other countries. As prices continue to drop on producing CD-recordable discs, think about regularly exchanging information via CD-ROM with another school in another part of the world. Pick a child whose family came from the community with which you want to communicate and involve him or her in any translation or cultural information you may need. Digitize pictures of the students, incorporate some of their classroom work, add any special projects or reports the class wants to include about your city, state, or country, and share with kids from around the world.

These are just some of the ways you might be able to justify or help convince your entire organization to purchase CD-ROM mastering equipment in your office or school. The best news is simply that prices are falling so rapidly that the justification becomes easier every few months.

But you probably have no shortage of great ideas for things to do with CD-ROM. Let's close with some specific suggestions for optimizing the file architecture for CD-ROM publication, whether on your own equipment or for working with a service bureau.

Tutorial: The Final Cut

So you've organized all your movies according to the figures earlier in this chapter to make sure that the application will be able to read them. You've tested this organization and you're sure it works. Now it's time to make sure that the CD-ROM you produce will work smoothly, run quickly, and look good for the millions of people you hope will buy it—or for the potential customers who will make a buying decision based on your interactive brochure, the students who will learn based on the content, or whatever your CD-ROM's intent is. These steps will help you make the best possible product and be the most successful with it.

1. **Test your title on a slower system than the one you used to develop it.**

   For some of us, this may take some doing; others who are using Power Macintosh or Pentium PC systems to develop the title will do well to heed this advice. If the speed looks too jerky on the slower computer, it's because the processor cannot ship the video frames to the screen rapidly enough; in QuickTime, this results in dropping frames from the playback. Find this out before you get technical support calls about how bad your title looks on a 386, a Macintosh Classic, or some other slow machine.

2. **Use a low-level disk format when preparing the CD-ROM disk for mastering.**

   Macromedia suggests the FWB Toolkit Primer as one source of this low-level format. The low-level disk format builds in the information about tracks, sectors, and file location that the CD-ROM will eventually use to provide access to your title. Low-level formatting of the kind provided by FWB improves the playback of QuickTime video from CD-ROMs.

3. **Pack your CD-ROM carefully, as the sequence and location of files will affect playback speed.**

   If you simply copy your files to the CD-ROM drive (or if your service bureau does), they are copied in alphabetical order by default. Organize your files (or load them sequentially, if you are using a multisession CD-R device for mastering) so that all related groups of files are located together on the CD-ROM. This reduces the amount of time the playback head has to shuffle from one spot on the disk to another to find related files. You can load the files in the same folder, or in separate folders that are near one another.

   Additionally, note that the first files you write to a multisession CD-R device will be the most quickly accessed from the CD-ROM that you produce, because these files are closest to the parked position of the read-write head. If you have data files or background images that your title will address repeatedly, put that file on the master first.

4. **Group files near the branching points to reduce the time the CD-ROM spends looking for them.**

   As for suggestion 3 above, the issue is that files near one another on the CD-ROM are easier for the drive to find when called for. When the branching of your title calls for an external file—for example, a movie or another presentation or some external form of data—you can save time by putting those files close to the files that call them.

5. **Have your users copy to their hard disk any files that must be changed during use.**

   For example, if you keep user profiles available to indicate how much of a training exercise your users have already performed, they will need to copy this onto their hard drives so that it can be updated as required.

   Also, if there are files that the user must access constantly (control files, player files, or the like), you may find that performance is enhanced by moving those files to the hard drive. The issue here is one of performance: most CD-ROM drives have an access speed of around 400 milliseconds—that is, four-tenths of a second. To put this in perspective, the blink of an eye takes about 40 milliseconds, or 1/25 of a second. Fast hard drives typically have an access time of 10 milliseconds or less.

More than anything else, though, remember this: Anything that can go wrong, will. Your job as CD-ROM producer—and mine as the author of this book—is simply to check everything that you know about in advance to reduce the number of things that will go wrong. You will encounter situations you didn't plan for, problems you haven't prepared for, and you'll have to use your own judgment many, many times during the final publication—just as you did during the development and design.

But with what you know now, and with the examples we've shared over the last couple of hundred pages, you're ready to take on the task of inventing a new medium of communication, a new art form, a new future for learning and fun. My real goal for this book was to light you up with your own creative power. Now take that light out into the world and let's discover what new things we can see.

Appendix A
Tips and Tricks

Brainstorming Ideas for CD-ROM Development

This appendix includes 84 suggestions for things you can do in the design, development, and publishing stages of your interactive CD-ROM. They're categorized by topic to help you find and structure them a little more clearly. Some of them encapsulate ideas you've already come across in this book, some of them are new. All of them can help you jump-start your multimedia project, so stick a Post-it Note on this page to help you find it again and have at it!

Making Digital Video Look Better

These tips are organized in increasing order of cost, beginning with some that cost nothing as long as you build them in from the start:

1. Use slow pans.

Move the camera slowly from side to side (called panning, short for panoramic shot) when shooting video to be digitized. Fast pans lead to jerky images because the digitizing sample rate at 15 fps can't get all the in-between frames that your camcorder does.

2. Use slow zooms.

Likewise, zooming in or out too quickly causes jerks in the sizes of images as they're digitized. Your eye is made to perceive differences in image size as changes in distance, and your brain automatically calculates a rate of change that's consistent with your expectations. When you add a frame in which the image is suddenly much smaller or much larger than the brain was expecting, your audience perceives this as a break in continuity.

3. Use lots of light.

You almost literally can't have too much light for video that you plan to digitize. Get as many lights as possible; I like to mount several directly on the tripod, but I also use as many as I can to fill in around the shadows in the image. On some of the examples on this CD-ROM, you'll see what happens when there isn't enough light.

Additionally, digitizers add noise to dark images, so even a static screen snapshot of a dark place in your image will look messy. Whenever possible, err on the side of too much light and let the camcorder adjust.

4. Use a tripod whenever possible.

Yes, there will be times when the hand-held look is just right, and you can learn to hold the camcorder pretty steady. However, for most work a tripod is going to make your shots look better for the simple reason that they won't shake around. Shaking looks bad enough at 30 fps, but when you introduce the noise of digitizing the images it's even worse.

A heavier tripod makes a better camera mount but is more of a pain to lug around if you're doing location work. So the added bonus tip here is to get a heavy tripod and hire someone with a strong back to lug it for you.

5. Use a remote on the camcorder.

I started using the remote on my camcorder when I was doing my first Toymation pieces, because for stop-motion you really can't shake the camera between frames. Then I reviewed places where I was making sequential shots of a stationary object in part of a series (the clip on opening and closing your computer, for example), and realized that the slight movements that I was making to the camera by turning it on and off manually were affecting the framing of the subsequent shots.

By switching to the remote, I was not only able to eliminate the shaking and consequential framing errors, but I also had a lot of freedom to set up a scene, manipulate the contents (or simply talk to the camera), and stop it later myself. It saves a little tape, too, but tape is cheaper than time.

6. Turn off your screen saver.

This tip is covered in the chapter on digital video, but it's worth repeating. The screen saver checks the mouse 60 times every second. That's a lot of interruptions for something as computation-intensive as video capture and digitizing. So as much fun as the Flying Toasters Anthem is to listen to (the first three or four hundred times, anyway), turn off your screen saver. Also turn off your mail program, if you use something like Eudora that checks mail every 15 minutes (or however long you set it for).

7. Put a CD-ROM and a diskette in the drive.

Again, this is confirmed on the Mac but not on the PC: the Macintosh's CD-ROM drive is set up so that the system checks regularly to see whether a CD-ROM has been inserted into the drive. Like the screen saver tip, this one saves you lots of cycles when it comes time to capture video.

8. Turn off virtual memory.

Oh, what the heck—try one short piece with virtual memory left on. It's good for a laugh, but more important, you'll never leave it on again. Why you want to turn virtual memory off: if you leave it on, the video looks jerky, but the most noticeable effect is that the sound is sampled at half-speed. It's amusing, unless you're working at 1 in the morning for a presentation you have to give to the board of directors at 9:30 and you have one more piece to digitize and now suddenly everybody in your QuickTime movie sounds like they've swallowed a bottle of muscle relaxants.

9. Buy more RAM.

You almost literally can't have too much RAM for doing a lot of video capture. You can squeak by with 8 Mb (all the video for this CD-ROM was digitized with 8 megabytes, on either the PC or the Macintosh), but having more gives you smoother images, better quality, and faster work. 24 Mb is good, 32 Mb is better.

10. Buy a faster processor.

I've become so spoiled by the pair of 66 MHz processors in my Apple Quadra 630 and my Compaq Presario 860 that anything short of a PowerPC or a Pentium seems slow by comparison. It's not just me: I loaded a short Director animation onto my PowerBook Duo, which uses a 33 MHz processor, and was amazed to see that things that were in perfect synchronization on the 630 were hopelessly out of time on the Duo. (Of course, the real lesson there is to test the timing and synchronization of your work on slower machines so that you will know what it looks like when your customers, students, or other end-users run the work you've made.)

11. Hire professional models and/or actors.

It's a simple trick, but a good one: professional actors and models are trained in holding themselves, speaking clearly, enunciating, and all the other tricks that make the difference between a Steven Spielberg movie and the local-access cable channel. Of course, it's expensive, but if you're going into the business of multimedia production (even if you're working on a professional or technical presentation rather than on what I've taken to calling "intertainment"), it's a logical expense.

Making Animation Look Better

In increasing order of cost:

12. Draw big and shrink.

This is an old-fashioned art-director's tip that works just as well on computer as it did in the darkroom. Graphic artists will often blow up a work by 200% or more to work on the fine details, then shrink them back down to the working size. The result is that uneven places in line, shape or form will be reduced by the shrinking process, often to regions so small the eye can't pick them up.

Most computer drawing programs have zoom-in and zoom-out features that will let you work on successively smaller regions of the image. If you're drawing bitmaps (for instance, changing the shape of a sprite in Macromedia Director), you will want to zoom in so that each pixel in the eventual image shows up clearly. If you're working in a more realistic medium such as Adobe Photoshop or Adobe Illustrator, zooming in gives you much finer control over what you do and how it looks.

13. Let go of the mouse button often.

This is surprisingly hard to do—and surprisingly important. If you hold the mouse button down while drawing the entire outline of something, you run the risk of having to lose the whole piece if you make an error. It's much easier to select (or undo, described in tip 14, below) a short section of a line than it is to erase part of something that goes through the entire image. I have learned this the hard way, by drawing something perfect in one long, sweeping, glorious set of curves that suddenly ends in a hiccup. In a bitmap editor, you can always retouch the hiccup, but in an object editor like Illustrator or Macromedia Freehand, you may be stuck. Let go of the button from time to time, every time you see something you like.

14. Remember Command-Z (or Control-Z).

It's better than Bestine, and noncarcinogenic too! Command-Z on the Macintosh and Control-Z on the PC are the "Undo" buttons. They will save the day when the mouse ball gets stuck on something, or the cord gets tangled up in those papers you've been meaning to clean up for days. Or, of course, when you simply decide you don't like the way something looks.

15. Don't use too many colors.

This is part of the KISS principle, short for "Keep It Simple, Stupid." It's still some of the best advice for designers, especially for those of us who find ourselves pressed into the position of designer after having gone to school to study English or electrical engineering or early childhood education and now find ourselves designing multimedia presentations for our school or our company.

A side comment about colors: if you're using a PC, save the color map. Macromedia Director, for example, lets you save a color map with each frame of your movie. You probably don't have to be that particular about it, but if you create your presentation at home or in your office and then take it to a meeting on someone else's PC, it will almost certainly look different. Windows programs load their own color maps, and then leave them in place for the next program to stumble over. (This is generally not the case on the Macintosh, and is therefore one additional concern for cross-platform developers to bear in mind.)

16. Copy the whole image and then change the part that moves.

Type Command-A to select the whole image, then open a new file or a new Cast member in Director and type Command-V to paste it in place.

What this gets you is identical images from one frame to the next, at least in the parts that don't change. For example, I recently worked on an animation of a cat stalking a bird. At one point, I wanted the cat's tail to flick, so I copied the drawing of the cat and changed the position of the tail in each of several successive frames. The result was a perfectly still cat with a wildly flashing tail, and a nice piece of animation.

17. Don't try to draw with a track ball.

I love my PowerBook Duo. I have gradually come to terms with its teeny trackball. It's just about useful for selecting text, it's fine for clicking on menus, but it's really difficult to draw with. If you're using a PowerBook, you might add an external mouse or see tip 18, below. If you're using a

Duo, the E-Machines extender is a neat way to get a lot of equipment connected to the back of your Duo. It's got a SCSI port for connecting to external drives, an ADB port for connecting to drawing or pointing devices, a VGA adapter for driving external monitors, and an RCA jack that takes out standard NTSC video signals so you can save your multimedia presentations to videotape or simply show them on the TV in the classroom, boardroom, or at home.

18. Use a pressure-sensitive drawing tablet.

In all the years I've been fooling around with computers, and in particular fooling around with drawing on computers, I've always used a mouse to do my illustrations. Most of what I do is line art, of the kind you've seen elsewhere in this book; the mouse is a fine way to draw a rectangle and to put some lines between it to make it a flowchart.

But a good friend who is now a computer animator said, the first time she was exposed to a graphics program on the Macintosh more than ten years ago, "Doing computer graphics with a mouse is like painting with a bar of Ivory soap."

Anyway, about a week ago I used a Wacom tablet for the first time and it's revolutionary to me. (Don't forget, I'm also the guy who didn't get an audio CD player till December of 1994.) Drawing tablets work with a pen that has a button on the shaft, about where my index finger falls; it's like the button you click on a mechanical pencil to make the lead advance. That's the mouse button; you hold that down to draw and the line on the screen matches the line on the tablet. It gives fine control, as fine as with a Rapidograph.

On the other hand, I experienced a little cognitive dissonance with it at first. If you've used a mouse with a large screen, you're no doubt accustomed to "scuffing," the motion you make to get the cursor all the way up into the opposite corner of the computer's desktop when you only have four linear inches on the physical desktop on which the mouse rests. Scuffing with a drawing tablet simply results in lines that stay in the same place; the corner of the tablet is the corner of the screen, so if you want to go from one corner to the other you pick the pen up and put it back down where you want it. Gee, just like a real pen. Amazing. I think I have to get one of my own now.

19. Make lots of tests.

Not only that, but save them, even the failures. To begin with, there's a fairly strong educational theory that says we learn more from failures than from successes; ask any kid who's touched a hot cooking implement about the inherent truth of that. More important, I've sometimes observed that a failure at one thing can be very successful at another, particularly when you're learning about multimedia. An effect, a piece of animation, or a design that just doesn't do what you thought it would may well end up doing exactly the right thing for something else.

Most important, though, is simply that by testing you learn what works, you learn to refine your animations, and you learn your own sense of style. Style is an illusory word for the subtle differences in presentation, timing, proportion, shading, and nuance that separate individual artists. It's as important in multimedia as it is in any other art form or any other creative method of communication. As you do animation tests, you'll see not only what works and what doesn't, but you'll see what you like, what you don't, what lights you up and what turns you off—in short, your style.

20. Never draw more than five frames before checking to see how they look.

Five frames represent a third of a second at typical CD-ROM frame rates. It may take up to an hour to draw those five frames, depending on how complex they are. Another hint: don't draw a complex frame in one picture; draw the primary dramatic action in one picture, the background in others, and complementary characters in their own pictures, then composite them together into the complete frame. Make each frame in modules for much the same reason you make your document design in modules: if you have to change, move, or redesign one module, you don't have to throw away the whole scene.

21. Hire a starving artist.

Remember what I said about actors and models in tip 11? It goes double for artists. As with actors, artists can be expensive, but the results can easily be worth the cost. A good artist can work faster than someone who isn't trained in the medium, and that can end up making you money if you can get your title to market sooner and hit a wave of interest in a particular topic. (Those of you who wondered how the heck they got the first O. J. Simpson CD-ROM out while the trial was still in session should file that thought under the same heading as this tip.)

Most important, a trained artist will be able to make your CD-ROM look good, which is critical in such a visual medium. Yes, there are books on design and layout, but there are times when having a dedicated professional working on your project will be worth the money. And speaking of money, consider carefully whether your artist will be doing work for hire or will be working for royalties. Work for hire is done on a contract basis and the rights to the work belong to the producer on publication. This is normally the model for layout artists and designers working on creative projects. When in doubt, consult a legal expert.

Tracking Interactivity While You're Working

22. Use a whiteboard.

Mine is always covered with block diagrams, arrows, letters, numbers, and pieces of printout (if not 8 x 10 glossies, for those of us who know the song *Alice's Restaurant*). At MacWorld 1995, I saw a device that I wish I could afford: the $2795 SoftBoard. It's a specially outfitted combination of a whiteboard and pens, designed so that what you draw on the whiteboard appears on your computer as a bitmap. (For the technically minded, they manage this feat by placing laser detectors around the top and side of the whiteboard, then provide coded rings that snap onto standard whiteboard pens.) The result is an input device that works with standard Macintosh and PC drawing tools, providing a way for you to capture whiteboard meeting notes electronically or use them as the pencil-test components of an early storyboard.

Even if you don't have three grand to sink into this system, you can still use a whiteboard for mapping out the flow of your document, then drawing lines between major components so that you can see where topics are connected, where they're dependent, and where your users can get added benefits out of knowing that some other module is available in your document. And in a pinch, you can videotape the whiteboard, framegrab the image as it displays on your monitor, and use the images directly in your prototype document.

23. Use index cards.

This requires more organization than the whiteboard approach, because you have to come up with some scheme for tracking the cards even when you can't see them; I find it much simpler to draw lines between boxes on the wall, but by the same token I run out of room. If you use index cards, you can implement some kind of numbering or naming convention that allows you to track and cross-reference topics. And you can sketch on the cards, make notes, and add to them wherever you are; those of you who commute by train or who are prone to waking up in the middle of the night can simply keep a few blank cards with you at all times.

24. Use a relational database.

This, of course, requires even more organization than using index cards. But in many ways it's the best approach. Many people characterize an interactive document as an information database to begin with; if you have a tool you like, one that allows you to create fields dynamically and make notes, you might want to track where your audience goes when they jump from topic to topic. The real advantage that a relational database (or RDBMS) has over any of the more ad-hoc systems proposed here is that it gives you an automatic way of sorting, selecting, and manipulating all entries of a particular type, or all entries that match the parameters you give it.

For interactivity, you probably want to track the modules themselves, plus any modules that connect to them. Then you'll have the ability to sort and print a list of all the modules that are affected when, for example, you change (or delete) an intermediate module.

The professional version of MediaWrangler, for example, comes with a built-in database that simplifies just this task, and also lets you build these sorting and selecting capabilities into the document you create. This could be a powerful way to combine interactive multimedia with database features, one that many CD-ROM projects can probably use to advantage.

25. Use a prototyping tool.

For quick tests of how something flows, I've become inordinately fond of Aldus Persuasion. You can see from the examples on the CD-ROM that it's possible to make sharp-looking presentations with Persuasion. What you'll see if you have the ability to work with the included examples is that it's the fastest way I know of to work out an interactive "pencil test" or prototype of your interactive document.

Even if you plan (and budget) for a more powerful tool like Macromedia Director for your ultimate project, Aldus Persuasion makes it easy to put together a quick sample to test out your basic user interface ideas. It's the interactive equivalent of sketching something on a napkin at a restaurant; it's really that easy to do.

26. Use an outline with cross-references.

Most of the slide presentation tools like Aldus Persuasion or Microsoft PowerPoint let you import text from word-processors, storing it in outline form in the document. With good cross-references to other outline bullets, you can track where your users will need to go while you're still developing the presentation.

27. Use Lotus Notes.

I have to admit I'm not a Notes power user by any means, but the work I've done with it impressed me for its ability to track all the elements of a running, collaborative conversation while it happens. If your environment consists of a number of people who will be working simultaneously on different elements of the same document, you might look into Lotus Notes or some other collaboration/workgroup tool as an aid to managing your project's flow from module to module, from team to team.

28. Use different colors for different kinds of links.

I first suggested this technique in *Multimedia Authoring*, after having used it with some success on a couple of interactive projects. It still works, whether you write the links on a whiteboard, a notepad, or an electronic drawing tool. Since then I've done considerably more research into the different kinds of links you may want to use in your documents; tip 31 discusses an important, and as far as I can see new, development in one-to-many links in hypertext or interactive multimedia.

29. Use HyperCard.

HyperCard is almost as easy to use as Persuasion, at least for jotting down quick interactive outlines. The best technique I've found is to create the link on one card where you have the context, make this link point to another card by name, then immediately create the new card with a name that matches the link you just created. You can then print out the HyperCard stack, stick it to your whiteboard, and map the whole thing out with different colors of ink, thereby combining several of these tips into one glorious master technique. Or at least making it easier for you to map out your project's interactivity.

30. Use a running index.

If you're working on a CD-ROM project that will be primarily text based, having a running index can be a lifesaver when you're designing your network of links. I'm particularly fond of the way that FrameMaker lets you create and manage different kinds of index, especially because of the way that Frame also lets you create hypertext links out of index entries by clicking a single check box on the menu when you set up the index document. Other types of indexing in Frame let you track headings at various levels, or for that matter any other kind of marker in your document. If you're a Frame user, look these up Frame Technologies' user's guide for that particular version.

31. Use IntellAssists.

IntellAssist is the name I give to my technique for managing multidirectional links in an interactive document. In the hypertext world, such links are also known as one-to-many links. The best example would be a reference (of which there are many in this book) to a particular piece of software, such as Macromedia Director. I refer to Director many times in this book, each in a different context.

An IntellAssist is a way of presenting the user with a list containing jumps to each place in the document at which I mention Macromedia Director. There would be just enough information on the IntellAssist itself to help the reader determine a little about the context of each of the jumps.

The key to using IntellAssists while designing your document is to understand that each time you make a reference in the document (whether in text or in a running video presentation) that belongs in an IntellAssist, you make a jump from the document to that topic's IntellAssist. In this way, each IntellAssist is like a miniature index, set up for interactive hypertext, that manages a particular conversation in your document. From any point at which you refer to this conversation in your document, your readers can jump to any other reference anywhere else in the information.

I'm still developing IntellAssists, in particular in the context of the electronic version of my previous book for AP Professional, *The CD-ROM Guide to Multimedia Authoring*. I hope that the concept makes life easier for you while you develop your own interactive projects, and that it makes possible a completely new way of accessing information for the future.

Questions to Help You Choose the Best Authoring System

32. What is my creative vision for the production?

This goes back to the first chapters of the book. Develop your creative vision as completely as possible. What does it look like? If it's a game, how do you play it? Don't just visualize the document—visualize people using it. If it's for kids, make a mental image of your title in use in a classroom, at home, at libraries, in computer labs, wherever you want it to be.

Picture it to yourself, then interview authoring system users, developers, and trainers so that you know which tool will let you build it to that picture.

33. Do I want a book with video or a movie with interactivity (or something completely new)?

Out of question 32 arises this more general question. A book that has a few digital video movies in it will require a very different kind of authoring system than a media-rich, highly interactive game. For the first, I know I'd choose FrameMaker: it's the premiere tool for creating electronic books, and with QuickTime now the de facto video standard across platforms, it's easy to import QuickTime movies into a Frame document and run it on Macintosh, Windows, and Unix workstations. For the second, I'd choose something like Macromedia Director, which has the ability to incorporate complex media elements, branch to anywhere in the sum of all the movies you include on a CD-ROM, and has a powerful programming language in Lingo, the interactive scripting language that Director supports.

34. How much money do I have to spend on it?

Believe it or not, the cost of the authoring tool has almost nothing to do with this question. What does matter is the cost of the learning curve for you or the price of consultants you need to hire to create your documents. If you have very little money to create your media components, for example (meaning your artwork, backgrounds, characters, sound effects, music, and the rest), then you don't need a media-rich package like Macromedia Director. In this case, you may be able to get by with a good, solid interactive tool like Aldus Persuasion or AltaVista MediaWrangler. You can then use framegrabbed digital photographs that cost nothing to produce and require inexpensive capture equipment such as a video camcorder and a capture card, which can run less than $1000 combined.

On the other hand, if you have an unlimited budget, please contact me directly through my publisher and I'll help you spend it wisely. Seriously, if you have a large budget, spend most of it on talent, not on hardware; a really talented artist, writer, and designer will do more for your package than ten of the hottest workstations. But you'll still need an authoring system that permits detailed design and animation, rather than something simple. Your creative vision (from tip 32) will help guide you as you look through the capabilities of different media tools.

35. Is this for internal use or for eventual sale, fame, and fortune?

One difference here is that if you're developing a multimedia presentation for training or marketing, and you intend it only to be used on computer systems that your organization actually owns, you can pick an authoring tool that doesn't have a cheap (or free) player. You may also want to build in some of your own capabilities to meet the specific needs of your organization. For example, if you're working on a project intended to support new employees as they learn your company's software or operating procedures, you may wish to integrate the multimedia directly into the product and run the content through your company's file server system. This means that proprietary or expensive software doesn't need to be distributed on the CD-ROM; you can set up your document so that it refers to the enterprise-wide file system. If you are developing a stand-alone title for entertainment or education, you'll have to make sure that any software required to see, play, or interact with your files are included on the disk.

36. Do I want this on Macintosh, PC, or both?

The world is gradually coming to the conclusion that there's room for both of these platforms, that there's value in the other system—whichever you use normally. This makes it much easier to develop multimedia titles that will work across platform. Version 4.0 of Macromedia Director supports development of cross-platform documents. It's surprisingly simple: you copy your Director file to the other workstation, then open it up in Director and edit it. You can't publish a Windows version of your Director title on the Macintosh, or vice versa, but you can finish your document on either platform, copy it to the other (either on floppies or across a network connector like MacLink), and then publish it on the other system.

There are some gotchas in that, mainly in the area of color maps; if you are planning to develop on the Macintosh and publish on the PC using Macromedia Director, make sure you explicitly save the color maps you want to use.

37. How much time do I need to finish this?

You'll also have to consider what you already know about the various authoring systems you're considering. The issue here is how much of your schedule will get eaten up by the learning curve of a complex new authoring tool. I've taught people to use Aldus Persuasion and Microsoft PowerPoint in a day, and sent them back to work with diskettes containing working examples of simple multimedia documents—but documents made with limited animation capabilities, and in the case of PowerPoint with no interactivity. If you want something with more power, such as

Macromedia Director, you'll have to budget more time to learn the tool. The trade-off is that you'll have more ability to do animation, better control over timing, faster performance of graphics on-screen, and better ability to do sound. Once again, these issues come from your original creative vision for the document you want to make.

38. What kind of content do I have to start with?

Many people are looking into publishing existing documents on CD-ROM as a less expensive way of doing business. It also has a slightly smaller ecological impact, as the paper cost on a huge document printed in many copies can be significant. If you already have documents in some electronic form, you may be locked into the authoring tool you want to use.

It's possible to convert most information from one tool to another. If you're publishing something that's mostly text, the Rich Text Format (RTF) is a fairly common way of converting from package to package; I use it to convert back and forth between FrameMaker for the Macintosh and Microsoft Word for Windows, for example. So if you have a FrameMaker document that you want to publish as an on-line help file using Microsoft WinHelp, RTF is part of the answer.

Note, however, that as of version 4.0.2 of FrameMaker for the Macintosh, RTF is unavailable as a Save As option; you'll need to transfer your Frame files to a Windows PC and then save them in RTF. From there you can import them into Microsoft Word for Windows and then use a tool like Blue Sky Software's RoboHelp to structure it for electronic publishing.

39. What kind of talent is already available to me?

Look carefully, and look creatively. You may find that people around you have hidden talents. Intuit Corporation recently held a talent show as a way their employees could learn to see their colleagues in new ways. You can not only learn new ways of interacting with the people you see every day, but you may also learn that the people around you have skills in writing, music, art design, or some other talent you need for your multimedia project. You may find that some of the people around you already have skills and abilities that can help you make one authoring system work more easily than another.

40. What else will I have to buy to make this authoring system work?

This book gives you some of those answers already, by outlining the different hardware and software packages that go into multimedia production. However, look carefully at the capabilities of the program you're examining. It's disappointing, not to mention expensive, to buy something only to find out that either it doesn't work with another tool you already have, or that you have to buy something else to make it function.

41. What literature, instruction, or consulting is available to get me started?

Look around, ask around, attend seminars and ask people questions. You may find that there's a wealth of information—some of it free, some of it for cost—that you can use to help you choose or implement one authoring system over another. Frame Technologies, for example, often gives free half-day seminars at which they introduce new solutions in electronic publishing. Some of these seminars are largely oriented toward building market awareness, but many of them have useful content that if nothing else can help you make an informed decision about the best tool for your task.

And of course, ask questions—not only of the people presenting these seminars, but of the people attending them. Some of my best ideas have arisen out of the need to answer questions from the people in the audience at presentations I've made; your input is valuable, no matter how new you are to a topic.

Simplifying Scripting

Scripting is still in use in many multimedia authoring tools—in fact, in virtually all the powerful ones—as a way of controlling interactivity, flow, sequence, and structure. It's also often used as a way to link your multimedia document to another external application.

I've paid little attention to scripting in this book, because the state of the art in multimedia now makes it possible to create surprisingly sophisticated multimedia presentations without typing a line of code. If you follow along with the exercises and examples here, you can generate sharp-looking multimedia presentations. If you follow multimedia as a profession, however, you will eventually reach the point at which you have to start writing scripts. Here are some suggestions for simplifying the scripts you write, and easing some of the pressure about writing them in the first place.

By the way, all these tips work equally well with conventional programming languages. In fact, I often contend that scripting is nothing more than a slightly less intimidating word for "programming," designed to get novice users of a tool into the job of writing programs without making them think they have to become—or hire—programmers. If you're using

Microsoft Visual Basic or Visual C to write control structures within which you display or manipulate your media, these tips work equally well in developing, debugging, and perfecting your code.

42. Visualize exactly what you want the script to do.

You literally cannot be too precise in your descriptions of what you want to happen. If you're scripting in Lingo, the scripting language for Macromedia Director, your precision will include decisions about:

- whether you want an action to occur when the mouse is pressed, or when it is released;
- what frame you want to jump to (if you're using scripting for interactivity); and
- whether you want your presentation to continue indefinitely from the frame you jumped to, or whether you want it to return after completing a defined action.

This is an example of the level of detail you'll need to consider when writing scripts. You may find it worthwhile to hire a programming consultant to help you with the scripts, if that's not already part of your professional experience.

43. Start small.

The first programming example in Brian Kernighan and Dennis Ritchie's industry-standard book *The C Programming Language* simply writes the words "hello, world" to the screen. Small scripts have a number of virtues:

- they take very little time to write, therefore wasting very little time if they're wrong;
- they are easier to understand later if you have to go back to one you wrote weeks before and figure it out; and
- you can always build them into more complex tasks later by hooking up several simple things you have already mastered.

Additionally, it's always nice to get positive feedback from having something work, and a small script is likely to be easier to get working if only because it has fewer components that could cause it to fail.

44. Break big tasks into little ones.

This is the flip side of the previous tip. Writing small scripts requires performing small tasks. This also makes debugging simpler, because you have less code to search through. The trick is scaling how much work you want a given script to perform. Make it do one thing—respond to a mouse click by changing a color map, for instance, so that the area that your user clicks on will blink—and then build that into the entire suite of interactivity scripts you're designing to manage the entire navigation system.

45. Start with something that works, even if it doesn't do what you want, and then change it in baby steps.

This tip also builds on the previous. I've often joked that the last new C program ever written was the one I referred to a couple of tips back, the one that says "hello, world." Most programmers begin learning a new language by typing in an example from the book and then modifying it till it does something like what they want it to do.

It's easy to see how this starts. The user's manual or trade book you're reading probably starts you off on a script that looks something like this (again using Macromedia's Lingo scripting language for example):

```
on mouseUp
  go to frame "MainMenu"
end
```

This will work, assuming of course that the Director movie you're working in actually has a frame that you've titled MainMenu. You may have an entirely different structure to your movie, but this script will work as long as you replace the word MainMenu with the actual names of the scripts in your movie.

46. If you get stuck, stop doing it for an hour or so and go do something else entirely.

This technique works on everything from troubleshooting hopelessly shot old British sports cars to writing multimedia scripts. Sometimes the real problem isn't that the task is too hard, it's that you're stuck in the same way of thinking about the problem. Get up (save your document first!), take a walk around the building, play with the cat, make a pot of coffee or tea, but most important, don't think about the problem at all. Put your mind on some other issue entirely—it's as if your mind were a pet gerbil, and you need to get it completely off the little exercise wheel.

This can be very hard to do, especially as a deadline approaches. But it's an important way to let your mind relax, open up, and solve the problem while you're involved in something else. It's surprisingly effective; try it.

47. Explain the task to someone else who has even less of a clue than you do.

Many medical schools teach procedures by following a three-part sequence that they call "watch one, do one, teach one." Students watch an instructor perform the procedure; shortly afterward they perform one of their own (under supervision); then finally they teach the procedure to a third party. It helps cement their understanding of the procedure they're learning. When you teach someone else how something works, they will ask questions that can help you frame your understanding of the issue in ways you hadn't previously considered. You'll be forced to give a structure to your understanding of the subject, a structure sufficiently robust to stand up to someone else's inspection of it.

You may also simply see something you missed in your own examination of the problem. I was recently stumped over a project using Macromedia Director, unable to work out from the user's guide the way that Lingo kept track of time-out values. After following tip 46 (I went out and worked on one of the cars for an hour to clear my head), I came back in and still couldn't figure out how to make it do what I wanted. So I brought in someone else and explained how I thought it worked. This pointed out to me what I'd been missing in the way that Director handled its time-out values, and I was able to proceed with the project.

48. Go back and redo the example out of the book, this time with your own words.

It's one thing to type in the example out of the book (meaning either the user's manual or the trade book you're reading), then change the words after you've been able to make it work. It can be quite another to try to generate your own version, using your own structures and your own media. A good intermediate step is to replicate exactly what works in the book, starting from scratch and using components from your own project. This can identify areas where you may not have seen something important to your understanding of the problem. Best of all, if you duplicate the book's example correctly, but use your own values and media, you should have a working example that displays your own pictures or uses your own structures.

After that, follow tip 45 and convert your now-working example that doesn't do quite what you want into a working example that does what you need your script to do. And remember, take baby steps; add single structures at a time, noting where they have an effect and where they don't.

49. Save anything that works, even if it doesn't do what you want.

Once you get something to work, save a copy of it. Use that one as the working basis for other scripts, following the principles of modifying known good examples until they perform the tasks you want.

As you become experienced in scripting, you will gradually develop the skills and abilities to make scripts that run from the beginning rather than having to duplicate existing work all the time. However, as you're still coming up the learning curve with scripts, or for that matter with any kind of programming, these tips will get you more effective in less time than anything short of returning to college for a computer science degree.

50. Ask your friends and colleagues.

The Xerox Corporation underwent a study a few years ago to determine the most effective way of transmitting information about the repair and servicing of their copy equipment. They were somewhat surprised to learn that a disproportionate percentage of this information was transmitted orally, in the form of stories told from technician to technician. Storytelling, anecdotes, and person-to-person contact are still the most effective way to get information on almost any topic. The trick, of course, is finding the right people.

So ask everyone you know. Often there's a commonly understood trick to manipulating a particular part of a scripting language that you simply haven't stumbled onto yet. Just as often, you may have friends and colleagues who have solved the same problem you have, and who can offer a simple and elegant solution for something that's been giving you trouble. If nothing else, Bob may know Susan who works with Janice who took a class with—you get the idea. Networking still functions face to face.

And speaking of networking, don't miss out on the Internet. Look for discussion groups on Usenet having to do with multimedia, or with the specific multimedia tools you are using or want to use. You may be overwhelmed with either the technical knowledge or the technical ignorance of other contributors to that newsgroup, but you may also get good advice, sometimes from the staff of the organization that made your authoring system. And of course, there's always technical support.

51. Ask a 14-year-old.

Okay, okay. Not all 14-year-olds are technically savvy, electronically sophisticated, and otherwise ready to convert your confusion into wisdom. But the early teen years are often a "sweet spot" between the ignorance of youth and the solidification of post-adolescence; they know enough to be helpful, but not too much to be of any use. Besides, many 14-year-olds have the time to do this stuff for fun, as a hobby. There's a completely different mental energy level that comes from doing something you love than the energy that comes from doing something for an employer.

52. Get a good night's sleep for a change.

This one's self-explanatory. Force yourself to shut down, stop thinking about the problem, and relax. Turn off the phone, the computer, the fax machine, the TV, the lights, the alarm clock, and all other distractions. Close your eyes, get some rest, and wake up naturally whenever you're refreshed. You may be surprised to find that you wake up with the answer to your problems.

Brainstorming Techniques for Interactive Story Development

I don't claim to have the single answer for developing interactive fiction. I also don't claim that any individual has it. What's opening up for me after several years of working in "intertainment" (a much more useful word than "infotainment," I believe) is that interactive storytelling is still developing as an art form and as a form of rhetoric. We don't have all the answers yet because so few people have spent any time looking into them.

So until I get around to editing Aristotle's *Poetics* to take interactive, nonlinear storytelling into account, here are some of my favorite brainstorming techniques, focused on interactive story development.

By the way, for those of you doing interactive nonfiction, this is for you too. You can tell just as compelling a story if it happens to be true as you can if you happen to have made it up. As Mark Twain said, "Truth is stranger than fiction because truth doesn't have to make sense."

These brainstorming exercises work well if you're by yourself; turn on the tape recorder or jot down your responses as you read the tip, and then start coming up with ideas. But they work best if you run through them in a group. Assemble your design team, everyone working on your project, and block out an hour or two of time during which you'll have their attention. (Project management tip 317: bring in lunch. If you really want everyone to show up, feed them. And make it something they like, too; pizza works in some corporate cultures, fruit salad in others, champagne in a few where I've been fortunate enough to work. You'll be amazed at the pulling power of $40 worth of pizza in the right environment.)

In a brainstorming meeting, assign one person to take notes, and do so on a whiteboard or on sheets of large paper on an easel. You want everyone to see everything. Creativity comes from seeing what's available and using it in ways that nobody has thought of before. So start by making sure everyone in the room can see what's available, and challenge them to come up with unimaginable ways to use what they have.

53. Think of famous historical (or fictional) characters and ask yourselves what they would do at this point in the story.

This stems from something my wife told me when looking at my high-school Senior Prom picture. I was wearing something that was considered quite stylish at the time, but which in retrospect was, well, the stylistic equivalent of putting all 147 fonts that came with your word processor onto every page of your document.

"In the future," Kim said, "when you're selecting clothes for a semi-formal event, ask yourself this question: Would James Bond wear this? If the answer is no, put it back."

The reality behind this tip is that we often have very powerful images of historical characters, real or fictional, that can help us visualize different ways of being. What would Mozart do in a given situation? How about Alexander the Great? How would Elizabeth I respond to the options in your plot at the point at which you're stuck?

By examining the behavior of a well-known individual, you can sometimes get ideas about how to make your own characters more individualized in your story. The trick is not to be inconsistent: if you write your story around someone who behaves like Attila the Hun in one frame and Calvin Coolidge in another, it's going to be hard for your audience to believe in the fiction.

54. Make up a list of different reasons (silly reasons, noble reasons, enlightened reasons, embarrassing reasons, spiritual reasons, evil reasons, stupid reasons, etc.) why the character would do one thing versus another at any point in the story.

We're all good at making up reasons to explain what we've done. It's one of humanity's greatest examples of creative power. If you doubt this simple truth, find a four-year-old child and ask her why she put the kitten in the refrigerator.

This exercise works best if you approach it in three parts. First, on your own and before the meeting, make a list of all the different kinds of reasons you want to propose. Start with the half-dozen or so up there, but add your own. Don't worry too much about making the kind of reasons fit the nature of your title: that is, it's okay to have funny reasons in a title that's about ghosts and mysterious deaths. The object is to open up your thinking, not close it down.

Second, call the meeting. For this part of the exercise, you may want to begin by stating the scenario or synopsis about which you're brainstorming so that everyone in the meeting will understand the plot so far. Remind them of the action, the back story (what's gone into the story before the title begins), and perhaps short character sketches of the main characters if you're working with people who may not be familiar with your title. Then read them the reasons, one at a time, and open the floor for discussion. Let as many people contribute as you can; get them to open up with suggestions for why your character may take the action you're interested in. This kind of group insight will help you explore the possible motivations for your characters, which in turn can open up new plot developments. It will also provide you in very little time with an almost unlimited number of possible courses of action to take at every branching point in your story.

Finally, as you record the reasons that your character takes a certain action, make a note about which reasons seem the most real to you, the most powerful. Write the reasons down as soon as the meeting ends and distribute them to all meeting attendees; let the reasons simmer for a day or two, then ask everyone to pick the ones that spoke the strongest to them. You may or may not get consensus on the most compelling, most realistic, or even most saleable reasons, but you'll begin to open your mind to your character's motivations, personality, and future courses of action. And you'll have keys to deciding what comes next down each of the many branches of your interactive story.

55. Think of how the situation would have played in an old "I Love Lucy" episode.

This is an expansion of tip 53. Here, instead of simply asking how an individual character would react in a given situation, you're asking how a whole set of characters, and more important a whole dynamic of interaction between those characters, would perform in that situation.

It doesn't have to be "I Love Lucy"; if there's a particular historical era that you're exploring, you may have real human beings whose actions and whose group dynamic you can explore within the structure of the plot (or plots) you are developing. The trick is to get out of your normal way of thinking about a situation, a characteristic, or a course of action and see what other ways are possible.

56. Explain the plot options to your cat.

Cats are good listeners, for the most part; as long as you scratch them under the chin (or whatever body part makes this particular kitty come unplugged), they'll let you ramble as long as you want. They don't interrupt, they don't tell you your ideas are stupid, and they don't make ludicrous points for the sole purpose of attempted self-aggrandizement. So sit down with your cat on your lap, find that spot (behind the ears is another good one; watch the eyes, when they narrow to slits and the cat's whole face gets wide, you've hit it), and start telling your story.

In case you hadn't guessed, the point of this exercise is not to get feedback from your cat. The only feedback you're likely to get from a cat is how really, really glad the cat is that you have opposable thumbs and can therefore operate the can opener. The point of this exercise is to tell your story. Explain your options, work them all through without being interrupted and without concerns about whether or not someone else will like them (for the time being). As in the watch one–do one–teach one exercise mentioned in an earlier tip, this exercise forces you to structure your own thinking about a particular topic, in this case the different actions your characters can take at a branching point in the story. Sometimes hearing them out loud, even from yourself, will make the stupid ones clearly sound stupid and make the potentially good ones develop into serious contenders.

If you don't have a cat, or if you're allergic to these finest creations of a sometimes quizzical evolutionary process (my own cat is at my feet now and from the look in her eyes I'd better say something nice about her and her species), other possible audiences include sleeping babies, watermelons, inflatable clown punching bags, the rearview mirror of your car, television talk-show hosts, and other objects blissfully lacking in sentience.

57. Have everyone in the team come up with the most implausible option at each point where the story could branch.

What's the goofiest, most nonsensical, least credible plot option you can think of for your character to do at this point? What's something so unbelievable that not even Ripley would print it? Is it for your hero and villain to start dancing the tango? Is it for a choir of angels to descend from heaven and take the heroine away in a chariot of gold? Is it for Congress to balance the budget while cutting taxes? You get the idea—pick something so far out there that there's no chance it could ever happen in real life.

Now let this serve as the backdrop for your story. Why is this particular scenario so implausible? What makes it unbelievable? And out of that understanding, what *is* believable? What is probable, plausible, or possible? Better still, what are some of the probable, plausible, or possible options that your characters could take at this time?

58. Have everyone come up with the most plausible option.

For this exercise, let's stand that previous tip on its head and see what falls out of its pockets. What's the most plausible, I-can-buy-that path for your characters to take at this point? What might even be so plausible that it's predictable, cliched, boring? Would that be for the hero and heroine to ride off into the sunset while Frankie Lane sings the theme song? Would it be for the villain to be disabled but not killed, vowing to return and wreak his revenge?

Now let this serve as your backdrop, as before. This time, however, consider why the action you've come up with here is so predictable. Why does it make so much sense? What is it about this course of action that makes it such an obvious response for your characters? And how can you change that aspect of this option in order to introduce a twist to the plot at this point in the story?

People love a balance between predictability and novelty. One of the reasons that Sidney Sheldon's TV series in the 1960s were so popular (these included *Bewitched* and *I Dream of Jeannie*) is that they took predictable, mundane situations and changed one rule—giving magical powers to the woman—which changed the entire setup. From the ridiculous to the sublime, consider that Shakespeare's audience knew well the stories he told. His historical dramas were events of public record; everyone knew the outcome of the Battle of Agincourt, but that makes Henry V's speech ("And gentlemen in England now abed/Will think themselves accursed they were not here/And hold their manhoods cheap whiles any speaks/Who fought with us upon St. Crispin's Day") that much more powerful for them. Even his fictional works (though serious historians sometimes account the histories as works of fiction as well) were familiar stories; the Danes had told the saga of Mad Amlothi for almost a thousand years before Shakespeare called it *Hamlet, Prince of Denmark*, and added "To be or not to be" to the language.

Predictability in itself is no vice. The trick is to see what's predictable, then cast it in a light that no one has ever seen before. Or in Hamlet's words to his mother, "You go not till I set you up a glass where you may see the inmost part of you." Look into the inmost part of the predictable, the plausible, and find the single facet of the jewel that makes it new, unique, unpredictable.

59. Act out the scene in charades and have someone jot down what the other members of your team blurt out.

In the very unlikely event you've never played charades, the game works this way: One person (or sometimes a team) has to act out a phrase, the title of a movie or book, or some other well-known saying; the other players have to guess what the first player is enacting. In practice, there's a lot of excited blurting-out going on while you play charades—exactly the right atmosphere for brainstorming.

So adapt charades to your creative sessions. Bring in your creative team, assign some of the prospective scenes out of your title to each person in secret, and then have that person act out the option in front of the rest of the team. Their task will be to determine what the action is, what's happening, or who's doing the action.

60. Ask your kids what they think would be cool.

If you're developing a story for children, start with your own if you have them. If you don't have children of your own, start asking your colleagues.

Even if you're not developing a story for children, ask kids for their input (assuming the story isn't inappropriate for their ages). Children live in stories to a degree that most adults have long since forgotten. Children haven't yet learned how not to be creative; give them an idea and let them go with it. You don't have to do everything they say, or even anything they say, but you may be surprised by the degree to which they can give you suggestions that light up your own creativity.

61. Ask your kids what they think would be dorky.

This question can be even more crucial than tip 60. Authors who want to do children's books learn early on that adults are far more forgiving than children when it comes to a book that doesn't keep their interest. Most adults will read the first chapter of a book before deciding they don't want to continue. Most children will read the first half of the first page and toss it back on the pile if it doesn't grab them.

If you're working on a title for kids, you've got a tough audience. Ask them whether they would lose interest in something you propose. Get an idea about whether your audience will really pay attention to the title you're developing. And remember that beautiful media, great sound tracks, and catchy music won't compensate for a story that doesn't catch and keep their interest or a game that isn't fun to play. When you create "intertainment," you merge storytelling with game-playing; both elements have to be present in order to keep your audience's attention.

If you're developing educational titles, you have an ulterior motive in mind: getting your audience to learn something. Here once again, remember my comment about soap operas versus programming a VCR: the soap opera tells its complex messages in the context of a story rather than as an abstract list of things you have to do.

62. Put words from the story on the wall and throw three darts at them, then make up a sentence using those three words.

Remember in school when you had to make up sentences about your spelling words? This is a little bit like that, but more fun. I like to throw darts because they're pointed, potentially dangerous, and only mildly random; if you don't like the idea of poking holes in your wall, you can put words from your story on cards, shuffle them, and pick three for your exercise.

Try to use mostly nouns, the names of people, places, or things in the story you're developing. A few verbs that reflect some of the action in your story can help, but if they're too specific they limit the interaction between the people or places in the story.

Not all of the sentences you come up with, of course, will be keepers. But this is another good tool, especially for use in a group, through which you can get people to start thinking about different possibilities for your story.

63. Define a specific, measurable result for your project.

Visualize the kind of change you want your document to make in the people who use it. If it's educational, think about what results your document's users will have in their academic career. If it's a home how-to, think about the money people could save by doing the tips you put into your document. If it's entertainment, think about how your audience will feel more relaxed, entertained, satisfied, excited, or whatever emotions you want to create for them. Don't just think of your document as the end result: visualize another result, something specific and something you can measure, that will occur for the people who use your story.

Visualize the people as well. What are they doing? Why are they using your title? What do they hope to get out of it? The answers to these questions, by the way, not only help you focus your own creative energies on the project at hand, they will also help you in the proposal, marketing, and publishing of your title. Publishers need to know that there is a market large enough to support the investment in creating, publishing, distributing and selling your title; bookstores and software outlets need to know who is going to buy your title. It will be much easier to do the sales and marketing of your title if you have a clear image of who will buy it and what they want to get out of it.

Publishing on CD-ROM

If you haven't already gotten this sense from the book, here it is in a nutshell: the actual technical side of CD-ROM publishing is merely the icing on the cake. Developing the content, capturing the images, generating the media, and preparing the story are far more time-consuming and far more important.

That being said, publishing on CD-ROM has to come at the end of the process, when you're already late and no other slip-ups can be tolerated. So here are some suggestions to help your actual publication go a little more smoothly.

64. Decide before you start whether you'll be going on both Mac and Windows.

If you want to publish on both platforms, rather than on one or the other, there are a number of things you need to look into. First, you'll probably want QuickTime and QuickTime for Windows; it is much, much simpler to digitize movies once, convert them, and then play them on the other platform than it is to digitize them, edit the clip, and rebuild them on the complementary system. Second, you'll want an authoring system that runs on both platforms with minimal fussing with your documents to get them to work; Macromedia Director, Aldus Persuasion, and Frame Technologies' FrameMaker are three such with which examples I'm familiar. (As more organizations adopt the Adobe Acrobat package, it may yet become the de facto standard for cross-platform CD-ROM output; keep your eyes open for more developments on this promising technology.)

More important, you'll need to start a consistent naming structure early on so that your documents all refer to the same video files. It's much easier to port your title to the complementary platform if you import video from a document that keeps its DOS-compatible filename, even if you're working on the Macintosh. That way you can simply copy all the information from one platform to the next, make any necessary adjustments to the control document in the authoring tool you selected, and most of the links, jumps, and references will work.

65. Learn the difference between ISO-9660 and hybrid CD-ROM formats.

It's simple: ISO-9660 is the CD-ROM format that is readable by both Macintosh and Windows CD-ROM drives. Hybrid means that there are separate partitions on the CD-ROM surface, one readable by Macintosh and one by Windows.

Why use one over the other? If your media files are readable by applications on either platform, then use the ISO-9660 format. This way you can include application programs for Macintosh and Windows, both of which can read the same data files. FrameMaker, Aldus Persuasion, and any custom application that pulls in QuickTime movies on the Macintosh and QuickTime for Windows on the PC work this way.

On the other hand, if you have completely separate applications, a hybrid CD-ROM may be the answer. Macromedia Director, for example, is something of a paradox in this regard; you can copy your working files from the Macintosh to a Windows PC and, as long as you have Director loaded on both machines, you can work on the files on the machine of choice and play them from within Director on that platform. But once you create a Projector, the playable executable file that Director produces from the movie or movies you have developed, that Projector is playable only on the platform on which it was prepared. So for doing cross-platform development with Director, you will need to have access to both kinds of machines, or at least one of the Macintosh variants that include a built-in 486 processor.

66. Structure your presentation so that all your movies are in the same directory or folder as your control document.

This holds true for any media that you distribute in their raw format: .AVI files on the PC, sound or graphics files, anything that your multimedia presentation will use as a resource. Chapter 11 gives more information about why this is important, but the short version is that with some tools, you build your interactive presentation in such a manner that the program looks for the media in a specific location. If you change the relationship between your media and your control document, your users won't be able to find the media when they play your title later.

67. Read the fine print in your authoring system's licensing agreement.

Make sure you understand whether there is a royalty for distributing the play-only version of your authoring tool. You may need to put the company's logo on your packaging material (see the back of the book for examples of this requirement). You may need to sign a license fee. You may need to get other permissions. Read the terms and conditions carefully so that you fulfill all that are required.

68. Spend the $150 and make an early test run to find out what you're going to screw up.

That's the going rate for making a CD-ROM master. By running an early test, you can determine whether or not your CD-ROM will work on various platforms, and you can get familiar with the process so that at the last minute you won't be knocking yourself out trying to learn something new on a deadline.

69. Make backups before you take your entire hard drive in to the CD maker.

Here's a horror story you don't even want to think about. Some friends of mine had been rushing to get their first release of a new product out the door in time for the Christmas buying season. They had lined up a CD-ROM manufacturer and were on the way there with a 500-megabyte hard drive. After it arrived at the CD-ROM vendor, who shall remain nameless for the reason you're about to hear, something happened involving the hard drive and a fall. The vendor couldn't get the hard drive to work, lost three days trying to get it to start, and only then called the customer back to let them know the CD-ROM would be late. When the customer picked up the hard drive with an obviously cracked case and several dislodged components inside it on further inspection, it became apparent what had happened. Needless to say, my friends found another vendor.

The happy ending here is that the customers had made backups and were able to give an intact drive to the new vendor in a few days. They did lose some time, however, time that could have been saved had the vendor been in better communication about the issues.

70. Ask your CD maker for advice.

Once when I was looking around for a print job, I called a number of vendors. It was depressing to have to explain what I thought was basic printing terminology to the people I was going to pay to produce some books for me. It didn't fill me with confidence in their ability to make good-looking copy.

The same rule should apply with your CD-ROM maker. They should know much more about the subject than you do, and be able to explain it to you clearly and without a lot of hand-waving and indirection. Ask them what media they use for input. Ask them what output formats they support. Ask them how long it will take. Ask them anything you can think of relating to the manufacture of your CD-ROM. The CD-ROM manufacturer can be for you what the printer is for a publications department: the difference between a failure and a great-looking document.

71. Test, test, test, test, test, test, test.

If your document doesn't work, it's going to make everyone unhappy: your customers, you, your investors, your managers, your students, whoever you come in contact with. Try it out. Try it on more than one machine. See what happens if you run it on Windows without storing the color maps first. The first effect of testing is to determine whether or not your multimedia application will load and run.

You can also do usability testing if you want to see how well your document performs the task you meant it to perform. That really requires a longer commitment of time and money. It's a worthwhile goal, especially if you are looking to produce a series of CD-ROMs on related subjects; your initial usability testing can help make subsequent CD-ROMs better, as well as making a convincing point in your marketing materials. If you can determine that users of your product learn 28% faster than people using some other method, that's a number that your potential readers can turn into dollars if you're working in the professional training market.

72. Digitize your video at a frame rate that's compatible with the kind of CD-ROM player you're planning to specify.

In general, this means 15 fps in a 160 x 120 window. This works out to approximately 150 kilobits per second, which is standard CD-ROM frame rate. Any faster and, paradoxically, CD-ROM playback can be jerky and out of synchronization. Any slower and the video will look jerky because it's been undersampled—that is, the pictures have been taken off the videotape from too far apart, and the resulting motion is jerky and ugly.

73. Play your presentation on a slower computer than you used to create it.

It was a shock to me the first time I ran a multimedia presentation on a 33 MHz Macintosh, after having developed it and lovingly timed it out on the 66 MHz Quadra 630. It was a fairly complex piece, with animated titles flying over animated video on a colored background. I had carefully timed the animations so that as the title uncovered the video frame, you could see the contents of the video—two race cars shooting out of Turn 11 at Laguna Seca Raceway—and it would all be synchronized with the sound of the cars' engines straining to be first away from the corner.

On the slower computer, the timing was completely off. The sound had finished long before the animation of the title had reached the point at which it was supposed to cross the path of the animated video. The net result was that the title covered the video during the entire action, and only the still frame was visible after the title passed over it.

The problem was that Macromedia Director, the tool I used to develop this multimedia piece, calculates the position of each element of the frame as it builds the presentation. If you move to a much slower computer, it will take significantly longer to calculate each position, at least for such a complex scene as this one with video, motion, sound, and composite images all in the same scene. And because one of my elements—the QuickTime movie of the two race cars—had a sound element to which I had synchronized the animation, I was bound for trouble. The problem is that sound plays at a fixed rate on the Macintosh, while the video frame rate and the speed of animation depend on the processor's capability. So my careful calculation of where the video frame would be when the cars shot out from behind the title was worthless as soon as I ran the presentation on a slower computer.

The general lesson from this is to remember to test your titles on a slower computer than the one you develop on and, in Macromedia Director at least, to slow down the frame rate to give you better timing control. Director lets you specify the frame rate between 1 and 120 fps; better yet, it can display the actual frame rate as a title plays, and then lets you lock in that frame rate to the title you're developing. This way you can play your title on a slow computer and lock in the frame rate, so that you will be sure the title will work on the less capable processor. Your other alternative is to specify that only computers of certain capabilities can run your title; this is probably only feasible if you're developing tools to be used in a single organization or enterprise, where you can be assured that your audience will be able to acquire the appropriate computer.

74. Design for the smallest screen you're likely to encounter.

Here's another heartbreaker. I had developed a short animation using Director, copied it over to a PowerBook from the 630, and then played it. I had put most of the action in the bottom third of the frame (it's a cat stalking a bird).

Unfortunately, the window is aligned from the top left corner of the screen. This means that I could see a little of the top of the cat's head and its ears, a flicker of the tail as it hunted, and then the escape of the bird as it flew off safely. (I knew you'd want to hear the thrilling conclusion.) No amount of fiddling with the screen size setting made it work on the PowerBook, because the pixel locations into which I'd dragged the art for the cat and the bird were outside of the physical locations visible on the PowerBook's smaller (640 by 400) screen.

For real fun, I should copy that piece over to my now-antique Macintosh Classic II 4/80, running a 15 MHz chip and using the original tiny Macintosh "periscope" monitor. That's the real triple-threat: black and white screen, slow processor, and small monitor size all in one.

75. Make sure that you clearly indicate what the system requirements are on the packaging.

Out of the last few tips comes this one, an important tip. Make sure that your audience has the opportunity to read what system specifications you require. This of course has no connection with whether they will actually read your specifications, much less follow them, but it will give your technical support people a certain feeling of smugness when the irate caller admits to not having read the requirements.

Tips for Cross-Platform Publication

As a side effect of working on this book, I've learned a lot about making applications work across the great Macintosh–PC divide. Much of this acquired wisdom comes across, I hope, in the text. Here it is encapsulated into a few short tips and suggestions.

76. There really is a good reason why people use the other brand of computer, whichever that may be; think about that instead of wondering why they're so brain-damaged.

While I use both the Macintosh and Windows PCs, as well as Unix workstations, I am more familiar with Mac applications, largely because they are generally a more mature multimedia platform at present. Early in this book's development process, I asked a friend who manages a university's PC network if he could tell me some of the things that he likes about using and working with the PC—not out of nonsensical platform competition, but as a way of understanding my readers and the needs you'd face.

Instead, I got a heated harangue about what he thought was wrong with the Macintosh. It was an interesting lesson about the Balkanization of the computer world: people take computers very, very seriously, attributing a great deal of importance to whether you have to hold the mouse button down while you make a menu selection or how many different spreadsheet applications you can buy for your computer.

Try to understand that there are good reasons on either side of the PC–Macintosh debate. The Macintosh is a hit in schools because Apple has always pursued the educational market with aggressive prices, and because the general ease of use of the Macintosh interface (especially in the days before Windows) made it a natural with young children. Conversely, the PC is a consistent winner among accounting groups in businesses because of the broad assortment of hardware and software available for Intel-based machines running Windows. Some people like to tinker with hardware, and most PCs make it easy for you to get at the insides so you can install new boards, new options, and make it all work together. Some people like the computer to be all but invisible, a tool that performs a task that they don't want to understand. There are many reasons for using a computer, but few for such hatred of the people who use the kind you don't. It really doesn't matter whether you use a Macintosh or a PC; what matters is whether it's the right tool for the part of the job that you do.

And the most important reason it doesn't matter is in the next tip.

77. You're not composing for a computer, you're composing for people.

When I tell people I write books about multimedia, the first thing out of their mouths is "Mac or PC?" That was one reason for the subtitle of this book.

The truth is, though, that you should never create an interactive CD-ROM for Windows or Macintosh. You should create an interactive CD-ROM for the people who will use it. Create your CD-ROM for human beings with problems, with questions, with desire for entertainment or education or just plain diversion. Some of those people have Macintoshes; some of them have PCs. Some of them are sophisticated users of various computing systems; some of them can barely find the File menu. Design your interactivity for them, and pick the tool that will let you do the best job. If you design primarily for the computer, you risk shortchanging the people who are, after all, going to pay for the title you develop.

78. Given enough time and enough money, you can come up with something.

Specifically for the arena of cross-platform development, just remember that at some level it's all ones and zeros. Eventually you can convert anything from one platform into its counterpart on the other.

The question is whether you have enough time or enough money. If you're developing a multimedia title with the intent of selling it at a profit, you have an upper limit on how much you can really spend on converting from one platform to another. At some point, you may discover that it's less expensive to redo a component on the new platform than it is to convert your existing media, application, or other component to run on the complementary system.

79. Someone else, somewhere, has probably already torn out much of his or her hair over the same problem.

There are millions of Macintoshes and PCs in the world, many of which run in adjacent offices. Your frustration at dealing with the problems inherent in doing cross-platform development work isn't unique to you. One company, DataViz of Trumbull, Connecticut, makes a product that works wonders in converting documents, graphics files, and other media between Macintosh and PC. The package is called MacLinkPlus and it's the only way to work in a mixed-platform environment.

MacLinkPlus allows you to translate not only between a number of popular applications, but also between standard formats. You can convert Microsoft Windows bitmaps (.BMP files) to Macintosh PICT files, to platform-independent TIFF files, or to and from a few other graphics standards. It's easy to use: you insert a PC diskette into the Superdrive on your Macintosh, then double-click on the file you want to convert.

There are only two problem with MacLinkPlus. First is that it doesn't convert between .AVI and QuickTime files, so you can't use it to port all your video files from the Macintosh to the PC. And the other, as you'll discover when you get into complex, detailed images, is that...

80. 1.4 megabytes isn't big enough.

Video files are big. Multimedia files are big. The combination of the two will eventually give you a file that's too big to put on a floppy and bring across from one machine to the other.

When that time comes, there are several things you can do. The most complex and expensive solution is a full-fledged local-area network. Several vendors sell heterogeneous networks, from which you can select PC file servers from your Macintosh for reading and writing files. Farralon's EtherWave transceivers are one solution I've used; they're a fast way to use drag-and-drop to transfer files across an Ethernet connection between Macintosh, Windows, and even Unix platforms. At about $100 per unit, they're a reasonable solution with good performance for the money.

A less expensive solution (about $100), suitable for small offices, small production facilities, and schools, is MacLink, also from DataViz. This is a cable that connects between the modem ports of your Macintosh and your PC. The product comes with software that runs at both ends of the cable so that you can transfer files cleanly. Once they're in place, MacLinkPlus will let you convert from PC to Mac. It's a seamless way of getting data across from one machine to the other.

81. Someday, when you least expect it, your window will show up with the wrong color map.

Macintosh users are accustomed to programs that set their colors correctly when you open the file. On the PC, this isn't always the case. Windows uses a color map scheme that says that the last program to load the color maps wins.

Color maps, in case you've never been aquainted with the term before, are the way in which many computer programs determine the color to display in an image. In effect, they're a digital paint-by-numbers scheme. The color map contains some number of slots, each one numbered and each one filled with the values required to make the electron guns in your monitor display the intended color. It is therefore a combination of the color map and the numbers in an image that determines the color of areas on the monitor. If color 0 is black, color 1 is white, color 2 is red, and so on, then any image that contains those numbers in its actual graphics area will show up with those colors when it displays.

The flip side of this is that if you change the assignments in the color map—making 0 blue, 1 yellow, 2 green, et cetera—then you completely change the look of your image. Everything that had been black is now blue, everything that had been white is now yellow, and so forth down the color map.

Now you may understand how the Windows convention can hang you up if you're not expecting it. Developers accustomed to the Macintosh will eventually load a Windows file, run the application, and have a mountain scene suddenly appear with green sky, purple faces, orange snow and magenta pine trees.

On the other hand, you can choose values in your color maps as a way of making fast animation. For example, it takes much longer to load a 640 x 480 graphic than it takes to load four or five memory locations in a color map. Some graphics programs let you change the locations in a few slots in the color map, for the purpose of creating the illusion of motion. You might, for instance, change the relative position of several orange, red, and yellow values while an image of a fire is displayed; changing the maps will make the flames appear to flicker. Of the tools discussed in this book, only Director lets you modify the color maps explicitly.

82. It's harder to assure compatibility among different configurations of Windows machines than it is from Windows to Macintosh.

I worked on an installation that used a particular brand of video overlay cards on the PCs. This overlay card required its own initialization file and its own software drivers, both of which were incompatible with the graphics card installed in some of that site's PCs. Those users who had this incompatibility spent days trying to get their systems to work properly with these mutually inoperable products.

The lesson here is that while the PC permits open competition among many vendors, both for hardware and for software, you need to remember that the computer is a system, in which all components need to work together. Without this synergy, it's just a lot of overpriced hardware.

The Macintosh isn't immune to this, by the way. The Macintosh loads system extension files when you boot it. Sometimes these files compete with one another for memory, for system resources, or for some other component that results in a crash. If your Macintosh won't start for some reason, try restarting it (power off and then power back on) while holding the Shift key down. This will start your Macintosh with no system extensions. On the one hand, you won't be able to see QuickTime movies or use your modem or built-in fax; on the other, you'll be able to run your computer while you develop a strategy for dealing with the conflicting extensions.

83. The Macintosh is better for initiating cross-platform work; as the minority, it has to be.

Simply put, if you want to publish on Macintosh and PC, it's much easier to use the Macintosh as the integration and development platform. As this tip suggests, this represents the Macintosh's position as the largest minority in a world dominated by DOS and Windows. But with the built-in ability to read PC disks, with the ease of handling color maps, and with the absolute consistency of user interface and interprogram communication, the Macintosh does more to make the Mac–PC connection work than the PC does alone.

84. With current CD-ROM standards and the software tools available now, you really can author one document and publish two.

If you've read this entire appendix, let alone the rest of the book, you can probably fill in most of the blanks by now. To develop a multiple-use CD-ROM, you need to make several decisions:

- Is my CD-ROM likely to have lots of common cross-platform data or media with comparatively little unique application development? If so, choose the ISO-9660 standard for your CD-ROM.
- Is my CD-ROM likely to have almost no common information, but rather different executables with embedded media in each platform? If so, you're a good candidate for a hybrid drive.
- Do I want identical content in my video, regardless of which platform it runs on? Then use QuickTime and QuickTime for Windows; digitize on the Macintosh and develop on either or both platforms.

Appendix B
Contents of the CD-ROM

This appendix describes the contents of the CD-ROM included with this book, and offers suggestions on the best way to enjoy and learn from the contents.

What Do You Get?

The CD-ROM includes two partitions: a Macintosh partition and a Windows partition. The Macintosh partition includes six directories, each containing files. Figure B-1 shows the files as they were loaded onto the 44-megabyte Syquest cartridge used to transfer the contents of the Macintosh files, which explains the "842K available" at the upper left-hand side of the figure. Your CD-ROM will look slightly different.

The following directories are available to Macintosh users:

- Persuasion Files
- PCVIDEO
- QuickTime Movies
- PowerPoint Files
- Director Files
- Still Images

Each of these directories is discussed individually below.

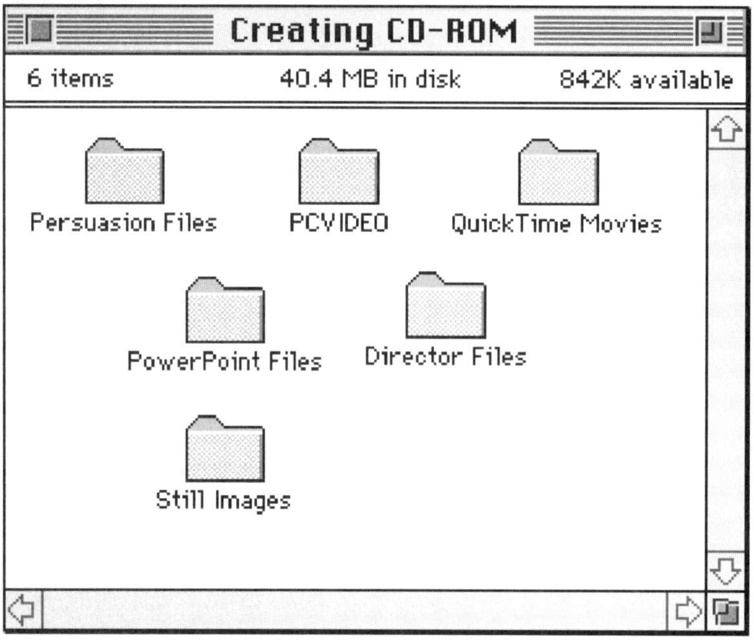

Figure B-1. The Macintosh files included on the CD-ROM

Persuasion Files

This directory contains the following files created using Aldus Persuasion.

Example 8-3

This file is an editable Persuasion document; if you have Aldus Persuasion on your Macintosh, you can copy this file to your hard drive and edit it to see how I constructed it.

The file demonstrates the use of transitions between slides in Persuasion as a method of pseudo-animation. Three things are noteworthy in this presentation:

- The transition in which the word "revealed" is revealed, along with the interior of the PC in the illustration. I copied all the content of the previous slide to the following, then added the word "revealed" and replaced the picture of the closed PC with a picture of the PC with its cover removed. Then the transition between these two pictures gave it the appearance of an animation in which the cover peels off the PC.

- The use of Persuasion animation to move the picture of the PC on and off the slide. I made that by selecting Auto-animate from the Persuasion Draw menu, then choosing an animation direction.
- The use of transitions to give the appearance of the arrows being drawn on the screen to show processor input and output. As with revealing the illustration in the opening of this example, the unchanged portions of the illustration appear not to move, while the added sections (the pink arrows leading into and later out of the yellow block representing the processor) look as though they are moving in the direction that they point.

You can experiment with other Persuasion animation and transition techniques if you have this program on your own Macintosh.

You can run Example 8-3 directly from the CD-ROM, but you will not be able to save the file unless you choose Save As... from the Persuasion File menu, then choose a folder on your computer's hard drive.

Example 8-3 Movie

This file is a Persuasion Player version of the file Example 8-3. You do not need Aldus Persuasion to play this file. You can run it in either of two ways:

- Click on the file Example 8-3 Movie to play. This opens Example 8-3 Movie and also opens Persuasion Player 3.0 to view the movie.
- Click on Persuasion Player 3.0, then choose Open from the File menu and select the Persuasion Player file you wish to view.

If you choose the second option, you can also change the speed with which the Persuasion Player file displays on your computer. If you have a slower or faster Macintosh than the Quadra 630 I used to generate these examples, you can adjust the speed with the Persuasion Player. This is also a useful technique if you rely on Persuasion for multimedia presentations at client's locations, where computer systems used for display may be faster or slower than those on which you authored the presentation.

F275GTB Movie

This is also a Persuasion Player document. You can open it in either of two ways:

- Click on the file F275GTB Movie to play. This opens F275GTB Movie and also opens Persuasion Player 3.0 to view the movie.

- Click on Persuasion Player 3.0, then choose Open from the File menu and select the Persuasion Player file you wish to view.

This document also contains digital media, included in the next file. No editable file exists for F275GTB Movie.

F275GTB Movie Movies

One of the features I like best about Persuasion is that it encapsulates the media for your Persuasion Player documents. This makes it easier for you to include your presentation on one floppy diskette, and media files such as QuickTime video or digitized audio on another floppy diskette. It also simplifies keeping track of the media content, as there is only one file containing all video or audio rather than a collection of files that you must track individually.

Persuasion Player 3.0

This is the royalty-free player that comes with Aldus Persuasion. If you have your own copy of Persuasion, you can create interactive multimedia presentations and distribute them with the Player file included here (or with the Player from your own copy of Persuasion) and let your clients, students, employees, or customers use your multimedia presentation.

Winter Animal v2.0

This is the editable Persuasion file containing excerpts from the interactive presentation created by Donna Haswell's first grade class at Cherry Chase Elementary School in Sunnyvale, California. Mrs. Haswell is one of Sunnyvale's 27 members of the Multimedia Specialists Program, a program made possible by grants from local industries and businesses. Training and support for the 27 multimedia specialists comes from Larry Liden, president of the Institute for Computer Technology (ICT), a Sunnyvale-based education center that provides classes to the community and extension courses associated with the University of California.

This project is described elsewhere in the book, but it deserves mention again here; it was a thrill to be part of this project and to see the reactions from the children.

Mrs. Haswell had prepared a lesson on animals and how they adapted to winter. She prepared a matrix of questions that her students would use to structure their learning about the animals they chose. The matrix was to include four pieces of information: the animal's name, where it lived, what it ate, and one interesting fact about it.

The children used traditional and electronic sources to research their animals, and came up with some great information about a variety of animals. (One boy reported the interesting fact about hedgehogs that "bees can't sting them.")

The children wrote their reports at home, then brought them in to class where they used a program called Storybook Weaver to create illustrations and to type their reports on the classroom's pair of Macintosh computers. Parent volunteers assisted the children, but the kids did all the work themselves, both preparing the illustrations and typing the reports.

Later, parent volunteers led by my wife, Kim Fisher, prepared an interactive presentation with Persuasion. I designed the structure and interactivity so that the presentation could be used in either of two ways:

- As a slide show: if left undisturbed, the presentation would run each slide in succession, then leave the last frame visible with a control button from which the children could start over; or
- As an interactive presentation: from any slide, the children could click on a button titled Choose A Name. This displays the list of all the names of children who participated, permitting each child to choose his or her name from the list.

We displayed this interactive presentation on March 23, 1995 at the school's Open House. The children were very excited to show their parents what they did on the computer, and even more excited that the presentation was displayed on the classroom's television.

Later, we recorded VHS cassettes of the slide show version of this presentation, using the Lapis LTV Card's output to the classroom's videotape recorder. At present, the school's video club is preparing a show using this presentation for Sunnyvale School District's community-access television station, provided as a public service by TCI Cablevision to the Sunnyvale, Cupertino, and Fremont Union High School districts.

Because of considerations over licensing, permissions, copyright, and other concerns, the version you can see on this CD-ROM contains only the stub of the interactive structure, as well as one piece of content: the report on weasels by Torrey Fisher. (This was the one child whose parents could be counted on not to cause legal problems for the publisher if we included her work on the CD-ROM.) If you or your school district are interested in learning more about this project, or in seeing how the actual interactive presentation worked, please contact me electronically on America On-

Line, SEFisher@AOL.com. I will be happy to give you more information about how you can create your own multimedia presentations in your own school, club, or organization.

Winter Animals Show

This is the Player file for the Winter Animals report. As with the other Player files, you have two choices:

- Click on the file Winter Animals Show to play. This opens Winter Animals Show and also opens Persuasion Player 3.0 to view the Player file.
- Click on Persuasion Player 3.0, then choose Open from the File menu and select the Persuasion Player file you wish to view.

If you do not have Aldus Persuasion, you can still see the structure, flow, and interactivity that we created for the Winter Animals presentation. As with the other file, most of the student artwork has not been duplicated out of legal concerns over copyright and permissions.

If for some reason the lesson inherent in that last statement has escaped you, here it is in black and white: If you are preparing a CD-ROM for publication, you *must* obtain permission from your contributors before you begin work. You cannot publish work from any other contributors who have not given you their permission.

PCVIDEO

This directory contains two QuickTime for Windows files. You can play these files on your Macintosh or you can copy them to a Windows PC with QuickTime for Windows installed and view the same files there.

isvrpro.mov

This file shows a digitized video of the Intel Smart Video Recorder Pro as it looks installed in a Compaq 860 Presario. Because dramatic irony is my life, I digitized this clip on the Apple Video System in the Macintosh Quadra 630. Yes, for aesthetic completeness I should have included a video clip of the Apple Video System that I digitized with the iSVR Pro.

waycool.mov

This is the output of Logomotion, a 3D "lite" program from Specular 3D. It's their low-cost tool, useful for creating flying 3D logos with various surface texture characteristics. The title will be obvious once you watch the movie.

QuickTime Movies

This folder contains some straight QuickTime Movies that you can import into your own sample presentations. They demonstrate several aspects of digitized video, and some of them are familiar from the text.

First Day

This is the video from which the three examples in Chapter 5 were derived. The sound track explains the name.

Terrorsaurus Rex

From the age of the carnosaurs comes unimaginable horror! SEE the peaceful village of teddy bears, lucky wishing trolls, and ceramic penguins flee in terror at the thundering approach of twenty feet of blood-crazed sauropod! FEEL the rippling waves of fear as the mightiest killing machine ever to tread the earth rips into the terrified community! CRINGE in horror as an innocent, defenseless teddy bear falls victim to bone-crushing mandibles of death! You'll shiver, you'll scream, you'll be unable to look away from *Terrorsaurus Rex,* filmed in glorious TOYMATION!

Producer: Scott Fisher

Director: Scott Fisher

Animator: Scott Fisher

Cinematographer: Scott Fisher

Toys courtesy of: Torrey and Bronwen Fisher

Digital Editor: Kim Fisher

"Not since Ed Wood has a single creative vision made such an unmistakable impact on a motion picture."—the critics

Made in Silicon Valley, U.S.A.

You get the point. This is in fact one of the silliest motion pictures ever made, a spiritual cross between *Bambi Meets Godzilla* and Art Clokey's *Gumby* shorts, and easily one of the most egregious examples of technology abuse so far this century. Edward D. Wood, Jr., in case you have been blissfully unaware thus far in your previously happy existence, was voted the Worst Director of All Time in 1980, and with good reason. His pictures include *Plan 9 From Outer Space*, the picture that marked Bela Lugosi's last appearance on film, which uses special effects such as flying saucers made of paper plates painted silver and dangled on fishing line across miniature sets. Tim Burton, the talented director of *The Nightmare Before Christmas* (a genuinely superb piece of computer-enhanced stop-motion animation) and other films, made a remarkable movie about Wood, starring Johnny Depp and Martin Landau in a breathtaking performance as a failed, dying, but still noble Bela Lugosi.

Look carefully at *Terrorsaurus Rex* and you can see the animator's hand actually holding the tyrannosaurus by its tail in one scene. It's the kind of movie that Spanky, Alfalfa, and the rest of the Little Rascals would have made if they'd had a camcorder, a Macintosh, and Bill Watterson's Calvin as screenwriter.

Yellow GT40

Just that; this one is heading out of the Corkscrew, turns 8 and 8A at Laguna Seca Raceway in Monterey, California. (If you're a fan of motorsports, you may have heard of the GT40, Ford's endurance-racing champion that broke the domination of Ferrari on international competition in the mid-1960s.) This clip was digitized at 7 frames per second, on a 320 x 240 video window. Compare it with the next video clip for smoothness and visual effectiveness.

Yellow GT40 Small

The same piece of video, but at 160 x 120 pixels and 15 frames per second. Notice how much more smoothly the cars move across the screen; even though the images are smaller, the motion is much more realistic.

PowerPoint Files

This folder contains the examples I created using Microsoft PowerPoint. Oddly enough, Microsoft themselves don't consider PowerPoint a multimedia authoring tool. While it does not permit interactivity, I've taught classes in beginning multimedia projects that start people with PowerPoint. It's easy to use, has a very short learning curve, and lets you get immediate feedback on the basic principles of creating multimedia presentations. You can learn about layout, screen design, information density, media selection, digital video frame rate, audio, pacing, and most of the other concerns that you'll have to face even if you go on to program your own multimedia titles in Kaleida's ScriptX or MIT's Athena Muse languages. But you can do it all with point-and-click simplicity while you work on your aesthetic sense of style and structure.

The following files are on the CD-ROM.

Sports Cars On Parade

What if you were part of a club in which everyone had a computer? Could you do your club newsletter in multimedia? It's not that far off—I do a number of social activities with a group of people who keep track of one another by electronic mail and the World-Wide Web. In fact, the video for this file came from a tour I hosted with my friends from the net.

One day, church newsletters will go out on diskette, on PCMCIA cards, or on some other electronic medium. When that day comes, presentations like this will be commonplace. Right now you still need economic justification for it, but when it's cheap and ubiquitous, multimedia will include presentations like this one.

Ch 5 Program Interface Tutorial

This is another example of using transitions between frames to create an imitation of animation. This is more likely the kind of work you'll be doing: teaching someone how to use a computer program by providing training tools on the computer itself. As with all the PowerPoint examples, if you have a copy of the program (rather than the royalty-free player included here) you can edit the files and see how I constructed them.

Ch4 Linear Example

Another example using builds, transitional animation, and digital video. In the second video clip, the little girl had just been caught spitting water back into the wading pool, and her squawk was in realization that she had not merely been busted, but that she was captured for all eternity on Mom's video camera. If there's ever an America's Funniest Home CD-ROMs, this one's probably worth $10,000...

Torrey2

The video used in Ch4 Linear Example. You can copy this onto your own computer and use it for practice in your own multimedia presentations, if you don't already have your own digitizing board.

Yaack!

More video used in Ch4 Linear Example. You can copy this onto your own computer also, and use it until you get your own digitizing board.

Old and New (video)

Pictures of lovely old cars, used in Sports Cars On Parade. The audio talks about "XPAGs" at one point—that's not the cars (the first two are M.G. TCs), but rather the model number of the engines used in the first two cars. The third car is an MGB-GT, which used a BMC B-Series engine, if you're interested in such things.

Raspberries

One of the fun parts about tours through the Santa Cruz mountains is just what this video shows: wild berry vines grow almost everywhere.

Winery Cat (video)

This is one of the hospitality experts at Bonny Doon Winery in California, the winery with the most highly developed sense of humor of any I know; if you're in the area just north of Santa Cruz, California, drop in and try a bottle of their Clos de Gilroy. No, it's not garlic wine; it's actually a very pleasant, informal red made predominantly from the grenache grape. Good served at cool room temperature with hearty picnic fare such as cold roast beef, rich cheeses, or my favorite, the sourdough artichoke bread from Norm's Market in Pescadero.

Sea at Pebble (Video)

This is Pebble Beach—not the one from the golf course, but another that is aptly named as you can no doubt see from the rocks visible in the video.

MS PowerPoint Viewer

The viewer file that enables you to see these sample documents. Double-click on this file, then select Open from the File menu and choose one of the viewer documents.

Director Files

This directory contains three files, each of which demonstrates something in Macromedia Director.

Shoyu Neko

(Translation: Soy Sauce Cat.) This demonstrates using text in Director. The buttons on the opening screens are instances in which a Lingo script is attached to a Cast member. If you click the button that says Read the

Whole Story, this Director movie presents a text box that you can scroll to read the entire text of the story all at once. If you click Next, the movie shows you essentially the next page of the storybook.

Tobiko

Macromedia Director is also a powerful animation program. This short cartoon was created by my daughter Torrey at age 7. I described what she needed to do in order to make the motion come out the way she wanted it, but she did all the work herself—I didn't touch the mouse or the keyboard. Tobiko, as indicated in Shoyu Neko, is the name of one of our cats. The green bird in this represents Aji, our South American grey-cheeked parakeet.

Winter Beta

From an early test for the Winter Animals program, I developed this interactive piece using Macromedia Director. I like the look of the book used as the "next page" button. Additionally, this piece demonstrates how much better Director makes transitions look between frames; the change from the red "Cherry Chase" frame to the blue and white "Winter Animals" frame looks like snow falling.

Still Images

The files in this directory are all Macintosh screen snapshots—PICT files created for SimpleText. You can import them into other graphics packages or other multimedia authoring tools. One of my favorites is Forest Blur, a picture I took of the forest at the ridge of the Santa Cruz mountains; I ran this through a screen saver that filters the image this way and makes it look as though it had been painted.

MediaWrangler on the PC

Windows PC users will be able to see a partition containing a number of files pertaining to AltaVista MediaWrangler. The CD-ROM contains a demonstration version of this simple multimedia authoring tool.

To run MediaWrangler, insert the CD-ROM into your D drive. You'll need about 10 megabytes of disk space to do an installation; for that, follow these steps:

1. Find the file SETUP.EXE on the CD-ROM (which is probably drive D:) in the File Manager.

2. Double-click the file SETUP.EXE. MediaWrangler asks you a number of questions about the directory you wish to use for installation. Answer according to your system's directory structure.

When you are finished, you should have a new directory on your hard drive (probably C:), called MWRANGLE. The file MWRANGLE.EXE is the executable file containing MediaWrangler. Double-click on that file.

MediaWrangler's user manual is duplicated in on-line help, so you can follow the tutorials in this book or you can use the electronic reference to find your way around. It's a very simple product, but you can begin making some entertaining, interactive documents within a few minutes. Additionally, you will enjoy browsing some of the data files and examples included with the MediaWrangler demonstration version.

Index

A

B

C

D

I

J

K

L

O

P

Q

R

S

T

LIMITED WARRANTY AND DISCLAIMER OF LIABILITY

ACADEMIC PRESS, INC. ("AP") AND ANYONE ELSE WHO HAS BEEN INVOLVED IN THE PRODUCTION OF THE ACCOMPANYING CD ROM ("THE PRODUCT") CANNOT AND DO NOT WARRANT THE PERFORMANCE OR RESULTS THAT MAY BE OBTAINED BY USING THE PRODUCT. THE PRODUCT IS SOLD "AS IS" WITHOUT WARRANTY OF ANY KIND (EXCEPT AS HEREAFTER DESCRIBED), EITHER EXPRESSED OR IMPLIED, INCLUDING, BUT NOT LIMITED TO, ANY WARRANTY OF PERFORMANCE OR ANY IMPLIED WARRANTY OF MERCHANTABILITY OR FITNESS FOR ANY PARTICULAR PURPOSE. AP WARRANTS ONLY THAT THE CD-ROM ON WHICH THE FILES ARE RECORDED IS FREE FROM DEFECTS IN MATERIAL AND FAULTY WORKMANSHIP UNDER NORMAL USE AND SERVICE FOR A PERIOD OF NINETY (90) DAYS FROM THE DATE THE PRODUCT IS DELIVERED. THE PURCHASER'S SOLE AND EXCLUSIVE REMEDY IN THE EVENT OF A DEFECT IS EXPRESSLY LIMITED TO EITHER REPLACEMENT OF THE DISC OR REFUND OF THE PURCHASE PRICE, AT AP'S SOLE DISCRETION.

IN NO EVENT, WHETHER AS A RESULT OF BREACH OF CONTRACT, WARRANTY OR TORT (INCLUDING NEGLIGENCE), WILL AP OR ANYONE WHO HAS BEEN INVOLVED IN THE CREATION OR PRODUCTION OF THE PRODUCT BE LIABLE TO PURCHASER FOR ANY DAMAGES, INCLUDING ANY LOST PROFITS, LOST SAVINGS OR OTHER INCIDENTAL OR CONSEQUENTIAL DAMAGES ARISING OUT OF THE USE OR INABILITY TO USE THE PRODUCT OR ANY MODIFICATIONS THEREOF, OR DUE TO THE CONTENTS OF THE CODE, EVEN IF AP HAS BEEN ADVISED OF THE POSSIBILITY OF SUCH DAMAGES, OR FOR ANY CLAIM BY ANY OTHER PARTY.

Any request for replacement of a defective disc must be postage prepaid and must be accompanied by the original defective CD-ROM, your mailing address and telephone number, and proof of date of purchase and purchase price. Send such requests, stating the nature of the problem, to Academic Press Customer Service, 6277 Sea Harbor Drive, Orlando, FL 32887, 1-800-321-5068. AP shall have no obligation to refund the purchase price or to replace a disc based on claims of defects in the nature or operation of the Product.

Some states do not allow limitation on how long an implied warranty lasts, nor exclusions or limitations of incidental or consequential damage, so the above limitations and exclusions may not apply to you. This Warranty gives you specific legal rights, and you may also have other rights which vary from jurisdiction to jurisdiction.

THE RE-EXPORT OF UNITED STATES ORIGIN SOFTWARE IS SUBJECT TO THE UNITED STATES LAWS UNDER THE EXPORT ADMINISTRATION ACT OF 1969 AS AMENDED. ANY FURTHER SALE OF THE PRODUCT SHALL BE IN COMPLIANCE WITH THE UNITED STATES DEPARTMENT OF COMMERCE ADMINISTRATION REGULATIONS. COMPLIANCE WITH SUCH REGULATIONS IS YOUR RESPONSIBILITY AND NOT THE RESPONSIBILITY OF AP.

About the CD-ROM

This CD-ROM contains examples, demonstration files, and sample video clips used in the procedures included in the text. Both Macintosh and Windows media are included so that readers can follow along on their own computers, using files like those they see in the book. In addition, a limited-performance version of the PC authoring tool MediaWrangler is available on the Windows portion of the CD-ROM. Windows users can try creating their own interactive catalogs, brochures, and slide shows with this simple and effective authoring system.

System Requirements

Macintosh: Color monitor, 68020 or better processor, 8MB of RAM, single-speed CD-ROM, sound and video built-in.

PC: Color monitor, 386 processor required (486 recommended), 8MB of RAM, 4MB hard drive space required for MediaWrangler; SoundBlaster CD-16 or equivalent sound card, SVGA video graphics, single-speed CD-ROM drive.